"This book captures, in Senator Paul Wellstone's own words, the very essence of how and why Paul was an extraordinary friend, teacher, mentor and public servant. Paul's own words connect with the reader as if he is right there before you pacing, gesturing, and on fire with passion for the people of Minnesota, the United States, and the world."
—Rep. Margaret Anderson Kelliher,
Speaker of the Minnesota House of Representatives

"Whether as a teacher, community organizer, or U.S. senator, Paul Wellstone always had a unique ability to communicate with people in a way that connected to their lives and called them to action in pursuit of a more just world. The passionate speeches Mark Ireland has collected in this book honor Paul's twelve years in the Senate and provide us with an inspiring guide to addressing our most relevant and pressing issues today."
—Jeff Blodgett, Executive Director of Wellstone Action!

"History always looks kindly upon individuals who had the courage to stand up and voice opposition to popular sentiment. This book—from No Child Left Behind to Iraq—is filled with examples of Senator Wellstone exhibiting such courage. His unique voice is terribly missed."
—Chris Coleman, Mayor of Saint Paul

"Finally, in one place, we have a memorable compilation of the words and thoughts that secured Paul Wellstone's place in history as one of Minnesota's most enduring leaders. Mark Ireland has given us an absorbing tribute. Paul Wellstone's floor speeches, which practically leap off the page, are a monument to his progressive passion."
—Representative Steve Simon, Assistant Majority Leader,
Minnesota House of Representatives

WELLSTONE
CONSCIENCE OF THE SENATE

WELLSTONE
CONSCIENCE OF THE SENATE

The Collected Floor Speeches of
Senator Paul Wellstone

Edited by
Mark Richard Ireland

with a Foreword by
Minnesota Secretary of State Mark Ritchie

NORTH STAR PRESS OF ST. CLOUD, INC.

ISBN 10: 0-87839-290-4
ISBN 13: 978-0-87839-290-2

First Edition, September, 2008

Published by:
North Star Press of St. Cloud, Inc.
PO Box 451
St. Cloud, MN 56302
www.northstarpress.com

Printed in the United States of America.

For my wife, Amy, and her patience and support.
—MRI

TABLE OF CONTENTS

> "This is no time for timidity."
> ~Senator Paul Wellstone ("Where are We Going?" an
> essay written in the early 1980s)

Contents

Contents

FOREWORD

by Mark Ritchie, Minnesota Secretary of State

Open this inspiring book to any chapter and just start reading. In moments you will discover one of the most honest, passionate and persuasive political voices from the latter half of the twentieth century—United States Senator Paul David Wellstone.

Mark Ireland has created an amazing gift for all of us by pulling together a collection of some of Paul's most powerful and poignant speeches made on the floor of the U.S. Senate. For those of us who knew Paul there are moments when you feel like you are sitting in the Senate gallery watching him wave his arms and move his whole body to convey the passion that comes from deep understanding and total commitment to making positive change. For those who did not have the privilege of knowing Paul there is an equally great reward awaiting you in the wisdom and experience that Paul brought to these statements that make them incredibly relevant even today. His goal, as he so often reminded us, was to make the world a better place, not to make it perfect.

In his masterful job of choosing the speeches to include in this book, Ireland has demonstrated a keen sense of the issues dominating public dis-

course in America today and how Paul used his floor speeches to address the complexity of these issues and to make proposals for working towards solutions. Taken as a whole, this collection of speeches brings to light facts, figures, ideas, and beliefs about the very same issues dominating the U.S. Congress and state legislatures today.

One of the best features of this book is the short and very carefully crafted brief introductions that author Ireland has written to begin each chapter. These words give key insight into Paul's thinking on a wide range of issues, including the national healthcare crisis, poverty and hunger, climate change, renewable energy, and foreign policy. To read this book is to hear Paul speaking in his own voice about his values, principles, experiences, and hopes for a country he dearly loved.

Like so many Minnesotans, what first drew me to Paul was his incredible ability to connect and communicate with people. The first time we met was at a rally during the farm crisis of the mid-1980s. Paul's speech that day deeply inspired me on a personal level. It gave me the hope, vision, and energy needed to get up every morning and continue working for social justice. Over the years, Paul not only became my representative in the U.S. Senate, he also became a close personal friend. He was someone I could talk to frankly when I was feeling discouraged about how difficult it can be to work towards effecting change in our community. Whether I was hearing him speak one-on-one or in a crowd of hundreds, Paul always cared deeply when speaking about these issues, and had many, many excellent ideas for solving problems.

Over the many years of our friendship I had the good fortune to hear Paul speak dozens of times, including twice from the pulpit of my church. While Paul truly had a gift for public speaking, he connected with people using more than just the emotional force behind his words. He was always diligent in his approach and never spoke without putting forth a well-researched, well-reasoned argument. The speeches were important to Paul as a politician in that they helped him win people over to his side in debates and campaigns, but they were also important to Paul as a professor and organizer in that he always wanted to make sure that we were teaching the teachers, training the trainers, and modeling the arguments and actions needed to advance the cause.

One of the unexpected delights of reading this book is being reminded that Paul was a deeply committed student of history and drew on his wide knowledge of the past and civil affairs to help make his case to policymakers, politicians, and everyday people. He could articulate a problem, place that problem within a context of shared values, and spell out a vision and course towards change.

In much of this book Paul is talking about what he called "kitchen table" issues such as education, health care, the environment and family-supporting jobs. He understood that these concerns, unlike the polarizing social issues of the so-called culture wars, are the concerns that dominate the day-to-day lives of ordinary people and deserve the

greatest attention; he understood that these issues would have the greatest resonance over time. From farm policy to mental health, he argued his case using stories of real people and facts from sources close to the problems. He tackled everything from campaign finance reform to the plight of coal miners with the same passion and care, including heartfelt acknowledgements for those who were leading the way on these issues.

Paul was a master at being able to listen and truly hear the concerns of Minnesotans. He would begin by listening to the private concerns spoken from the hearts of the people who trusted him. He would then turn those stories of real challenges and difficulties into a public discourse about how to tackle these concerns, whether they were large or small. Paul served as a political bridge in many situations because he was uncommonly able to connect the individual concerns and problems of his constituents with the larger context of politics and policy, and in so doing was able to truly serve the public.

Even though many of the speeches included in this collection were delivered on the floor of the U.S. Senate over a decade ago, the issues Paul raised have remained relevant to the trials we face today. Particularly on matters of foreign policy—ranging from the ethics of China hosting the Olympic Games, given their human rights record, to the devastating effects of the North American Free Trade Agreement on family farms—Paul's words are prescient.

He had the prophetic insight to know that unilateral, preemptive military strikes by this country would have wide-reaching and long-term consequences. He understood that the deadly arrogance of invading Iraq without adequate preparation or planning would lead to disaster, and he was unwavering in his opposition to this war. Paul's message about the continuing need to strive for peace found throughout this book comes with a painful reminder of what little progress we as a nation have made on some of the issues that Paul held dear.

Among the many gifts left to all of us by Paul was his consistency. While specific issues may come and go—and they do—fundamental values, principles, and objectives should not. Paul's allegiance was not to one narrow partisan agenda or political ideology, but to core beliefs that were deeply and intrinsically Minnesotan. Paul and I occasionally talked about what brought us both to Minnesota, he from North Carolina and I from Iowa via Alaska and California. We shared the same story, that the Minnesota values of political openness, the respect for history and tradition, the value of hard work, the spirit of cooperation, and the unquestionable equality of all drew us both to the state. It was this fidelity, this faithfulness to his principles that won Paul such support from Minnesotans and electrified crowds of all kinds. In this book, Paul's words address those same values, the ones that attracted him to the state and that he articulated so well.

The enduring legacy of Paul Wellstone is one of optimism and hope. Even when speaking on difficult and dark topics, such as the invasion of Iraq , he spoke with the conviction that we as a people and country, could do better, could be better. Paul had ambitious goals, ones that inspired and challenged us. And on some of these there has been remarkable progress since Paul's passing, such as the recent passage by the U.S. House of Representatives of the Paul Wellstone Mental Health and Addiction Equity Act. Through the speeches in this book, it becomes apparent that Paul wholeheartedly believed in the transformative power of the democratic process. He knew that politics could be a force for good, and that—in his own words—that politics is "what we do, politics is what we create, by what we work for, by what we hope for and what we dare to imagine."

INTRODUCTION

PAUL DAVID WELLSTONE
July 21, 1944 to October 25, 2002

A simple black cloth covered his desk in the rear of the empty senate chamber. Covering a senator's desk with a black crepe has been a tradition since the eighteenth century. It indicated that there had been a death in the family. The senator who had occupied that desk would not return.

It was an aisle desk. According to Senator Barbara Boxer of California, it was a desk he loved. Senator Wellstone could see everyone come and go from this vantage point. It also allowed him to leave his papers behind, step easily into the aisle and speak from the heart. He could gesture and pace, and fight for what he believed in.

He had left that desk to return to Minnesota.

In the midst of a close campaign for re-election, he told other senators: "I want to be with my people. I need to touch them. I need to look them in the eye. I can't wait to get home."

On October 25, 2002, Senator Paul Wellstone, his wife, Sheila Wellstone, and daughter, Marcia Wellstone, along with three campaign staff—Will McLaughlin, Tom Lapic, and Mary McEvoy—were traveling in a small airplane flown by two pilots, Richard Conroy and Michael Guess. They were traveling to a funeral in northern Minnesota.

It was a cold and overcast morning with freezing rain. Just southeast of Eveleth, Minnesota, the plane crashed in a heavily wooded area. There were no survivors.

Paul Wellstone was born in Washington, D.C., on July 21, 1944, and raised in nearby Arlington, Virginia. His father, Leon, was a Jewish immigrant from Russia who fled persecution three years before the Russian revolution. Leon Wellstone was a government civil servant who worked for the United States Information Agency. Paul Wellstone's mother, Minnie, was the daughter of Jewish immigrants from the Ukraine.

In his memoir, *The Conscience of a Liberal*, Paul Wellstone described his mother as follows:

"I was ashamed of my mother for all the wrong reasons. She was a cafeteria worker at Williamsburg Junior High in Arlington, Virginia. Kids would make fun of these low-income, working-class women—especially their looks and the way they talked. I didn't want my friends to know that they were making fun of my mother. Of course later on—much later on—I came to cherish my mother, to love her for how hard she worked to take care of me, to appreciate her obvious working-class background (the ultimate compliment my mother could pay a person was, "She is a good worker"), and to deeply resent elitist put-downs of ordinary people."

Paul Wellstone had similar feelings toward his father, which also changed over time:

"With my father, it was different. By age and appearance, he just didn't fit in. And his immigrant background could cause frustrations for me as a kid. . . . By high school age, I came to treasure my parents, especially my father. He spoke ten languages fluently. Most important, he was a fountain of wisdom and knowledge."

Paul Wellstone also had a brother, Stephen, who was eight years older. Although being an excellent student, Stephen suffered from mental illness and was hospitalized in a psychiatric institution during his first year of college. Even though Stephen was eventually discharged, finished college, and taught fifth grade, Paul Wellstone's experience of visiting his brother at the Virginia State Mental Institution as an eleven-year-old boy haunted him.

He described the psychiatric hospital as a "snake pit." And, later described his experiences with the mental health system a "radicalizing experience."

At age sixteen, Paul Wellstone met his future wife, Shiela Ison, at the beach. They dated for approximately three years, and, just after turning nineteen, the two were married over the objection of many family members.

Paul Wellstone studied political science at the University of North Carolina, Chapel Hill ("UNC"). He was soon a father, while also competing as a wrestler, taking additional classes to graduate early, working, and becoming active in the civil rights movement.

After obtaining his undergraduate degree, Paul Wellstone and his young family remained at Chapel Hill, where he began graduate work in political science. At twenty-four, he obtained his doctorate degree, and then accepted a teaching position at Carleton College in Northfield, Minnesota.

In 1969 Paul Wellstone was, in his own words, "determined not to be an outside observer but to use my skills as a political scientist to empower people and to step forward with people in justice struggles." Neither the college nor rural Rice County, where it is located, were prepared for the young professor. After three years of identifying the needs of rural poor and agitating for change, Paul Wellstone was fired. It was a unanimous decision by the political science department, the president, the dean, and the board of trustees.

Paul Wellstone, now with three children, was given one year's notice. During that year, the students rebelled. Fifteen hundred out of sixteen hundred students signed a petition, demanding that Carleton College retain Paul Wellstone. An older mathematics professor, Sy Schuster, stepped forward and began challenging the way the decision to fire Wellstone had been made. At the end of the year, that decision was reversed. In addition to being reinstated, Paul Wellstone was given full tenure.

Twelve years later, in 1982, Paul Wellstone ran for Minnesota State Auditor and lost. His loss, however, did not deter him from politics. He remained active in the Democratic-Farmer-Labor Party ("DFL"). In 1988, he was the state co-chairman of Reverend Jesse Jackson's presidential campaign, and then state co-chairman for the eventual Democratic presidential nominee, Massachusetts Governor Michael Dukakis.

Two years later, in 1990, Paul Wellstone beat two much better known candidates to win the DFL endorsement for the United States Senate as well as the opportunity to challenge incumbent Senator Rudy Boschwitz. Few took Paul Wellstone's campaign seriously. Wellstone was a short (five feet, five inches), liberal, college professor with minimal financial resources. Initial polls indicated that Senator Boschwitz led by twenty percentage points.

Over the course of the summer, however, Wellstone organized at the grassroots level, while Senator Boschwitz remained in Washington, D.C. Senator Boschwitz was working on a budget agreement. This limited the amount of time he was spending in Minnesota.

Paul Wellstone traveled around the state in a battered and often broken green school bus. His visible and scrappy effort, combined with unconventional television advertisements, created a sharp contrast to the campaign being run by Senator Boschwitz. Although Paul Wellstone was outspent by a seven-to-one margin, the race slowly began to tighten, and he ultimately won with 50.5 percent of the vote.

Paul Wellstone was the only senate candidate to unseat an incumbent in 1990. His victory was one of the first signs that voters were longing for change, and it foreshadowed the difficulty that President George H.W. Bush would have against then-Arkansas Governor Bill Clinton. Indeed, Paul Wellstone's message about the economy, education, and universal health care was incredibly similar to the themes successfully used by the Clinton campaign.

Paul Wellstone arrived in Washington, D.C., as an optimist. Although he made mistakes, such as talking to reporters about his opposition to the Gulf War in front of the Vietnam Memorial, he learned from these experiences. Over time, he found opportunities to create bi-partisan coalitions related to domestic violence, trafficking in women, and parity for mental health and chemical dependency treatment. He did not, however, waiver from his beliefs or the "politics of the center."

Senator Wellstone did not define the politics of the center in the same way as typical politicians and Washington, D.C., pundits, but rather the "center" referred to the center of people's lives. It entailed affordable child care, good education for children, health security, living-wage jobs that would support families, respect for the environment and human rights, and clean elections and clean campaigns.

In 1996, former Senator Rudy Boschwitz ran against Paul Wellstone to reclaim the senate seat he had lost. In a barrage of negative television advertisements, Senator Wellstone was repeatedly called "embarrassingly liberal." One television advertisement featured a caricature of Senator Wellstone speaking to a group of burned-out, dope-smoking hippies. The months of negative advertisements eventually back-fired. Senator Wellstone was re-elected by a nine percentage-point margin. Among voters who labeled themselves as "moderates," fifty-nine percent voted for Senator Wellstone.

His second term was similar to his first, although he continued to become more familiar with the rules of the United States Senate and comfortable with his role. In 1998, Senator Wellstone briefly considered running for president. Unofficial student groups began to form on college campuses, and Senator Wellstone retraced Robert F. Kennedy's 1966 poverty tour. Ultimately, Senator Wellstone decided not to run for health reasons. His bad back made the constant travel incredibly painful.

Although he had initially promised to limit himself to two terms, Senator Wellstone decided to seek a third-term in 2001. He also disclosed that he had Multiple Sclerosis in February 2002.

Nearly every poll taken in 2002 indicated that the race between Senator Paul Wellstone and Norm Coleman, the former mayor of Saint Paul, was close. Norm Coleman relied heavily on the support of President George Bush, who was still popular in the wake of the September 11th terrorist attacks on the World Trade Center in New York and Pentagon in Washington, D.C.

On October 11, 2002, just one month before the election, Senator Wellstone joined with a small number of other Democratic senators and voted against the Iraq war. The vote was seventy-seven to twenty-three. Senator Wellstone was the only senator facing reelection to vote against the war. At the time, the vast majority of Americans supported the invasion of Iraq. Minnesotans, however, rewarded Wellstone for his courage. His poll numbers slightly rose.

Just fourteen days later, the plane carrying Senator Wellstone, his wife, daughter, and campaign aides crashed in northern Minnesota. Paul and Sheila Wellstone were survived by their two sons, Mark and David.

Senator Wellstone and Sheila Wellstone's work is now continued through Wellstone Action, a national center for training and leadership development for the progressive movement. Founded in January 2003, Wellstone Action is training, educating, mobilizing and organizing a vast network of progressive individuals and organizations.

1

THE PERSIAN GULF WAR

> "One of the reasons I opposed this war was that I feared the administration had no strategy for achieving long-term political objectives in the Middle East. Indeed, I feared the administration had little conception of the potential political consequences of a war."
>
> ~Senator Paul Wellstone, April 9, 1991

When Paul Wellstone was initially sworn-in as a United States senator, the first order of business for the new Congress concerned authorization of the use of military force in the Persian Gulf. Approximately five months earlier, on August 2, 1990, Saddam Hussein had invaded the neighboring country of Kuwait. The invasion and occupation of Kuwait was condemned throughout the world, and many leaders feared that the Iraqi military would continue its offensive into Saudi Arabia.

United States forces amassed in Saudi Arabia to deter such further action, and military leaders began planning offensive measures. Secretary of State James Baker built an international coalition to support an end to the Iraqi occupation through military force.

On January 10, 1991, Senator Paul Wellstone made his first floor speech as a United States senator in opposition to the use of military force. Senator Wellstone believed that the military action was premature. He believed that it would have unintended consequences, such as threatening Israeli security, as well as increasing the num-

ber of radical militants and the amount of anti-American sentiment in the Middle East. He asked: "What kind of victory will it be?"

Despite opposition by Senator Wellstone and others, the United States Senate passed the resolution in support of military action in the Persian Gulf. Five days later, the Persian Gulf War began with an Apache helicopter strike.

By March 3, 1991, just a month and a half later, military operations had largely ceased. Coalition Forces declared victory, and a decision was made not to continue into Baghdad and overthrow Iraqi President Saddam Hussein. This decision was controversial, particularly in relationship to the Kurds in northern Iraq and Shiite population in southern Iraq. At the time, both groups were attempting to overthrow Saddam Hussein.

Because there was no active support from the United States, their uprising was brutally repressed by Saddam Hussein. It caused a humanitarian refugee crisis in northern Iraq and showed that the problems in Iraq were not over. In a floor speech in support of humanitarian aid, Senator Wellstone stated, "One of the reasons I opposed this war was that I feared the administration had no strategy for achieving long-term political objectives in the Middle East. Indeed, I feared the administration had little conception of the potential political consequences of a war."

WAR MEANS DEATH AND DESTRUCTION
January 10, 1991

Mr. President, this is not the speech that I wanted to give. I rise to speak in this chamber for the first time with a very heavy heart. I wanted my first speech to be about children and education, and health care, and a credible energy policy and the environment.

I never thought that the first time I would have an opportunity to speak in this chamber the topic would be such a grave topic: Life and death, whether or not to go to war, to ask America's men and women, so many of them so young, to risk life and limb, to unleash a tremendous destructive power on a foreign country and a faraway people.

This is the most momentous decision that any political leader would ever have to make, and decide we must. Let no one doubt that the Congress has the responsibility to make this decision. The Constitution is unambiguous on this point. Congress declares the war, not the president.

Mr. President, I give no ground to any of my colleagues in my condemnation of Saddam Hussein. It is a bedrock principle of world order that no country has the right to go in and swallow up another country, and that is why I supported the president's policy at the beginning, a policy that I think the president has abandoned.

It was such a successful policy. The economic sanctions were working, rallying the international community, isolating Saddam Hussein and, most important of all, I believe the initial policy was well on its way to prove the point that

we can respond to aggression without the slaughter that modern-day warfare brings. Mass slaughter. I mean to say just that, Mr. President.

War means death and destruction, and there are some in this chamber who may believe that this truth is so obvious that it need not be said. I think it needs to be said over and over again.

I have observed this debate, and it seems to me that all too often in the theorizing about strategy and politics, it is forgotten what war means in human terms: The terrible loss of life, broken dreams, broken lives, broken families. I will tell my colleagues something, Mr. President, the fathers and mothers of young men and women from Minnesota who are now in the Persian Gulf have not forgotten what war means in personal terms, and we must not forget either. Town meeting after town meeting after town meeting, citizens would stand up, quite often a Vietnam vet, point a finger at me and say: "Senator, how many of the Senator's children are in the Persian Gulf?"

And I would respond this way. I would say: I'm the son of a Jewish immigrant from the Soviet Union, and if I believe Saddam Hussein was a Hitler and that we must go to war now to stop him, if I believe we must do that for the defense of our country or the defense of this world, I am a citizen in this world, then as much as I could hardly stand the thought, I could accept the loss of life of one of my children, ages twenty-five, twenty-one, and eighteen. I would rather it be me, but I could accept the loss of their life. But this is the truth. I could not accept the loss of life of any of our children in the Persian Gulf right now, and that tells me that in my gut I do not believe that it is time to go to war. I do not believe the administration has made this case to go to war, and if I apply this standard to my children, then I have to apply this standard to everyone's children. I have to apply this standard to all of God's children.

President Bush appears to be on the verge of making a terrible mistake that will have tragic consequences for the whole world. Life is so precious.

War is an option that one pursues when all other options have been tried. We have not given sanctions a chance. The policies that I am afraid the administration is pursuing, the rush to war that I am afraid is so much a part of what is now happening in our country and in the world will not create a new order, Mr. President. It will create a new world disorder. What kind of victory will it be, what kind of victory will it be if we unleash forces of fanaticism in the Middle East and a chronically unstable region becomes even more unstable, further jeopardizing Israel's security?

We are the ones, as my colleagues have said so well, who will pay the largest part of the price with loss of life. What does it mean? What kind of victory will it be if we shoulder this responsibility, if the alliance fractures and if there is an explosion of anti-American fury throughout the Arab world, accompanied by widespread violence and terrorism, what kind of victory will that be?

What kind of victory will it be if our already fragile economy is fractured? Whatever happened to the war on poverty, the war against drugs, the war against illiteracy, the war to make sure our citizens do not go without adequate health care? Whatever happened to the war against the poison of the air and land and the water? What kind of victory will it be if we are so paralyzed economically we cannot deal with any of these pressing domestic needs? What kind of victory will it be if our country, a country I love dearly, is torn apart again? What kind of victory will it be if tens of thousands of people die in the Persian Gulf, so many of them—and I need to state this point carefully because I mean no disrespect—so many of them disproportionately men and women of color, low and moderate income? What kind of victory will this be?

Some causes are worth fighting for. This cause is not worth fighting for right now.

We must stay the course of economic sanctions, continue the pressure, continue the squeeze, move forward on the diplomatic front, and, Mr. President, we must not rush to war. Very large and long-term interests of our country and the world are at stake in the decision we are about to make. Our options are not simply war or appeasement.

I very much resent any discussion which suggests that anybody who says, as I am saying today, that we must not rush to war is in any way, shape or form talking about appeasement. Negotiations are not appeasement. Every diplomat knows this. Our options are not simply war or peace. We have an opportunity to stay the course with sanctions, and we have an opportunity in the international community to show that there is a new way to respond to aggression, where conflicts can be resolved without resorting to war. It is too early to give up on that approach. It is the mark of a great nation that it has the patience and the conviction to pursue its highest goals. We stand on the brink of catastrophe if we allow domestic politics, self-imposed deadlines, or military logistics to rush us into a war that no one wants and a war that even in victory will so severely damage our national interests. An agenda for war has been laid out. It is time to develop an agenda for peace.

I leave you, Mr. President, with a wonderful Hebrew word, *tikkum*. It means to understand and to heal and to transform the world.

Voting Against Authorizing the Use of U.S. Armed Forces Pursuant to U.N. Securty Council Resolution

(January 12, 1991)

Mr. President, I have sat in on many administration briefings. There have been so many graphs and charts and figures about planes and bombs and economic sanctions. But I have asked the questions over and over and over again: Can you tell me how long will the war last? What will be the casualties? What will be the loss of life? And the silence is deafening. Not one graph, not one chart, not one set of figures.

This administration is unable or unwilling to provide us with information about the most precious commodity of all—life. And yet it asks for a blank check to initiate war. We must not give this administration that blank check.

I hope I am wrong. But I speak with a sense of foreboding. I am chilled. I believe that if we rush to war, it will be a nightmare in the Persian Gulf. Our country will be torn apart and, Mr. President, very little good will happen in the United States of America or in the world for a long, long, long time.

Thank you.

Phone Saddam Hussein

January 15, 1991

Mr. President, yesterday many parents of men and women in the Persian Gulf were here.

They are so frightened that their children will die in a war in the Gulf, and I believe that every single citizen in our country can understand their fear. I remember not too long ago at a gathering of Woodbury, Minnesota, guardsmen who were to leave for the Gulf. I did not know what to say, but these were the words that come to my mind.

I said to those men and women: "We are proud of you and we will support you." I said to those men and women: "We hope and pray that you never have to go to war." And then I said, "I will do everything as a U.S. senator to make sure that you do not have to go to war."

It is in this spirit that I rise to speak today. I heard Senator Harkin say to the president of the United States—and I think he said it with eloquence and power—President Bush, pick up the phone, pick up the phone and call Saddam Hussein and talk directly to him.

There are those who say it is too late. It can never be too late. It can never be too late to avoid war and the resulting massive loss of life. The president of the United States has been very clear to Mr. Hussein about what will happen if he does not end his unlawful occupation of Kuwait. I believe we have made it very clear what war will be all about. But I hope the president of the United States today, as we approach war, can pick up the phone and also be clear with Mr. Hussein [about] what will happen if he does leave Kuwait. He should be clear what this war is not about.

We should be clear [with] Mr. Hussein that this is not a war in opposition to a peace conference in the future. We are not opposed to a peace conference that will deal with a variety of important fundamental disputes and problems in the Middle East. In fact, we have gone on record supporting such a conference.

We should make it clear that we are not going to be involved in fighting a war, which would prevent a just settlement of disputes between Iraq and its neighbors. In fact, the very first United Nations resolution makes that very point.

We should make it crystal clear to Saddam that we will not be fighting in a war to remove Mr. Hussein from power. We have already assured Saddam Hussein that if he leaves Kuwait—and he must leave Kuwait—there will be no such attack on his country.

Mr. President, it is very late. There were those in our debate who said they were not voting to go to war. They did not want to go to war. I know they meant that. Many of my colleagues said we are voting to give the President full strength to negotiate. We are not voting to go to war. But as I speak today, it does not feel that way to me. It feels as if we are very close to war and to a terrible loss of life.

So I rise today to echo the words of Senator Harkin and to say to the president of the United States, take that last step, take that last step. Pick up the phone and make that call and speak directly to Mr. Hussein. No harm would come from that. It can only do good, and it is never wrong to do everything you can to avoid war.

I thank the Chair.

CONDEMNING IRAQ'S UNPROVOKED ATTACK ON ISRAEL
January 24, 1991

I rise to support the resolution condemning Iraq's unprovoked attack on Israel. I want to condemn this attack in no uncertain terms. I want to condemn this attack as the senator from Minnesota. I want to condemn this attack as an American citizen. And I want to condemn this attack as the son of a Jewish immigrant from the Soviet Union.

My heart goes out to the Israeli people. Upon hearing of this attack, chills ran down my spine, Mr. President, and I believe it is very important at this moment that we express our full support for the State of Israel.

Let me also at this moment, at this time, express my concern about an ever-widening war. Let me also appeal to all those who are involved in this hostility that every effort be made to make sure that innocent civilians do not become the casualties of this war, innocent civilians wherever they live.

Thank you, Mr. President.

DESERT STORM SUPPLEMENTAL AUTHORIZATION AND MILITARY PERSONNEL BENEFITS ACT
March 13, 1991

Mr. President, I fully support—and indeed have worked to help put together—the legislation for military personnel benefits. This benefits package justly recognizes the contributions of the men and women who served so honorably in the Persian Gulf and recognizes the hardships of the families—the wives, the husbands and the children—of our service personnel.

I was proud to work as a member of the task force which helped shape this bill. I thank Senator Glenn for his leadership on the task force and the leadership of both parties which forged the leadership agreement.

This bill provides for a wide range of benefits for the troops, including increased hostile fire or imminent danger pay, transitional medical coverage and clarification of employment rights. The bill also provides for a range of benefits for the families of the troops, including child care assistance and education and family support services.

I am pleased that these essential veterans and personnel benefits will be funded out of Department of Defense accounts to pay for incremental costs of Operation Desert Shield. I hope we can welcome the troops home in another way, too, by focusing our energies and our commitment to moving forward on the home front to address urgent domestic issues—to health care, to education, to energy policy, to the economy.

There would be no better reward for the troops coming home than to show them and their fellow citizens that we are committed to a better, fairer America.

HUMANITARIAN RELIEF FOR THE KURDS IS THE LEAST WE CAN DO
April 9, 1991

Mr. President, I thank the senators from New York for their bill authorizing the provision of medical supplies and other humanitarian assistance to the Kurdish people and to Iraqis seeking refuge in the allied occupied zone. Their speedy effort to address a horrific situation is to be commended. I am pleased to join them on this legislation.

In reprisal for a short-lived Kurdish uprising, Kurdish people are being driven from their homes and slaughtered wholesale by forces loyal to Saddam Hussein. Hundreds of thousands of Kurds—civilians and rebels alike—are desperately trying to escape Saddam Hussein's genocidal rampage. For the refugees massed at the Iraqi border, food is scarce, medicine unavailable, and fear and cold are pervasive.

This bill represents a first modest step, but it is an important step which will set U.S. policy on the right and moral path. The fifty million dollars in humanitarian assistance authorized by this bill is the very least we can do. Unfortunately, fifty million dollars won't go very far in meeting the needs of the refugees.

The United States, and the international community, did not react in the past when Saddam Hussein massacred Iraqi Kurds or violated basic human rights of the whole population. But this time the United States has a special responsibility and a special opportunity.

The United States actively encouraged the Kurds and the Shiites to rebel against Saddam Hussein. The United States bombing campaign—that, in the words of a U.N. report, pounded Iraq back into the pre-industrial age—created the conditions for Iraq's collapse into internal war and chaos. During the early phases of the uprising, President Bush made much of the fact that the cease-fire forbade Hussein any military use of the Iraqi Air Force. He promised to shoot down any Iraqi aircraft used to attack the rebels.

But as the Kurdish and Shiite insurrections were brutally suppressed and the civilians populations slaughtered, the United States turned its back. As forces loyal to Hussein made extensive use of helicopter gunships to shell civilian populations, the United States stood by.

The reason offered by President Bush for our lack of response to Hussein's slaughter is that he does not want to intervene in Iraq's internal affairs. But we are already deeply involved. The United States extensively bombed the country, invaded it, killed 100,000 conscripts and thousands of civilians, and called on its people to overthrow its dictator. American forces now occupy 20 percent of Iraq, we control all of its airspace and we are proposing to regulate by fiat all their oil revenues and arms trade. We are deeply involved.

I am encouraged by the European Community and the United Nations' efforts to provide relief for the victims of Iraq's civil chaos. The European Community has pledged 180 million dollars in assistance, and the United Nations is going to appoint a senior diplomat as coordinator of a widespread humanitarian effort. Britain and other nations are proposing the establishment of a Kurdish enclave under international protection. I would hope that the United States would assume a leadership role in addressing this tragedy. But short of that, the United States can encourage these efforts with a generous pledge of U.S. aid and military troops for a multilateral peacekeeping force.

One of the reasons I opposed this war was that I feared the administration had no strategy for achieving long-term political objectives in the Middle East. Indeed, I feared the administration had little conception of the potential political consequences of a war.

The bill proposed by Senator Moynihan and D'Amato will start to address these consequences. Finally, Mr. President, I want to go on record expressing my concern that the funding provided in this bill will not put at risk existing refugee disaster assistance and relief funds.

RELATIVE TO MEDICAL AND HUMANITARIAN ASSISTANCE TO IRAQ
July 16, 1991

Mr. President, I rise today to offer a resolution with Senator Dodd and several others of my colleagues, which responds to the human tragedy unfolding daily in Iraq. I am pleased to be a member of the Subcommittee on Children and Families, chaired by Senator Dodd. Our shared concerns have motivated our efforts to find a means of alleviating the horrible suffering of the children and families of Iraq.

In America, the Persian Gulf war is long over. But in Iraqi hospitals and homes, it is still being fought against epidemic disease and starvation. When the world community imposed economic sanctions against Iraq, it did not intend for them to cause prolonged, profound suffering among the people of Iraq. How many times did President Bush state that our problem was not with the Iraqi people, but with its political leadership. Certainly our quarrel was not with babies and children. Yet that is who has suffered most and continues to suffer most.

A top-level U.N. mission sent to Iraq to assess that country's civilian needs returned over the weekend. The team found that without massive imports of food, medicine, and essential supplies, the country is headed for "a major catastrophe." The U.S. envoy, Prince Sadruddin Aga Khan, reported to the U.N. Secretary General the team's strong recommendation to ease sanctions in order to make funds available for these essential imports.

The findings of the U.S. team, included in a report scheduled to be released later this week, are further corroboration of findings of other recent investigations. A medical team from Harvard that visited Iraq in April estimated that 170,000 children under the age of five will die in the coming year from the delayed effects of the Gulf War. The Harvard team, and others, say these projections are conservative.

The youth of Iraq is perishing daily as most of the world stands by unable or unwilling to respond. The immediate cause of death in most cases is waterborne infectious diseases in combination with severe malnutrition. The prevalence of acute malnutrition is so high that a nationwide famine is quickly becoming a likelihood if food shortages are not relieved.

Until the imposition of U.N. sanctions, Iraq imported over seventy percent of basic foodstuffs. Currently, shortages exist in all of the basic commodities needed for everyday survival. Supplies of baby milk are particularly scarce. Those food supplies that are available are priced out of reach for most Iraqi families. Due to the shortages, food prices now average 1,000 percent higher than prices a year ago.

Safe drinking water also is in dangerously short supply, especially outside of the major cities. When allied bombing destroyed the national electrical grid in January, water treatment plants throughout the country ceased to function. Iraqi civilians turned to polluted rivers for drinking, bathing and disposal of sewage. Today, less than thirty percent of Iraq's pre-war electrical generating capacity is available. What this has meant for Iraq's children is epidemic conditions of waterborne diseases such as cholera, typhoid, and dysentery.

The U.N. team has recommended two formulas for easing the sanctions—allowing Iraq to sell oil or unfreezing its assets abroad. At least $3.75 billion of Iraqi State assets is frozen in foreign banks, of which about forty percent is in American banks. If private assets are included, the total is closer to five billion dollars. Last May, Iraq requested permission to export 900 million dollars worth of oil to raise funds for the importation of food, medicine, and equipment for reconstruction. The Security Council has not acted on Iraq's request.

Whichever method is used to make available large sums of money, says Prince Aga Kahn, it should not be too complex or too bureaucratic. The Iraqi Government's recent lack of candor concerning the existence of nuclear weapons production facilities has rightfully reinforced the world community's unwillingness to place any trust in the government. Given this, I believe that Iraq's frozen State assets represent the most readily available source of funds and the most readily managed funds by U.N. officials.

The resolution we are introducing today calls on our government and others to immediately transfer to the United Nations that portion of Iraq's frozen State assets necessary to help meet the medical and humanitarian needs of Iraq's families and children in greatest need. A similar resolution has already been introduced in the House of Representatives by Congressman Tim Penny from my State of Minnesota.

I believe that the United States and other countries should also begin devising the procedures for allowing the exportation of Iraqi oil to raise funds for emergency needs. Effective means must be established to monitor the importation and distribution of goods and services to ensure that they are reaching Iraq's needy civilian population.

Our resolution also asks the U.N. donor nations, including the United States, to fulfill their pledges made to the United Nations in response to its earlier appeal. From the beginning of this crisis, the United Nations has had to beg for resources. The United Nations issued a revised appeal for 400 million dollars for humanitarian assistance in Iraq, including assistance for the refugees. Less than half of this total has been received. The international relief agencies on the ground immediately should receive international resources necessary to provide to the most needy such essentials as baby milk, wheat, sugar, rice, and cooking oil.

I urge my colleagues to join Senator Dodd, Senator Simon, Senator Cranston, and myself and our House colleagues in this effort to respond to a calamitous situation in Iraq. The Persian Gulf war continues to claim victims—innocent families and children. Immediate action is required if the world is to protect these innocent victims.

2

HEALTH CARE

> "My basic starting principle is that every citizen in the United States deserves access to affordable, dignified, humane, and quality health care regardless of employment status, regardless of income regardless of age and regardless of current or prior health care condition."
> ~Senator Paul Wellstone, September 16, 1991

Universal health care for all Americans was an issue that Senator Paul Wellstone felt deeply about. It was personal. He campaigned on the issue, and spoke about it often. Although the hope for universal coverage dimmed in 1994, when Republicans gained the majority in Congress, Senator Wellstone continued to press the issue. He also spoke in favor of more modest proposals, such as the Family Medical Leave Act, health care for children, and easier access to prescription drugs. Even when other senators stopped talking about health care, Senator Wellstone continued to push for reform. According to Senator Wellstone, universal health care was not an entitlement program, it was a fundamental human right.

STATES AS LABORATORIES FOR UNIVERSAL HEALTH CARE
September 16, 1991

Mr. President, everywhere I travel in Minnesota and around the country, health care is the most pressing issue on the minds of people I meet. Everywhere I go, health care is what people want to talk to me about, and it is what they want me to talk to them about.

In small towns it is the issue; cafes, it is the issue; farms, it is the issue. At the Minnesota State Fair, day after day after day, it was the issue. In the cities, on street corners, in the neighborhoods, it is the issue.

Mr. President, it is clear to me that in the last six months there has been a dramatic change in what people in our country collectively are feeling and thinking and hoping for and angry about in our country, and there is no question in my mind that health care is a very, very central issue to peoples' lives. Increasingly the voices that are calling for reform here in the U.S. Congress represent every segment of our society.

The astronomical increases in health care costs bring us all together, and a crisis, which once affected the poor, now affects all of us in our country.

Mr. President, I think it is interesting for someone who has always cared fiercely about this issue to look at the way in which the political dynamic is changing. So many people in our business communities, small businesses and larger businesses, are calling for major health care reform. And so many providers, the doctors and the nurses and the nurses' assistants are calling for health care reform.

Mr. President, this crisis increasingly unites us all. My basic starting principle is that every citizen in the United States deserves access to affordable, dignified, humane, and quality health care regardless or employment status, regardless of income, regardless of age and regardless of current or prior health care condition. But increasingly, Mr. President, the economics of health care, the cost of health care, and the unavailability of private health insurance has put this goal out of reach for many, and more and more Americans.

There is no doubt that the health care system is in a state of crisis, all spelled in capital letters, and that this is a national crisis demanding a national solution. Yet, in Washington, I hear so often from my colleagues, colleagues that I respect and that I work with every day, about the so-called political realities, that we really cannot push forward any major health care reforms in our country. But I do not hear this talk in towns, in cafes. It is the talk I hear in Washington about the political realities.

And the question, Mr. President, is this: Can we make universal health care a reality? That is the question that we ask right here in the U.S. Senate. And to answer that question, can we make it a reality, let us look at some other realities.

Our health care system is in a state of crisis. That is a reality. More than thirty-four million people in our country have no health insurance whatsoever. That is a reality. Double that number are underinsured. That is a reality. The number of underinsured and uninsured are growing daily. That is a reality. The United States of America, a country I love very much, is the only advanced economy in the world without a form of universal health care coverage. That is a reality; I think a disgraceful reality.

Families can be bankrupted by long-term illness at any time, and that is a fate that could befall any of us—a reality. The United States spends more on health care than any other country, twelve percent of our GNP—a reality. Automobile manufacturers spend more money for health care coverage for workers per car than the cost of steel. That is a reality. A quarter of our health care bill, a 750 billion-dollar bill, is spent on administration instead of caring for people who are in need; one-quarter of the health care dollar is spent on administration. That is a reality. The number of health care administrators is rising three times as fast as the number of physicians or health care workers. That is a reality.

Mr. President, it is because of all these realities that health care reform must become a reality right here in the U.S. Senate.

The question is not whether we are going to have any health care reform. The question is no longer whether or not we are in crisis. The question is no longer whether or not there are problems. The question is what kind of reform will we have. What shape will it take?

In the Senate this year, the debate over reform is centered to a large extent on S. 1227, the legislation introduced by the Democratic leadership, Senators Mitchell, Kennedy, Riegle, and Rockefeller. This legislation is an employer mandate, or pay-or-play proposal. And it is coupled with a new, expanded public health care program, to provide universal health care coverage for our citizens. The leadership bill also proposes to control spiraling health care expenditures by establishing a mechanism, which would make recommendations on costs in different sectors of the health care economy.

I commend my colleagues, the sponsors of S. 1227, for their efforts to address one of the key imperatives of our day. And I share the goals of the sponsors of this legislation: Universal access to health care and cost containment. But I differ with them in some of the goals. And I want to lay out some of my critique and some of my proposals.

The leadership bill is an important bill, but I think we need to do even more to control health care costs. The bill mandates the establishment of a health expenditure board as an independent agency of the executive branch and the bill gives this board a broad mandate to look at expenditures and to establish expenditure goals. But it has no power. It has no power to enforce these recommendations.

Given the crisis in health care costs, I think it is essential that this board be given more enforcement power. I worry about cost containment. I worry about state governments that are being hit by these costs. I am worried about the ability of our businesses to continue to absorb these costs. And I am worried about the cost to our society of these increased health care costs.

More fundamentally, I am concerned about the way in which this legislation links health care coverage to employment status. My concern is that this could very well lead to a two-tier system, which is inefficient and inequitable. And I am also concerned that this employer-mandate may be putting too much of a burden on our businesses and our workers for the financing of health care.

Achieving universal health care coverage and some cost control through an employer mandate system may be an interim solution to our crisis. It may be an important step in the right direction. But I am convinced that the ultimate answer to our crisis of access and the crisis of cost is a single-payer system, a national health insurance program. It is the simplest. It is the most efficient. And it is the most equitable path to health care reform.

The concept is to streamline and simplify the administration and financing of health care

and to preserve consumer choice in the delivery of health care. In other words, the federal and state governments would finance the system. But the government does not run the clinics. Government does not run doctors' offices. Government does not run the hospitals. Services will be delivered through the same sources that we have today, the same sources: Private doctors and nurses; health maintenance organizations, HMOs, clinics, nursing homes, and hospitals.

The goal is to make the system simpler. Everyone will be covered by the same system instead of this confusing and inefficient system we have today. And administrative costs will drop dramatically with a single payer. Capital costs will be budgeted at a regional or state level. And there will be some control over what has become a spiraling medical arms race.

Such a system can work and it does work. We only need to look to our neighbor in Canada. We need to study the Canadian example, borrowing from what works well there and not using what does not work. No one is saying we should adopt the Canadian system in the whole. But many are saying that we ought to take advantage of this system and study its successes and see what we can learn.

There are several features of what we have in the United States today that I would fight to the very end to preserve. I come from a state where managed care is very important. We need to preserve those HMOs. I spent time and visited with the Mayo Clinic in Rochester, Minnesota, and no one needs to tell me about the importance of education and to continue to have these centers of excellence. I took part in a two-day internship, spent time in hospitals, two major hospitals in Minnesota. Nobody needs to convince me about the importance of technologies that save lives and in the long run lead to less expense.

In large measure, I believe that the cost of a national health insurance program could be borne by the savings gained from the administrative efficiencies and other cost control measures. And these savings which come from single payer may be the way in which we finance long-term health care as well. In fact, a report introduced and published by the General Accounting Office in June pointed out that we can save an estimated sixty-seven billion dollars a year if we move to single payer: sixty-seven billion dollars a year.

The *New England Journal of Medicine* pointed out that we could save 136 billion dollars a year. I firmly believe that what is going to drive this debate is how we control these health care costs and how we make quality health care available to people. I firmly believe otherwise we will never be able to address this crisis of long-term care; that people toward the end of their lives should live in such fear of catastrophic expenses—that is wrong. For citizens, older Americans, not insured by private insurance—and our public system is woefully inadequate, and you only receive public assistance when all of your resources, or just about all of your resources of depleted—and that is wrong.

I am convinced that only with a universal health care coverage program, single payer, with these huge savings in administration will we be able to have a serious, long-term health care program. As a matter of fact, I would argue that a single-payer system has the ability of bringing together the broadest coalition of citizens. I am talking about the vast majority of people in this country, united behind a universal health care coverage for our country.

The point is this. Health care reform is not a liberal issue. And it is not a conservative issue. It is not a Democratic issue. And it is not a Republican issue. It is not a business issue. And it is not a labor issue. It is an issue that unites the people in this country.

The *Wall Street Journal* pointed out this summer a poll that found that sixty-nine percent of the Americans in our country support a Canadian style national health system; almost seventy percent of the people. We have to listen to voices of people. We have to make this reality. This is a national crisis that demands a national solution.

But if Washington is not ready to act decisively with a national single-payer bill, if we are not ready to act decisively and enact national health care reform, if there is gridlock here in Washington, then I think at the very minimum if we cannot be a part of the solution, we should not be part of the problem, and it is important that we encourage states to move forward with their own health care reform.

There are dynamic ideas and dynamic forces for change coming at the state level. That should not surprise anyone. We live in a grassroots political culture. And the states are closer to the crisis that people face. I have seen these forces in Minnesota and I have seen these forces in other states as well.

* * *

We should tap into the ideas and creativity and commitment of those people working in the state level on health care reform. In the history of our country, states have often served with distinction as the leaders and the laboratories for reform.

And so, Mr. President, it is in this spirit that I have developed an amendment to the leadership health care legislation. My proposed amendment encourages individual states to set up single-payer systems on a statewide basis as model demonstration projects. The amendment specifies minimum requirements that states must meet to qualify for federal financial incentives. But the states will be given maximum flexibility to design their own single payer systems.

* * *

But I would conclude, Mr. President, by saying in as strong a way as I can, in the last analysis we must understand that this is a national crisis and it certainly requires a national solution. In no way, shape, or form should we put the burden on the states. I am talking about enabling legislation that allows states to move forward with their own proposals, backed by some federal waivers and incentives, because I think that may be the way we move our country forward.

As I said earlier, this is a national crisis. Too many people in this country have no health insurance, too many people in this country have too little health insurance, and too many businesses in our country cannot afford to cover their employees with health insurance. Virtually no one in this country—no one in this country, including everybody in the gallery today—is immune from the crisis that could affect them if there is a catastrophic illness and expense in their own families. Too many individuals and too many businesses and the vast majority of people in our country are affected by our failure to move forward with serious national health care reform.

Roosevelt talked about it in 1935. That was over a half a century ago. But I will tell you something, Mr. President. There is no question in my mind that we could do much better, much better in a country which spends more on health care than any other country in the world and in a country which has the best medical services and the best research in the world, the tragedy being that it is not for all the citizens who live in our country. It is time for a fundamental change to address a fundamental problem. There really is no other choice but to enact major health care reform in the United States of America. This time of crisis requires no less.

* * *

This is what it is all about. This is why you put so much sweat and tears to a campaign to get elected, so you can come to Washington and develop legislation, and you work with your colleagues. So you never give up; you keep on pushing and you keep on pushing until you pass legislation that you know will lead to the improvement of people's lives. That is what I think this health care legislation is all about.

HEALTH CARE REFORM HEARINGS AND A CALL FOR ACTION
November 13, 1991

Mr. President, health care has become a very popular issue. Polls show it; commentators are talking about it. The electrifying victory of Harris Wofford in Pennsylvania last week proved it. Now everyone wants to talk about health care. Let me emphasize those words: talk about health care; talk about health care.

But we need more than talk. We need to act. We need legislation which fundamentally changes the way we finance and deliver health care in the United States of America. And the fundamental change will only come and make a difference when we address two crises: the crisis of access, and the crisis of costs. These two fundamental issues have to be dealt with in any piece of legislation if that legislation is to pass the test.

Two questions, Mr. President: First of all, does the proposed legislation guarantee full access for citizens in our country to health care? Will there be health care for all citizens? We must start with that premise, that each and every citizen in the United States of America deserves dignified, affordable, high-quality health care regardless of income, regardless of age, regardless of employment status, and regardless of prior or current health-care condition.

The second question: Does the proposed legislation control rising health-care costs? Because if we do not control the costs, then we are not going to be able to provide access to all citizens within our country. We cannot lose sight of these two issues, and no amount of rhetoric, no amount of speeches should be able to obscure the fact that these are the two fundamental questions that have to be addressed.

Mr. President, the Democrats have introduced—and we will be introducing more—proposals which at the very minimum guarantee access to health care for every citizen, and which control health-care costs. Those are the two issues that have to be dealt with. We may differ on details, but we are united in our commitment to the fundamental principle that every American deserves—every American deserves—health care.

Meanwhile, from the White House, the silence is deafening. Meanwhile, we get a proposal from the Republicans, which does not address the question of whether or not there will be access to health care for every citizen, which does not address the fundamental question of cost control. I am afraid, Mr. President, that the proposal that we have received from the Republicans on the other side of the aisle does not represent a step forward, but represents a great leap sideways. That is what we have so far.

Mr. President, speaking for myself, I believe the ultimate answer to the question of access and to cost is a single-payer system of national health insurance. It is the simplest, it is the most efficient, and it is, I think, the most equitable reform. What we do is we have one insurer, and, therefore, we simplify the administration of the program.

By the same token, we make the system simpler: not all sorts of different forms and rules and regulations, but we enhance and preserve consumer choice. The delivery of the health care has to be state and local, it has to be through a pluralistic framework, and consumers should choose from a range of different options.

Mr. President, I want to point out on the floor of the Senate today that if we are serious about cost control, and that will drive any reform, we have to understand that there are two reports to pay attention to: GAO, the General Accounting Office—I did not say Democrat or Republican—GAO, in June, with a report that said with single payer, we could save sixty-seven billion dollars in one year just in administration, not in deliver[y] of services to people; and the *New England Journal of Medicine*, with an article that said with single payer, we could save up to 137 billion dollars in one year, just from administration.

Now, Mr. President, we have a model just a little bit to the north. It is the Canadian health-care plan. I did not say it was Heaven on Earth. I did not say it was perfect. I think we have to study that plan and draw from its strengths, and then, of course, add to our own American experience. We will do more with HMOs; we will do more with centers of excellence; we will do more with technology.

But that single payer, that notion of cutting out the bureaucracy and getting right to the administration and financing of health care is an extremely important proposal. That, Mr. President, will be, at the national level, what I would be pushing very hard.

* * *

The final point, Mr. President, let us make sure we do not just talk. I really think talking about health care these days has become the functional equivalent of politicians kissing babies. Everybody is going to do it. But let us look for the substantive proposals, let us be willing to offer our proposals, let us be willing to offer our legislation, and then let those proposals be scrutinized and let us have the debate and let us move forward with fundamental reform that will make a real difference in the lives of Americans all across this country.

There are lots of powerful, I mean really powerful, economic interests who are going to oppose the national health insurance plan. But I think at this point we can concern ourselves, first and foremost, with the national interest, and the national interest is to move forward with a national health insurance program that, once again, will provide dignified, humane, affordable care for every citizen within this country.

THE FAMILY AND MEDICAL LEAVE ACT
August 11, 1992

Mr. President, I rise today to express my support for the conference report on the Family and Medical Leave Act of 1991. If we work at it, Mr. President, this bill can be the first step in the development of a comprehensive policy designed to support American families. I hope that adoption of this conference report will signal a shift in our priorities as a nation regarding families and children.

This is not a complicated piece of legislation. It is not hard to explain. S. 5, the Family and Medical Leave Act, is designed to protect the jobs of American workers when they are faced with a family crisis. It says that you should not have to choose between having a family and having a job. It says that we believe in families in America, that we are willing to pay the small price, as a nation, for making families possible for people who work. It signals that we recognize that many American workers have trouble supporting their families and keeping them together in difficult times, concerned about the effect of taking leave time on their jobs. It is not television sitcoms that are destroying American families. It is our unwillingness to help people support their families. With enactment of this long-awaited conference report, we can begin to change that situation.

I want to make it clear, Mr. President, that I consider this legislation to be just a beginning, a modest start toward a more comprehensive family policy. We provide, with this act, twelve weeks of unpaid, job-protected leave per year for employees who are faced with the birth or adoption of a child, or who need to take care of an immediate family member who has fallen seriously ill. This is not much and it is very late—in the United Kingdom, the first policy of this sort was instituted in 1911, and the current leave policy there dates back to 1946. Canada's policy dates to 1962. Sweden has had a sickness and maternity leave policy since 1891. It is true, we can be a conservative, prudent country when it comes to adopting social legislation. But now that we have had close to a century in which to observe how these policies work around the world, I believe we must adopt our own, modest plan.

We are still the only developed country in the world with no family leave policy. If our observation of other nations tells us that this bill is hardly a radical new idea, it also tells us that it is hardly a family leave policy either. In Canada, workers are provided with eighteen total weeks of leave and they receive ninety percent salary during the first sixteen weeks of that leave. In France, employees can take up to sixteen weeks leave, including six before giving birth, and they typically receive eighty-four percent of their pay during that period. Two of the nations most often cited as our major competitors for international markets, Germany and Japan, provide family leave policies—in Germany it is fourteen weeks, paid at one-hundred percent of salary and in Japan, twelve weeks at sixty percent of salary. So we have a long way to go, if we are to catch up. And I must admit, Mr. President, that I do not understand why we must settle for anything but the best policies in this country.

So here, with this bill and this conference report, we will begin to update American family policy, to catch up with the rest of the developed world. This may be a minimal family leave policy, Mr. President, but it is a step in the right direction. It could not come at a more critical time for this country. More and more, Mr. President, we are a country of working families. Currently, ninety-six percent of all fathers and sixty-six percent of all mothers with school-aged children are in the work force. Over half of all women with infants work outside the home. What little progress we have made in the past twenty years on average incomes in this country has been due to the increase of two wage-earner families. If we are not going to make it possible to support a family on one income any longer, then we must make it possible for at least one family member to take some time out of work in case of emergencies.

If the lessons we have learned from other countries, and from studies of our own, prove correct, this policy will prove to be good for American business as well as for American families. According to a 1990 study by the Institute for Women's Policy Research, workers who suffer bouts of serious illness and who have no job-protected leave lose about 12.2 billion dollars in earnings every year. Taxpayers pay an additional 4.3 billion dollars annually through various support programs for workers who have lost their jobs due to lack of this sort of leave. A 1990 study from the Small Business Administration concludes that "the net cost to employers of placing workers on leave is always substantially smaller than the cost of terminating an employee."

As discussed in the conference report we have before us, this policy is expected to cost about $5.30 per covered employee. Keep in mind, however, that the only employees who are covered are those who work in firms that employ fifty or more workers, so that ninety-five percent of employers are not covered by this policy. In 1989, the General Accounting Office [GAO] estimated that this policy would cost about 244 million dollars annually. That is clearly a bargain.

Mr. President, we do not have to look to foreign countries for examples of the effectiveness of family leave policies. We can look at several of the states for examples of the benefits of this policy. In my own state, we have a parental leave law that requires an employer to provide up to six weeks of unpaid parental leave to a mother or father upon birth or adoption of a child. A 1991 study by the Families and Work Institute of our policy along with similar policies in Oregon, Rhode Island, and Wisconsin, found that employers were able to implement the law easily and inexpensively, with little or no impact on other benefits. It did not lead to increases in the cost of health insurance, or unemployment insurance, training or administration, as some critics have predicted. It did promote healthier practices among parents, especially mothers, who were able to take medically recommended leaves to recuperate from childbirth and to be with their children.

By voting for this conference report, we are making a commitment, as a nation to support families, in all their forms. We are making a commitment to children. We are making it possible for parents to work and provide for their families. If we are serious about families, we will take this initial step. If we are serious about competing with Europe and Japan, we will take this step. If we want to make it clear that the values we believe in are rooted in the family, then we will begin by helping to shore up that family. This is, I hope, the first of a new set of policies that will show that we are, in this country, committed to putting our immense national resources behind our children and our families.

CHILDREN'S HEALTH CARE
January 21, 1997

Mr. President, children's health care coverage needs to be a priority in this Congress. We need to be committed to providing access to affordable coverage and care to all working families in America. We also need to provide coverage for uninsured pregnant women, in order to ensure that children get a healthy start in life. All children should have access to services that provide for their basic health care needs such as immunization, preventive services, acute care, and dental care services, regardless of whether they live in rural or urban areas.

Employers are rapidly cutting health care coverage for children of their employees. When a family earning $16,000 each year is required to pay over ten percent and sometimes as much as one-third of their income to purchase health insurance for their children, they are forced to make very difficult choices. They must choose between providing their children with basic needs such as food and shelter, and paying for health insurance.

Health care coverage for children is an investment in the future. Children with undiagnosed or untreated health problems may have difficulty learning in school. A child with poor vision that has not been diagnosed or treated may be unable to see the blackboard. A child who is in pain from preventable tooth decay may not be able to eat an adequate diet, and the pain may make it difficult for the child to concentrate. A child with asthma who has poor access to care may spend many hours in an emergency department and many days in the hospital for treatment of problems that could have been prevented. This occurs at a significant cost not only in terms of dollars, but also in terms of lost opportunities to attend school, and loss of work time and income for the child's parents. These situations can be prevented with adequate health care coverage and access for children.

Children in rural areas are especially vulnerable, as there are fewer services available in these areas, and some needed services are located at significant distances from their homes. In addition, these children often live in homes where their parents work for small employers, who are unable to offer dependent coverage at a low cost.

Several states have demonstrated the cost savings available by providing assistance to working families. My home state, Minnesota, operates its own program that helps families buy private health insurance. Ninety-thousand people are covered, including 50,000 children. Over the years, more than 41,000 families have used MinnesotaCare to leave or stay off welfare, saving the taxpayers twenty-six million dollars per year.

It is essential that we address this issue and provide low- and middle-income families with the option to purchase affordable private insurance coverage for their children. These families must be provided with the means to purchase this coverage in a timely manner, so that they do not have to delay the purchase of coverage for their children.

We need to build on successful private, state, and federal efforts to help working families afford to provide health coverage for their children. Providing coverage for children through age eighteen and pregnant women is the next logical step in incremental health care reform. It is sound policy and makes economic sense. It will ensure that all children in America have a healthy start in life.

Personal Prescription Drug Import Act

July 24, 2001

Mr. President, I rise to introduce legislation that helps to correct the injustice that finds American consumers the least likely of any in the industrialized world to be able to afford drugs manufactured by the American pharmaceutical industry. The reason is the unconscionable prices the industry charges only here in the United States.

I am under no illusion that this legislation provides comprehensive or ultimate relief to Americans who are struggling to afford the prescription drugs they need. However, this bill does expose and highlight the problem American consumers face, and it provides a certain measure of immediate relief for individuals struggling with the high cost of prescription drugs.

When I return to Minnesota, which I do frequently, I meet with many constituents, but none with more compelling stories than senior citizens struggling to make ends meet because of the high cost of prescription drugs, life-saving drugs that are not covered under the Medicare program. Ten or twenty years ago these same senior citizens were going to work every day—in the stores, and factories, and mines in Minnesota, earning an honest paycheck, and paying their taxes without protest. Now they wonder, how can this government, their government, stand by, when the medicines they need are out of reach.

It is not just that Medicare does not cover these drugs. The unfairness which Minnesotans feel is exacerbated, of course, by the high cost of prescription drugs here in the United States, the same drugs that can be purchased for frequently half the price in Canada or Europe. These are the exact same drugs, manufactured in the exact same facilities with the exact same safety precautions. A year ago, most Americans did not know that the exact same drugs are for sale at half the price in Canada. Today, you can bet the pharmaceutical industry wishes no one knew it. But the cat is out of the bag, and it is time for Congress to begin to address these inequities.

Legislators, especially from northern states but also from all around the country, have heard first-hand stories from constituents who are justifiably frustrated and discouraged when they can't afford to buy prescription drugs that are made in the United States, unless they go across the border to Canada where those same drugs, manufactured in the same facilities are available for about half the price. It is time to codify the right of Americans to go to Canada and certain other countries to buy the prescription drugs they need at a price they can afford. And it is time to allow Americans to obtain those necessary medications through the mail as well.

Driving to Canada every few months to buy prescription drugs at affordable prices isn't the solution; it is a symptom of how broken parts of our health care system are. Americans regardless of party have a fundamental belief in fairness, and know a rip-off when they see one. It is time to allow Americans to end-run that rip-off.

While we can be proud of both American scientific research that produces new miracle cures and the high standards of safety and efficacy that we expect to be followed at the FDA, it is shameful that America's most vulnerable citizens, the chronically ill and the elderly, are being asked to pay the highest prices in the world here in the U.S. for the exact same medications manufactured here but sold more cheaply overseas.

That is why today I am introducing with Senator Stabenow the Personal Prescription Drug Import Fairness Act, a bill which will amend the Food, Drug, and Cosmetic Act to allow Americans to legally import prescription drugs into the United States for their personal use as long as the drugs meet FDA's strict safety standards. With this legislation, Americans will be able to legally purchase these FDA-approved drugs in person or by mail at huge savings.

What this bill does is to address the absurd situation by which American consumers are paying substantially higher prices for their prescription drugs than are the citizens of Canada, and the rest of the industrialized world. This bill does not create any new federal programs. Instead it uses principles frequently cited in both houses of the Congress, principles of open trade and competition, on a personal level, to help make it possible for American consumers to purchase the prescription drugs they need.

The need is clear. A recent informal survey by the Minnesota Senior Federation on the price of six commonly used prescription medications showed that Minnesota consumers pay, on average, nearly double, 196 percent, than paid by their Canadian counterparts. These excessive prices apply to drugs manufactured by U.S. pharmaceutical firms, the same drugs that are sold for just a fraction of the U.S. price in Canada and Europe.

Now, however, federal law allows only the manufacturer of a drug to import it into the U.S. It is time to stop protecting the pharmaceutical industry's outrageous profits, and they are outrageous, and give all Americans the legal right to purchase their prescription drugs directly from a pharmacy in a limited number of countries with regulatory systems the FDA has found meet certain minimal standards.

Last year, the editors of *Fortune Magazine*, writing about 1999 pharmaceutical industry profits, noted that "Whether you gauge profitability by median return on revenues, assets, or equity, pharmaceuticals had a Viagra kind of year." In 2000, drug company profits were just as excessive.

Let's take a look at the numbers, so there can be no mistake:

Where the average Fortune 500 industry in the United States returned 4.5 percent profits as a percentage of revenue, the pharmaceutical industry returned 18.6 percent.

Where the average Fortune 500 industry returned 3.3 percent profits as a percentage of their assets, the pharmaceutical industry returned seventeen percent.

Where the average Fortune 500 industry returned 14.6 percent profits as a percentage of shareholders equity, the pharmaceutical industry returned 29.4 percent.

Those record profits are no surprise to America's senior citizens because they know where those profits come from, they come from their own pocketbooks. It is time to end the price gouging.

We need every piece of legislation we can get to help assure our senior citizens and all Americans that safe and affordable prescription medications can be legally obtained from countries with a track records of prescription drug safety. The Personal Prescription Drug Import Fairness Act is one such step.

We all know that the giant step this Congress should be taking is the enactment of a comprehensive Medicare prescription drug benefit. Such a benefit should address two issues. First, Medicare beneficiaries are entitled to a drug benefit as good as Congress provides for itself. That means a low deductible, twenty-percent copay, a cap on out-of-pocket expenses of about $2,000, and affordable premiums. Second, we need seriously to address the outrageously high prices that Americans are forced to pay for prescription drugs. If we address those high prices, we can provide a comprehensive benefit at a price that is affordable to Medicare beneficiaries and to the federal government. I have already introduced a bill, S. 925, the Medicare Extension of Drugs to Seniors Act of 2001, that provides affordable comprehensive benefits and makes it possible to enact them by reigning in the ever increasing cost of pharmaceuticals using three complimentary approaches.

But, while we wait for the Finance Committee and this Congress to act on a Medicare drug benefit, we should not lose the opportunity to provide some needed relief. That is why I am introducing the Personal Prescription Drug Import Fairness Act today.

This bill includes specific protections, which were not included in a recent House-passed amendment to the Agriculture Appropriations bill. These protections include: one, importation for personal use only of no more than a three month supply at any one time; two, limitation on country of origin; three, no importation of controlled substances or biologics; four, requirement that imported drug be accompanied by a form prescribed by the Secretary of HHS in consultation with the Secretary of the Treasury that makes clear what overseas pharmacy is dispensing the drug, who will be receiving it, and who will be responsible for the recipients medical care with the drug in the United States.

The only things that are not protected in this bill are the excessive profits of the pharmaceutical industry. My job as a United States senator is not to protect those profits but to protect the people. Colleagues, please join in and support this thoughtful and necessary bill that will help make prescription drugs more affordable to the American people.

3

MENTAL HEALTH AND CHEMICAL DEPENDENCY TREATMENT

> "What we were simply saying is, for gosh sakes, do not put people in a position where they cannot work because they will not get the coverage, and they have to be on medical assistance. Do not put people in a position where they could do well in school, but they cannot do well in school. Do not put people in a position where they are homeless, and they should not be homeless. Do not put people in a position where they wind up incarcerated, where that is not where they should be."   ~Senator Paul Wellstone, June 12, 1996

Conservative Republican Senator Pete Domenici of New Mexico became one of Senator Wellstone's closest allies in the fight to obtain parity for mental health and chemical dependency treatment. Struggling with the mental illness of a loved one was an issue that they both had in common. Senator Wellstone's brother, Stephen, had been hospitalized and treated for mental illness, and Senator Domenici's daughter had also struggled with mental illness.

They formed a "mental health working group" comprised of thirty-five senators, and, in 1996, Congress passed the first federal mental health parity law. The law, however, was far weaker than the legislation that Senator Wellstone and Senator Domenici wanted. In 2001, they proposed a new parity law. Although there were many calls to pass the legislation immediately in honor of Senator Wellstone after his death, the legislation was delayed and blocked. Eventually, in the spring of 2008, the new parity law passed the United States House of Representative.

MENTAL HEALTH PARITY
June 12, 1996

Mr. President, I rise to talk about what I hope will be a bipartisan approach, but I speak with a considerable amount of concern. I have worked very closely with my colleague from New Mexico, Senator Domenici, a Republican, and very closely with my colleague from Wyoming, Senator Simpson, on a mental health amendment to the insurance reform bill.

That amendment passed, Mr. President, by a sixty-eight-to-thirty vote. What that amendment said was that as we look at insurance reform, we do not mandate benefits, but once plans are put into motion, and once there is an agreement about a particular plan for employees or for citizens, this ought not to be discrimination against people who are struggling with mental illness, illness that is diagnosable and treatable. That amendment passed by a sixty-eight-to-thirty vote.

What we were simply saying is, for gosh sakes, do not put people in a position where they cannot work because they will not get the coverage, and they have to be on medical assistance. Do not put people in a position where they could do well in school, but they cannot do well in school. Do not put people in a position where they are homeless, and they should not be homeless. Do not put people in a position where they wind up incarcerated, where that is not where they should be.

Mr. President, we had strong bipartisan support. It then went to what will, hopefully, be a conference committee. It is with profound disappointment and some indignation that I say on the floor of the Senate that what has now happened on the part of my Republican colleagues on the House side is they have essentially knocked out the whole amendment.

Mr. President, working with Senator Domenici, Senator Simpson, people like Senator Conrad, we came up with a pared-down formulation that said at least for lifetime limits, at least for annual limits, have the same caps as for physical illness, so that people who are struggling with mental illness are not put under economically, so that people can receive the care that they need. We should end this discrimination.

This particular compromise would cost, according to CBO, 0.2 of a one-percent increase. That is it. Mr. President, there is no good policy reason, I say to my colleagues on the floor of the Senate today, there is no good policy reason why this compromise that we presented to members of the conference committee on the House Republican side should not have been accepted. It is fair. It is equitable. It economically makes sense. It is just. It is the right thing to do. There is not one single argument that can be made against it. Not one single argument that can be made against it.

Now what we hear on the House side from Republicans is that what we will get is a commission to study the problem. Senator Domenici does not consider that acceptable. I do not consider that acceptable. Senator Simpson does not consider that acceptable. That is not even the point. It is not acceptable for families all across this country who thought we were going to finally end this discrimination.

Mr. President, there will be a press conference this afternoon at two o'clock. A lot of the families, men and women and children who are struggling with mental illness, will be there. Several of us will be there. I think what they will say is they are going to visit with every member of that conference committee on the House side, Republican and Democrat alike. They are going to visit, I say to my good colleague from Mississippi, Senator Lott, they are going to visit with leadership, and they are going to say to leaders and they are going to say to Democrats and Republicans alike: "Tell us why it is still not time to end the discrimination. Tell us why you are unwilling to end this discrimination against our children, against our wives, against our husbands. Tell us when it is not time to end discrimination."

Mr. President, I say to my colleague from Mississippi, if I could get his attention, I want to mention this afternoon at two o'clock we will have a press conference with some wonderful families who have been struggling with mental illness. You know Senator Domenici cares so much about this. They are going to meet with leadership and say, "Look, [at] the formulation that we now came up with," not the commission. . . . It helps end the discrimination. Please do not shut our families out.

I hope you will give them your utmost consideration.

THE PASSAGE OF THE MENTAL HEALTH PARITY AMENDMENT

September 27, 1996

Yesterday, President Clinton signed the VA/HUD appropriation bill and the Mental Health Parity amendment which was included in the appropriated bill into law. For all of us who worked so hard to achieve passage of the parity amendment, the enactment of the provision represented more than the insurance policy changes that the provision will actually require.

Passage of the legislation is a symbol of fairness, progress, and hope for millions of Americans and their families who, for far too long, have been victims of discrimination—families who for far too long have been thrust into bankruptcy, or denied access to cost-effective treatments because their illness was a mental illness and not a physical illness like cancer or heart disease. Mental illness has, in one way or another, touched the lives of many of us who work here on Capitol Hill, and I am pleased that the 104th Congress was able to take this first and very necessary step toward parity.

I want to take this opportunity to say that while the passage of this amendment was a historic step forward for people with mental illnesses, the amendment was a fist step and a first step only. It does not require parity for copayments or deductibles or inpatient days or outpatient visit limits. It also does not include substance abuse services. My State of Minnesota has passed legislation, which goes much further than what we were able to accomplish in this Congress. Minnesota requires that health plans provide full parity coverage for mental health and substance abuse services. The cost impact of this legislation in Minnesota has been minimal according to a recent study based on preliminary data.

Without full parity coverage for mental health and substance abuse, health plans will continue to discriminate against individuals and families in need of services. The responsibility for and cost of care will continue to be shifted from the private to the public sector. For children and adolescents, the burden and cost of care will continue to be shifted to the child welfare, education, and juvenile justice systems. These overburdened systems are often not able to provide needed services, and many are forced to go without treatment. This will continue to be the case.

I have seen first hand in my state at facilities like Hazelden and others, the benefits that drug and alcohol treatment can bring to the lives of millions of Americans. Alcohol and other drug addictions affect ten percent of American adults and three percent of our youth. Untreated addiction last year alone cost this nation nearly 167 billion dollars. Ultimately, we all bear the cost of delays or gaps in mental health and substance abuse services. Sadly, that fact has not been changed by the passage of Senator Domenici's and my amendment.

We have much more work to do, and I look forward to consideration of legislation which would provide full parity coverage for mental health and substance abuse services. I am grateful for the advocacy, hard work, and compassion of the mental health and substance abuse community. Without them, we could not have achieved such success this year. This victory was made possible because families and friends of people struggling with mental illnesses were willing to speak out in public. This issue has a human face now and that made it possible to win votes and enact legislation.

MENTAL HEALTH EQUITABLE TREATMENT ACT OF 2001

March 15, 2001

Mr. President, I am pleased today to join my colleague from New Mexico once again to introduce a bill for fairness in health coverage for those with mental illness. The Mental Health Equitable Treatment Act of 2001 will take the critical next steps to ensure that private health insurance companies provide the same level of coverage for mental illness as they do for other diseases. This bill will be a major step toward ending the discrimination against people who suffer from mental illness.

In 1996, I was proud to introduce the Mental Health Parity Act, a law which broke new ground, placing mental health alongside other medical and surgical coverage for parity in insurance coverage. Although the 1996 bill was limited to parity in annual and lifetime limits in care, the message was clear: there is no place for discrimination against those with mental illness.

Since the Mental Health Parity Act became law, we have seen that the costs have remained low and manageable, but, unfortunately, we have also seen that employers and insurance companies have taken advantage of the gaps that remain in coverage for mental illness. Patients have faced increases in copayment and deductible costs, more problems in gaining access to care, fewer approvals for hospital stays and outpatient days, and refusals to cover care. The suffering of people with mental illness has grown, and the time to end this discrimination is now.

For too long, mental illness has been stigmatized as a character flaw, rather than as the serious disease that it is. As a result, people with mental illness are often ashamed and afraid to seek treatment, for fear that they will lose their jobs or friends, for fear that people will not recognize the suffering that they endure, for fear that they will not be able to receive help. We have all seen portrayals of mentally ill people as somehow different, as dangerous, or as frightening. Such stereotypes only reinforce the biases against people with mental illness. Can you imagine this type of portrayal of someone who has a cardiac problem, or who happens to carry a gene that predisposes them to diabetes? And yet, we have all known someone with a serious mental illness, within our families or our circle of friends, or in public life.

Many people have courageously come forward to speak about their personal experiences with their illness, to help us all understand better the effects of this illness on a person's life, the ways in which effective treatments have helped them, or, sadly, the ways in which a loved one died through suicide as a result of untreated mental illness. I commend those who speak out on this issue, for their honesty and courage to come forward about their experiences, to help the world to understand the reality of this disease.

The statistics concerning mental illness, and the state of health care coverage for adults and children with this disease are startling, and disturbing. A watershed in our understanding of the impact of mental disorders is the 1996 Global Burden of Disease, GBD, study, conducted for the World Bank and World Health Organization by experts at Harvard University.

The GBD defined a very useful concept, called the Disability Adjusted Life Year, DALY, which refers to healthy years of life lost to either disability or premature mortality. Based on this measure of disease burden, mental disorders—which are prevalent worldwide, often begin early in life, and frequently are characterized by recurrent episodes, as in depression, or chronicity, as in schizophrenia, produce a disproportionate share of DALYs, much of which is due to the disabling nature of mental illness. According to the GBD study, in the U.S. and throughout the developed world, depression is the leading cause of disability, and three other mental disorders are among the top ten causes of disability, bipolar disorder, schizophrenia, and obsessive-compulsive disorder.

The National Institute of Mental Health, a NIH research institute within the U.S. Department of Health and Human Services, describes serious depression as an extremely critical public health problem. More than eighteen million people in the United States will suffer from a depressive illness this year, and many will be unnecessarily incapacitated for weeks or months because their illness goes untreated. The cost to the nation is in the billions of dollars. The suffering of depressed people and their families is immeasurable.

The situation is worse for children. The 1998 Surgeon General's Report on Mental Health estimates that between five and nine percent of those under age eighteen have mental disorders so severe that they face overwhelming difficulties in their efforts to function well with their families, friends, and teachers. For children, mental illness carries a double burden: both the suffering of the disorder itself, as well as the lost period of healthy learning and social development needed to help children live up to their potential. The recent tragic episodes of violence in our schools remind us that inadequately treated emotional and behavioral disorders in our children can literally have lethal consequences in terms of suicide and murder.

Our investment in mental health research is paying off well. We know so much more now about brain disease, behavioral and emotional disorders, and treatment. But without access to care, such treatments cannot help those who are suffering from mental illness. We know from NIH-funded research that available medications and psychological treatments, alone or in combination, can help eighty percent of those with depression. But without adequate treatment, future episodes of depression may continue or worsen in severity. Yet, the steady decline in the quality and breadth of health care coverage is truly disturbing.

The inequities related to the status of mental disorders in health insurance is indisputable. The U.S. General Accounting Office issued a report in May 2000, that verified that despite passage of the 1996 mental health parity law, fourteen percent of employers failed to comply with even the limited protections required by that law. Of the eighty-six percent that did comply, most (eighty-seven percent) continued to limit their mental health benefits, thus violating the spirit, if not the letter, of the law.

In other words, the majority of employers who claim to provide mental health benefits restrict actual care through limitations on coverage or access, or by increasing the cost to the patient. And they do this despite the fact that costs are low. According to most reports on parity, including the most recent analysis requested by Congress from the National Advisory Mental Health Council, when mental health coverage is managed appropriately, premium increases can be as low as one-percent.

Yet inequities in coverage continue, despite the 1996 law and the numerous state laws that have tried without success to finally put an end to this health care discrimination. The discrimination continues despite the fact that there is no biomedical justification for differentiating serious mental illness from other serious and potentially chronic disorders, nor for judging mental disorders to be in any way less real or less deserving of treatment. What does exist and continues to grow is an extensive body of rigorous research that has demonstrated that treatment for mental disorders is both precise and cost-effective.

Although the costs for coverage have been shown to be low, the consequences of untreated mental illness in our society are very serious and far-reaching—especially when one looks at how it affects individuals, families, employers, corporations, social service systems, and criminal justice systems. I have seen firsthand in the juvenile corrections system what happens when mental illness is criminalized, when youth with mental illness are incarcerated for exhibiting symptoms of their illness. To treat ill people as criminals is outrageous and immoral. We must make treatment for this illness as available and as routine as treatment for any other disease. The discrimination must stop.

The Mental Health Equitable Treatment Act of 2001 is modeled after the Federal Employees Health Benefit Plan, and provides full parity for all categories of mental health conditions. Group health plans would be prohibited from imposing treatment limitations, including restricting numbers of visits or covered hospital days, or financial requirements, such as higher copayments, that are different from other medical/surgical benefits. This bill is a major step forward in coverage for mental illness by private health insurers. It does not require that mental health benefits be part of a health benefits package, but establishes a requirement for parity in coverage for those plans that offer mental health benefits. This bill goes a long way toward our bipartisan goal: that mental illness be treated like any other disease in health care coverage.

The Mental Health Equitable Treatment Act of 2001 is designed to take a large step toward ending the suffering of those with mental illness who have been unfairly discriminated against in their health coverage. The time to pass this bill is now.

4

DOMESTIC VIOLENCE AND VIOLENCE AGAINST WOMEN

> "Last year Congress passed the first most comprehensive package of legislation to address gender based violence— the Violence Against Women Act. It was a great step forward in stopping the cycle of violence. But, it is not enough. We cannot stop at reforming and improving the judicial system and think it will solve the problem. The entire community must be involved in the solution—we all must be involved in stopping the cycle of violence."
>
> ~Senator Paul Wellstone, March 9, 1995

Senator Wellstone's advocacy for programs that help the victims of domestic violence and prevent violence against women reflects the dedication and passion of his wife. Sheila Wellstone had spent twenty years focused on raising their children and working as an aide at the local high school library. Now, suddenly, a public figure, she dedicated herself to raising awareness about the issue. Over ten years, she became one of the nation's leading experts on the problem of domestic violence.

Sheila Wellstone played a key role in the drafting and passage of the Violence Against Women Act and other legislation, including legislation related to the trafficking of young women and girls for sex. She was also appointed by the U.S. Department of Justice and the U.S. Department of Health and Human Services to the Violence Against Women Advisory Council in 1995. Senator Wellstone often referred to his wife as his partner, and in no other area is this partnership more reflected than in Senator Wellstone's work to end domestic vilence and violence against women.

END THE STONEWALLING
June 29, 1994

Mr. President, yesterday, I held a press conference with representatives Torricelli, Schroeder, DeLauro, and Maloney from the House. Our focus was on the conference committee dealing with the crime bill. What we spoke to was the stonewalling, I am proud to say, not by Senate conferees but by some House conferees, on some family antiviolence provisions which we believe are critically important.

Mr. President, I speak on the floor today to convey the following message to some of my colleagues in the House on this committee. It is so crystal clear that it is time for the Congress to take domestic violence in our nation seriously, to understand that domestic violence is a crime, and to understand that it must be treated as such.

Mr. President, in November, the Senate approved, with the support of both Senator Biden and Senator Hatch, an amendment I introduced called the Domestic Violence Firearm Prevention Act. I wish to describe it for those who are listening.

It would, first of all, prohibit anyone who has been convicted for abusing a spouse or a child from owning or possessing a gun. It is very interesting, Mr. President, the National Rifle Association—and I am not on the floor, by the way, to attack the NRA at all—has said over and over again, look for us for support in making sure that guns are not in the hands of people who have committed crimes.

That is really what this amendment says.

It would prohibit anyone who has a restraining order issued against them from owning or possessing a gun. Finally, it would prohibit anyone from selling or giving a gun to someone they knew had been convicted of abusing a spouse or a child.

Mr. President, I have said it once. I have said it twice. I have said it ten times. All too often the only difference between a battered woman and a dead woman is the presence of a gun. Let me repeat that. All too often the only difference between a battered woman and a dead woman is the presence of a gun. We are trying to get the guns out of the hands of those people who have been convicted of an act of violence within their families. It is a most reasonable amendment.

This amendment was severely weakened on the House side. Statistics, Mr. President: every twelve seconds in the United States of America—FBI statistics—a woman is battered; every twelve seconds. Over 4,000 women are killed each year at the hands of their abusers. Please remember, Mr. President, this is the most underreported crime in America. An estimated 150,000 incidents of domestic violence involve a weapon. The *New England Journal of Medicine* in a recent article pointed out that with the history of battering, if there is a gun in the house or in the home, that woman is five times more likely to be murdered.

The problem is this: We have some conferees on the House side who are saying, yes, if somebody has been convicted of a felony, then of course, we would take a gun out of their hands. That is the law of the land. But domestic violence is a misdemeanor quite often. They are right. So if I or you or someone, God forbid, beat up our neighbor's wife, it would be a felony. If we beat up our own wife, it is a misdemeanor.

What happens in state after state after state, Mr. President, is that the charges that are brought against abusers are essentially limited and brought down to fifth-degree assault or misdemeanor charges. Even in those states which say domestic violence is indeed a felony, sometimes the standards are so strict, permanent physical impairment has to happen as a result of it, or there had to be a use of a weapon, or there have to be broken bones—what I am saying is the fact that we do not treat domestic violence seriously. We do not treat this violence against a spouse or a child as a felony. All too often we treat it as a misdemeanor, and, therefore, the perpetrators are able to continue to own a gun. Then what happens all too often, and it is tragic and it is unnecessary, is that a woman is no longer battered, she is dead.

We are just simply saying that under federal law we have a list of circumstances where we say you cannot own a gun or a firearm if you have committed a felony, and we should include domestic violence within this category.

Mr. President, it is amazing to me that this stonewalling is taking place on the part of the House conferees. There is such a disconnect to the position that some of them are taking and what people in the country are saying. I did not argue that this particular amendment is a be-all or end-all. But I am telling you one more time, it clearly is an important step in making the home a little bit safer place. It clearly is reasonable. It clearly speaks to some of the violence that is taking place, not just in our streets but in our homes. To me it is absolutely outrageous.

I give Senator Biden—and I know we are going to have Senator Hatch with us because he is supporting this—great credit. But we have to have this provision passed as a part of this crime bill.

Mr. President, if we pass the Violence Against Women Act provisions that Senator Biden has done such a great job for years and years in speaking about as a part of the crime bill, and we pass some of the other family violence provisions, whether it be safe visitation centers, whether it be getting the guns out of the hands of those people who have committed an act of violence against a spouse or child, we will be sending a very, very powerful and positive message to women in this country. This is the message: This violence is not your fault. There will be support for you in your community, and perpetrators will be held accountable.

I hope that the stonewalling ends, and I hope this provision is not dropped late at night. I know that we have support from Senate conferees. Hopefully we will have support from the House conferees. I am convinced that, if the House conferees hear from the public in this country about this amendment—and I know there is overwhelming support for it—it will be passed. But that is probably the only way it is going to happen, and that is why I speak on the floor today.

INTRODUCING THE VICTIMS OF ABUSE ACCESS TO HEALTH INSURANCE ACT
March 9, 1995

Mr. President, today I am introducing the Victims of Abuse Access to the Health Insurance Act. This bill would outlaw the practice of denying health insurance coverage to victims of domestic violence.

In Minnesota three insurance companies denied health insurance to an entire women's shelter because "as a battered women's program we

were high risk." The women's shelter in Rochester was told that it was considered uninsurable because its employees are almost all battered women.

A woman sought the services of Women House in St. Cloud because the abuse during her twelve-year marriage had escalated to such an extent that she was hospitalized for a broken jaw and spent two weeks in a mental health unit of a hospital. She was subsequently denied coverage by two insurance companies—one said they would not cover any medical or psychiatric problems that could be related to the past abuse.

These are just a couple examples of women who have been physically abused and sought proper medical care only to be turned away by insurance companies who say they are too high of a risk to insure.

Victims of domestic violence are being denied health insurance coverage. This is an abhorrent practice. It is plain old-fashioned discrimination. It is profoundly unjust and wrong. And, it is the worst of blaming the victim.

We must treat domestic violence as the crime that it is—not as voluntary risky behavior that can be easily changed and not as a pre-existing condition. Insurance company policies that deny coverage to victims only serve to perpetuate the myth that the victims are somehow responsible for their abuse.

Domestic violence is the single largest threat to women's health. Denying women access to much needed health care must be stopped.

The Victims of Abuse Access to Health Insurance Act is a very simple and straightforward bill. It would prohibit insurance companies from "engaging in a practice that has the effect of denying, canceling, or limiting health insurance coverage or health benefits, or establishing, increasing or varying the premium charged for the coverage or benefits" for victims of domestic violence.

It would prohibit insurance companies from considering domestic violence as a preexisting condition. Under the bill, domestic violence is defined as any violent act against a current or former member of the family or household, or someone with whom there has been or is an intimate relationship. This could mean spouse, partner, lover, boyfriend, or children. If an insurance company, or even a company that is large enough to self-insure, violates this act, it could be held civilly and criminally liable.

Reporting domestic violence and seeking medical help is often the first step in ending the cycle. Oftentimes health care providers are the first, and sometimes the only, professionals in a position to recognize violence in their patients' lives. Battered women should be encouraged to seek medical help. We should not be discouraging this by allowing insurance companies to use this information against them. Women should not have to fear that when they take that first step they could lose their access to treatment.

Doctors and other health care providers need to be encouraged to properly diagnose, treat, and document domestic violence. Denial of health insurance coverage will cause doctors not to document it accurately if only to protect the victim.

Domestic violence is the leading cause of injury to women, more common than auto accidents, muggings, and rapes by a stranger combined. It is the No. 1 reason women go to emergency rooms. And research indicates that violence against women escalates during pregnancy.

Last year during the health care reform debate, I raised this issue in the context of requiring insurance companies to make insurance available to all people who wanted it. We should certainly all be moving toward that goal. However, this is a real immediate need and it must be addressed.

Last year Congress passed the first most comprehensive package of legislation to address gender based violence—the Violence Against Women Act. It was a great step forward in stopping the cycle of violence. But, it is not enough. We cannot stop at reforming and improving the judicial system and think it will solve the problem. The entire community must be involved in the solution—we all must be involved in stopping the cycle of violence.

Insurance companies should not be allowed to discriminate against anyone for being a victim of domestic violence. This is an abhorrent practice and should be prohibited.

I urge my colleagues to support it.

THE SAFE HAVENS FOR CHILDREN ACT OF 1997
July 31, 1997

Mr. President, I rise today to introduce legislation that will provide safe havens for children who are members of families in which violence is a problem. I am pleased to have my distinguished colleague from Illinois, Mr. Durbin, join me in this effort.

The prevalence of family violence in our society is staggering. Studies show that twenty-five percent of all violence occurs among people who are related to one another. Data also indicate that the incidence of violence in families escalates during separation and divorce. In fact, over seventy percent of women who are treated for domestic violence in emergency departments have already separated from the person who has inflicted their injuries. Many of these assaults occur in the context of child visitation. This clearly places children at risk not only of witnessing violence, but also of becoming victims of violence within their own families. Children who are exposed to violence suffer many long-term effects of this exposure.

In addition to the obvious physical consequences of violence, there are innumerable psychosocial effects. For example, a child who learns from his parents, his role models, that violence is a way of resolving differences, or controlling another person, will grow up believing that it is normal to use violence in everyday interpersonal relationships. As a consequence, he will grow up believing that it is acceptable to physically hurt those people he loves the most. A young girl who watches her mother being beaten up by her father may come to understand that physical injury is just one aspect of a "normal" relationship. Children who are exposed to violence are at risk for mental health problems and substance abuse problems as they grow up. When we allow children to grow up believing that violence is normal and acceptable, we do a great deal of damage to their lives and decrease their chances for healthy futures.

In order to prevent the risk of exposure to violence, I am introducing this legislation, to provide funding for the creation of child safety centers. These centers will provide a safe environment in which children can visit with their parents without risk of being exposed to violence in the context of their family relationships. This bill will protect children from the trauma of witnessing or experiencing violence, sexual abuse, neglect, abduction, rape, or death during parent-child visitation or visitation exchanges, protect victims of violence from experiencing further violence during child visitation or visitation exchanges and will provide safe havens for children and their parents during visitation or visitation exchanges.

This act will provide grants to states to enable the states to enter into contract and cooperative agreements with public or private nonprofit entities in order to establish child safety centers. These centers will operate for the purpose of facilitating supervised visitation and visitation exchange. The services provided by the centers will be evaluated each year, so that we will learn how many people are served by the centers and what types of problems are encountered by the clients of the centers. The act will authorize appropriations of $65,000,000 for each of the fiscal years 1998 through 2000.

Mr. President, this legislation will go a long way in protecting children from family violence and in providing support for families that are experiencing violence. We need to do this to protect our children and give them the chance to grow up without believing that violence is normal.

THE VIOLENCE AGAINST WOMEN ACT II
May 21, 1998

Mr. President, I rise today as a proud co-sponsor of this Violence Against Women Act. I was a co-sponsor of the original Violence Against Women Act of 1994 and will work hard to see this Violence Against Women Act pass as well. As you well know my wife, Sheila, and I do a lot of work trying to reduce violence in homes. That is a big priority for us. And the passage of the 1994 Violence Against Women Act was a first big step and an historical occasion.

It was the culmination of over twenty-five years of hard work by local and national organizations. It was an acknowledgment that this kind of violence within families is everybody's business. It was the public recognition that for all too many women the home, rather than being a safe place, is a very dangerous place. And finally it sent a clear message that violence against women was a crime that would not be tolerated. It sent a clear message that we as a nation were committed to ending violence against women. At that time we thought we were introducing a comprehensive bill to end violence against women. We have learned a great deal since the passage of the first Act and with that knowledge we know we can and must do better.

We have also learned that violence against women is a multi-faceted problem that must be addressed in many ways. While the first act provided important funding to improve services to abused women and improve the criminal justice system, the statistics show we must do more. In my own state of Minnesota, at least seventeen women were killed in 1997 by their intimate partners. In that same year, over 4,000 women and over 5,000 children used domestic violence shelters in my state. I am sure that the provisions provided in VAWA allowed so many women to be served. I am sure that the provision in VAWA allowed law enforcement, in my state and across the country, to better address cases of domestic abuse. But now we must broaden our approach to this critical problem.

And so today we introduce the Violence Against Women Act II. This legislation not only reauthorizes and improves the initial commitment set forth in VAWA, but also addresses the impact of violence against women in areas of child visitation, sexual assault prevention, insurance discrimination, as well as violence in the workplace and on campuses. The initiatives in this bill, as I'm sure my colleague Joe Biden will attest, were developed as part of a collaborative effort with researchers, advocates and service providers alike. Seeing the problems that victims face on a daily basis, they have helped us to develop legislation that will assist women who have been victims of violence.

I have worked hard at addressing the severe economic consequences of domestic abuse on working women and am proud to say that VAWA II includes provisions to ensure access to family and medical leave coverage. With the passage of this act women will be allowed to be absent from

work so that they can deal with the domestic violence in their lives. Under this legislation, victims of abuse could use family and medical leave to attend court hearings and go to appointments with health care providers. In addition this legislation specifies that unemployment compensation should be provided if employment is terminated due to domestic abuse. If a woman loses her job because of the abuse she is experiencing in her home then she will be assured access to unemployment compensation. In other words, this legislation addresses the fact that the cycle of violence will not be interrupted unless victims of abuse are assured of economic security and independence.

Another facet of domestic violence that has been recognized since the passage of the 1994 Violence Against Women Act is the discrimination that victims of abuse face. I have worked hard at ending discrimination by insurance companies against victims of abuse and am proud to be able to say that this issue is well addressed in VAWA II. After years of work by advocates, encouraging women to come forward and report their abuse, we now find that they are being discriminated against based on their status as victims of that abuse. We all know that denying women access to insurance they need to foster their mobility out of an abusive situation must be stopped. Under this legislation insurance companies could no longer discriminate against victims of abuse in any line of insurance.

And finally, I would just like to mention the provision to provide safe havens for children. It is time we address the danger that children and victims of abuse are subjected to during visitation sessions with former partners. Let us stop further violence from occurring by providing safe centers for children who are members of families in which violence is a problem. These centers will provide a safe environment in which children can visit with their parents without risk of being exposed to violence in the context of their family relationships. These centers will also save the lives of mothers by providing secure and supervised environments where they can drop off their children to visit with their abusers. Stopping the cycle of violence means providing safe places for women and children inside and outside the home.

While we worked hard in the first Violence Against Women Act to make streets and homes safer for women by investing in law enforcement initiatives, we have learned that a woman's safety is dependent on her ability to achieve economic as well as physical security. The measures that I have mentioned are only some of the pieces that show the comprehensive nature of this bill. It is a reflection of what we have learned and the acknowledgment that we can and must do better. The Violence Against Women Act II is an impressive piece of legislation that deserves serious attention in this Congress. I look forward to the hearings and debates on this bill and look forward to working on and seeing it pass.

VICTIMS OF TRAFFICKING AND VIOLENCE PROTECTION ACT OF 2000
October 11, 2000

I thank my colleague, Senator Brownback, for his very gracious remarks. It has been an honor to work with him on this legislation. I think a very strong friendship has come out of this effort. There are some times when we can work and reach out and have the most interesting and I hope important coalition. Working with Senator Brownback, Sharon Payt, and Karen Knutson has been the best legislative work.

At the end of the day, I believe today we will pass this legislation. Members can feel they have done something really good. They can make a positive difference. I thank Senator Brownback

for his great leadership and his great work for each step along the way. In all the negotiations, all the work that has been done, the Senator has been there. I thank the Senator.

I want to talk about Charlotte Oldham-Moore and Jill Hickson, who have worked with me and our staff, who have done a great job. There are other people who will be on the floor who put this together—especially the Violence Against Women Act—Senator Leahy, Senator Biden, Senator Hatch, and others, and Sam Gejdenson and Chris Smith have been phenomenal. I thank them for their yeoman work on the House side. I also thank Frank Loy and Harold Koh at the State Department for their work.

The trafficking of human beings for forced prostitution and sweatshop labor is a rapidly growing human rights abuse. It is one of the greatest aspects of the globalization of the world economy. The Victims of Trafficking and Violence Protection Act of 2000 is the first piece of legislation to address the widespread practice of the trafficking of men, women, and children into sweatshop labor and sexual bondage.

My wife, Sheila, urged me to do something about this problem several years ago. Consequently, she and I spent time with women trafficked from the Ukraine to work in brothels in Western Europe and the United States. They told us after the breakup of the Soviet Union and the ascendancy of the mob, trafficking in women and girls became a booming industry that destroyed the lives of the youngest and most vulnerable in their home countries.

We began work on the bill then, and three years later, after extraordinary bipartisan effort, tremendous leadership from Senators Brownback and Leahy, and Sam Gejdenson and Chris Smith, and others, it passed the House with a vote of 371 to 1. Now it is poised to pass the Senate.

Our Government estimates that two million people are trafficked each year. Of those, 700,000 women and children, primarily young girls, are trafficked from poor countries to rich countries and sold into slavery, raped, locked up, physically and psychologically abused, with food and health care withheld. Of those, as many as 50,000 immigrants are brought into the United States each year, and they wind up trapped in brothels, sweatshops, and other types of forced labor, abused and too fearful to seek help.

Traffickers exploit the unequal status of women and girls, including harmful stereotypes of women as property and sexual objects to be bought and sold. Traffickers have also taken advantage of the demand in our country and others for cheap, unprotected labor. For the traffickers, the sale of human beings is a highly profitable, low-risk enterprise as these women are viewed as expendable and reusable commodities.

Overall, profit in the trade can be staggering. It is estimated that the size of this business is seven billion dollars annually, only surpassed by that of the illegal arms trade. Trafficking has become a major source of new income for criminal rings. It is coldly observed that drugs are sold once while a woman or a child can be sold ten or twenty times a day.

In the United States, Thai traffickers who incarcerated Thai women and men in sweatshops in El Monte, California, are estimated to have made eight million dollars in six years. Further, Thai traffickers who enslaved Thai women in a New York brothel made about 1.5 million dollars over one year and three months.

Last year, Albanian women were kidnapped from Kosovo refugee camps and trafficked to work in brothels in Turkey and Europe. Closer to home, organized crime has trafficked Russian and Ukrainian women into sexually exploitive work in dozens of cities in the United States of America. Just next door, law enforcement authorities suspected mafia involvement in the gruesome murder of a Russian woman trafficked to Maryland.

All of these cases reflect a new condition: Women whose lives have been disrupted by civil wars or fundamental changes in political geography, such as the disintegration of the Soviet Union or the violence in the Balkans, have fallen prey to traffickers.

Seeking financial security, many innocent persons are lured by traffickers' false promises of a better life and lucrative jobs abroad. Seeking this better life, they are lured by local advertisements for good jobs in foreign countries at wages they could never imagine at home. However, when they arrive, these victims are often stripped of their passports, held against their will, some in slave-like conditions, in the year 2000.

Rape, intimidation, and violence are commonly employed by traffickers to control their victims and to prevent them from seeking help. Through physical isolation and psychological trauma, traffickers and brothel owners imprison women in a world of economic and sexual exploitation that imposes a constant threat of arrest and deportation, as well as violent reprisals by the traffickers themselves to whom the women must pay off ever-growing debts. That is the way this works.

Many brothel owners actually prefer foreign women, women who are far from help and from home, who do not speak the language, precisely because of the ease of controlling them. Most of these women never imagined they would enter such a hellish world, having traveled abroad to find better jobs or to see the world.

Many in their naiveté believe nothing bad can happen to them in the rich and comfortable countries such as Switzerland or Germany or the United States. Others are less naive, but they are desperate for money and opportunity. But they are no less hurt by the trafficker's brutal grip.

Trafficking rings are often run by criminals operating through nominally reputable agencies. In some cases overseas, police and immigration officials of other nations participate and benefit from the trafficking. Lack of awareness or complacency among government officials such as border control and consular offices contributes to the problem. Furthermore, traffickers are rarely punished, as official policies often inhibit victims from testifying against their traffickers, making trafficking a highly profitable, low-risk business venture for some.

Trafficking abuses are occurring not just in far-off lands but here at home in America as well. The INS has discovered 250 brothels in twenty-six different cities which involve trafficking victims. This is from a CIA report. This is the whole problem of no punishment—being able to do this with virtual impunity.

In a 1996 trafficking case involving Russian and Ukrainian women who answered ads to be au pairs, sales clerks and waitresses, and were forced to provide sexual services and live in a massage parlor in Bethesda, Maryland, the Russian-American massage parlor owner was fined. He entered a plea bargain and charges were dropped with the restriction that he would not operate a business again in Montgomery County. The women, who had not been paid any salary and were charged $150 for their housing, were deported or left the United States voluntarily. There was no charge at all.

Teenage Mexican girls were held in slavery in Florida and the Carolinas, and they were forced to submit to prostitution.

Russian and Latvian women were forced to work in nightclubs in the Midwest. According to charges filed against the traffickers, the traffickers picked the women up upon their arrival at the air-port, seized their documents and return tickets, locked them in hotels and beat them. This is in our country. The women were told that if they refused to work in sexually exploitive conditions, the Russian Mafia would kill their families. Furthermore, over a three-year period, hundreds of women from the Czech Republic who answered advertisements in Czech newspapers for modeling were ensnared in an illegal prostitution ring.

Trafficking in persons for labor is an enormous problem as well. The INS has also worked on cases involving South Asian children smuggled into the United States to work in slavery-like conditions. In one case, about 100 Indian children, some of them as young as nine or ten, were brought into New York and shuffled around the country to work in construction and restaurants—ages nine and ten, in the United States; today, in the United States—2000.

Some of the children appear to have been sold by their parents to the traffickers. In Woodbine, Maryland, a pastor bought Estonian children, ages fourteen to seventeen, promising them they would attend Calvary Chapel Christian Academy, but then forcing them to clean roach-invested apartments and to do construction. The children worked fifteen hours a day. The children were threatened and punishments included denial of food and being forced to stand in one spot for prolonged periods.

The bitter irony is that quite often victims are punished more harshly than the traffickers because of their illegal immigration status, their serving as prostitutes, or their lack of documents, which the traffickers have confiscated in order to control the victims.

A review of the trafficking cases showed that the penalties were light and did not reflect the multitude of human rights abuses perpetrated against these women.

In a Los Angeles case, traffickers kidnapped a Chinese woman, raped her, forced her into prostitution, posted guards to control her movements, and burned her with cigarettes. Nevertheless, the lead defendants received four years and the other defendants received two and three years. That is what they received.

In a tragic case involving over seventy Thai laborers who had been held against their will, systematically abused, and made to work twenty-hour shifts in a sweatshop, the seven defendants received sentences ranging from four to seven years with one defendant receiving seven months.

In another case where Asian women were kept physically confined for years with metal bars on the windows, guards, and an electronic monitoring system, and were forced to submit to sex with as many as 400 customers to repay their smuggling debt, the traffickers received four years and nine years—in the United States of America, in the year 2000.

I thank Senator Brownback for his work. It is important.

A review of the trafficking cases showed that the penalties were light, and they did not reflect the multitude of the human rights abuses perpetrated against these women. The statutory minimum for sale into involuntary servitude is only ten years, whereas the maximum for dealing in small quantities of certain drugs is life.

Let me repeat that. The statutory minimum for sale into involuntary servitude is only ten years, whereas the maximum for dealing in small quantities of certain drugs is life.

Few state and federal laws are aimed directly at people who deliver or control women for the purpose of involuntary servitude or slavery in sweatshops or brothels. Consequently, prosecutors are forced to assemble cases using a hodgepodge of laws, such as document fraud and interstate commerce, and accept penalties that they believe are too light for the offense. Up until this legislation, there was no way for the prosecutors to go after these traffickers.

The Victims of Violence and Trafficking Protection Act of 2000 establishes, for the first time, a bright line between the victim and the perpetrator. It punishes the perpetrator and provides a comprehensive approach to solving the root problems that create millions of trafficking victims each year.

This legislation aims to prevent trafficking in persons, provide protection and assistance to those who have been trafficked, and strengthen prosecution and punishment for those who are responsible for the trafficking. It is designed to help federal law enforcement officials expand antitrafficking efforts here and abroad, to expand domestic antitrafficking and victim assistance efforts, and to assist nongovernment organizations, governments and others worldwide, who are providing critical assistance to victims of trafficking. It addresses the underlying problems which fuel the trafficking industry by promoting public antitrafficking awareness campaigns and initiatives in other countries to enhance economic opportunity, such as microcredit lending programs and skills training, for those who are most susceptible to trafficking, and have an outreach so women and girls as young as ten and eleven know what they might be getting into.

It also increases protections and services for trafficking victims by establishing programs designed to assist in the safe reintegration of victims into their communities and ensure that such programs address both the physical and mental health needs of trafficking victims.

Imagine what it would be like to be age twelve or thirteen, a young girl, to go through this. We have, in Minnesota, the Center for the Treatment of Torture Victims. It is a holy place. I have had an opportunity to meet with staff and meet with many men and women who have been helped by this center. These girls, these women, have gone through the same living hell.

This legislation also increases protections and services for trafficking victims by providing community support. Furthermore, the bill seeks to stop the practice—and this is so important. I am sitting next to Senator Kennedy who has done so much with the immigration work. This bill seeks to stop the practice of immediately deporting the victims back to potentially dangerous situations by providing them with some interim immigration relief. Victims of "severe forms of trafficking," defined as people who were held against their will—"for labor or services through the use of force, fraud, or coercion for the purpose of subjection to involuntary servitude, peonage, debt bondage or slavery"—would be eligible for a special visa letting them stay in the country at least through the duration of their captors' prosecution, and perhaps permanently.

Right now, if you are a Ukrainian girl or woman in a massage parlor in Bethesda, and you step forward to get some help, you are deported. The trafficker is hardly prosecuted. The victim is automatically deported. This provides temporary visa protection.

I will give an example. In a 1996 trafficking case involving Russian and Ukrainian women who had answered ads to be au pairs, sales clerks, and waitresses but were forced to provide sexual services and live in a massage parlor in Bethesda, Maryland, two miles from here, the Russian American massage parlor owner was fined. He entered a plea bargain and charges were dropped with the restriction that he would not operate his business again in Montgomery County. The women, who had not been paid any salary, were forced into prostitution, and were charged for their housing, were deported.

This legislation toughens current federal trafficking penalties, criminalizing all forms of trafficking in persons and establishing punishment commensurate with the heinous nature of this crime. The bill establishes specific laws against trafficking. Violators can be sentenced to prison for twenty years to life, depending on the severity of the crime. Yes, if you are trafficking a young girl and forcing her into prostitution, you can face a life sentence. They can also be forced to make full restitution to their victims, paying them the salary that would have been due for their months or years of involuntary service.

This bill requires expanded reporting on trafficking, including a separate list of countries which are not meeting minimum standards for the elimination of trafficking.

It requires the President to suspend "nonhumanitarian and nontrade" assistance to only the worst violators on the list of countries which do not meet these minimum standards and who actively condone this human rights abuse. This is a major piece of human rights legislation. This is a major human rights bill.

These are the rare governments which are openly complicit in trafficking people across their borders. It allows the Congress to monitor closely the progress of countries in their fight against trafficking, and it gives the administration flexibility to couple its diplomatic efforts to combat trafficking with targeted enforcement action. Finally, the bill provides three generous waivers.

By passing the Victims of Violence and Trafficking Act today, this Chamber will take a historic step toward the elimination of trafficking in persons.

Thanks to the partnership of Jewish and Evangelical groups, women and human rights organizations, and others, we will take a historic and effective step against organized crime rings and corrupt public officials who each year traffic more than two million people into desperate, broken lives of bondage and servitude.

Something important is in the air when such a broad coalition of people, including Bill Bennett, Gloria Steinem, Rabbi David Sapperstein, Ann Jordan, and Chuck Colson work together for the passage of this legislation. I am thankful for their support, I am thankful for the support of the administration, and I am thankful for your support today in seeking to end this horrible, widespread, and growing human rights abuse.

By way of conclusion, I say to my colleagues, starting with Senator Brownback, I believe with passage of this legislation—I believe it will pass today and the President will sign it—we are lighting a candle. We are lighting a candle for these women and girls and sometime men forced into forced labor. I also think because of the work of so many in the House and the Senate, this can be a piece of legislation that other governments in other parts of the world can pass as well. This is the beginning of an international effort to go after this trafficking, to go after this major, god-awful human rights abuse, this horrible exploitation of women, sometimes men, and of girls.

I am very proud of this legislation. I thank my colleague from Kansas. I thank other colleagues as well.

INTRODUCTION OF THE CHILDREN WHO WITNESS DOMESTIC VIOLENCE ACT
October 2, 2001

Mr. President, I introduce this legislation today because, as I have said before, nowhere is violence more isolated from view, more difficult to combat and more far reaching in its impact than violence in the home. To turn a blind eye to the suffering of the victims of domestic violence and their children is to be, however unwittingly, complicitous in the crime because it is out of sight and behind closed doors that domestic violence thrives.

This bill reflects the fact that the effects of domestic violence extend far beyond the moment when violence occurs. One of the most compelling marks that violence against women leaves is on our children. I am reminded of the voice of Quinese Robinson, a teenager from Minneapolis, who just last year, came home to find that her mother's husband had brutally murdered her mother. Quinese simply said, "My mom is the most important person in our life. When he killed her, he basically killed all four of us because we do not have a mother."

This is one story among millions. It is estimated that as many as ten million children witness violence in the home each year, and much of this violence is repetitive. As many as seventy percent of children who witness domestic violence are also victims of child abuse. If we are serious about helping children and reducing youth violence, we cannot ignore the impact of domestic violence on children.

Studies indicate that children who witness their fathers beating their mothers suffer emotional problems, including slowed development, sleep disturbances, and feelings of hopelessness, depression, and anxiety. Many of these children exhibit more aggressive, anti-social, and fearful behaviors. They also show lower social competence than other children.

Children in homes where their mothers were abused have also shown less skill in understanding how others feel when compared to children from non-violent households. Even one episode of violence can produce post-traumatic stress disorder in children. Children who witness domestic violence are at higher risk of suicide.

Jeffrey Edleson and others at the Minnesota Center Against Violence and abuse at the

University of Minnesota collected multiple studies on the devastating results of this trauma. The examples are painful, but they deserve telling. One four-year-old girl named Julie witnessed her father stab her mother to death. In describing the event, Julie consistently placed her father at the scene of the crime and recounted her father's efforts to clean up after the crime. She could not describe her father's actions but when the district attorney saw Julie stabbing a pillow and crying "Daddy pushed Mommy down," he was sure that the father had committed the crime.

A child who was being treated at San Francisco General Hospital saw his father cut his mother's throat. For a period of time after the crime, the child could not speak.

Not surprisingly, Edleson found that children growing up in violent families are more likely to engage in youth violence and that the social and economic risk factors for youth violence correspond to the risk factors for domestic violence and child abuse.

The Office of Juvenile Justice and Delinquency Prevention at the U.S. Department of Justice identifies family violence as a major risk factor in the lives of serious, violent and chronic juvenile offenders. It is estimated that as many as forty percent of violent juvenile offenders come from homes where there is domestic violence.

In addition to increasing violence, witnessing domestic violence directly hinders school achievement. Child witnesses have higher incidences of impaired concentration, poor school attendance, being labeled an underachiever, and difficulties in cognitive and academic functioning.

As this overwhelming research indicates, domestic violence and violence against women permeate our entire society. People who try to keep family violence quiet and hidden behind the walls of the home ignore its tragic echoes in the hearts and minds of our children, in our schools, on the streets and in our human relationships.

In the face of this devastating situation, I call on my colleagues to say to these child witnesses around the country that they will not suffer in silence, for that is what their abusers want them to do. Their cries will not be muffled behind closed doors and by the fear inflicted by abusive parents. We need to provide these children with a way out of violence and a way to deal with the pain of violence.

This bill represents a modest step to address this devastating problem. I urge my colleagues, in the names of all of these children, to support this critical legislation.

5

MEDICARE AND SOCIAL SECURITY

> "For my mother and father, neither of whom are alive, Leon and Minnie, the Medicare Program, I think, was the difference at the end of their lives between dignity and just economic disaster. It is a terribly important program."
> ~Senator Paul Wellstone, July 27, 1995

In 1994, just two years after President Clinton was elected, the Democrats lost control of both the House and Senate. It was a major set back for President Clinton. Often referred to as "The Republican Revolution," the Democrats lost fifty-four seats in the House and eight seats in the Senate. Congressman Newt Gingrich became the first Republican Speaker of the House in forty years, and immediately began implementing the Republican's Contract with America.

On January 23, 1995, during his third State of the Union Address, President Clinton began implementing a strategy called "triangulation." He attempted to position himself between the new Republican majority on the right and the Congressional Democrats on the left. In that speech, he declared, famously, that "the era of big government is over."

Medicare and Social Security were considered by many to be the epitome of "big government." Senator Wellstone, however, viewed both programs differently. He spoke often about the important role that Medicare and Social Security played in preventing poverty, and he fought efforts by the new Republican majority to privatize or dismantle either program.

MEDICARE'S THIRTIETH ANNIVERSARY
July 27, 1995

Mr. President, on July 30, 1965, President Lyndon Baines Johnson traveled to Independence, Missouri, and he signed Medicare into law. That simple ceremony marked the beginning of a new era of health and economic security for America's seniors.

Prior to Medicare, only half of America's elderly had health insurance. Today, more than thirty-six million elderly and disabled Americans, including more than 630,000 Minnesotans, are protected by Medicare. Mr. President, Medicare is a program with overwhelming support in Minnesota among seniors, their children, their grandchildren, and all Minnesotans.

Many of us remember what it was like for seniors before Medicare. Many seniors lost everything paying for necessary health care, and many others simply went without it.

Mr. President, the Medicare Program, imperfections and all, made the United States of America a better country. Prior to Medicare, what often happened was that as people became elderly and no longer worked, they then lost their health care coverage. Many people could not afford good health care.

This was a program, along with Medicaid, that made our country more compassionate. It made our country a fairer country. It made our country a more just country.

I can say, Mr. President, having had two parents with Parkinson's disease—and the Presiding Officer and I have talked about Parkinson's disease before, and we both have a very strong interest and support for people who are struggling; I think the Presiding Officer has a family connection also with Parkinson's disease— for my mother and father, neither of whom are alive, Leon and Minnie, the Medicare Program, I think, was the difference at the end of their lives between dignity and just economic disaster. It is a terribly important program.

Mr. President, Medicare also is important to Minnesotans because we, as a state, I think, have had a great deal to do with its creation. Hubert Humphrey, Walter Mondale, and Don Fraser, among others, worked tirelessly on its creation.

This was a project of countless Minnesotans, advocates for seniors from all across our state, our universities, our communities, all came together during the early part of the decade of the 1960s, and finally culminating in 1965 on July 30, when we passed this hallmark legislation.

In many ways, I argue today on the floor of the Senate, Medicare is a product of Minnesota. It reflects Minnesotans' values. It reflects the tradition of my state: A tradition of respect for seniors and a commitment to those members of our community who need a helping hand. As Hubert Humphrey, a great Senator, said in support of Medicare, "Our country's strength is in the health of our people." That was the premise of the Medicare Program.

This year, the thirtieth anniversary of the Medicare Program, all too many Republicans have resolved to cut the program by 270 billion dollars over the next six years. While the budget deficit clearly needs to be reduced, the Republican proposal to finance a tax cut to the tune of 245 billion dollars—most of it going to high-income and wealthy people—and at the same time putting into effect severe and, I think, draconian cuts in the Medicare Program, a program which has played such a central role in improving both access to and quality of health care services for our country's elderly and disabled, is unacceptable, I argue—and we will have a debate about this, as time goes on—and unconscionable.

Mr. President, while I believe the Medicare Program could and should be improved, I want to be quite clear that I do not think that this program will be improved by cutting 270 billion dollars over the next six years.

Mr. President, a dramatic restructuring of Medicare not based on sound public policy would be a grave mistake. A dramatic restructuring of Medicare of the kind that has been proposed now by too many Republicans, not based on sound policy, would not be a step forward for Medicare beneficiaries in Minnesota or across the country, but would be a huge step backward.

Republicans have proposed, Mr. President, to fundamentally change the program from universal health insurance for seniors to a fixed amount of cash, which each Medicare beneficiary could use to purchase coverage in the marketplace. This would effectively transfer the risk of Medicare inflation and medical inflation to the elderly, in order to relieve the government from bearing the risk.

Mr. President, seniors would be expected to pay the difference between the cost of a health plan and the Medicare voucher amount. The elderly in our country, Mr. President, already pay four times more out-of-pocket expenses for medical costs than those under sixty-five years of age. This does not include the enormous cost of nursing homes, which is now nearly $40,000 a year.

While Republicans claim that they want to use a voucher system to emulate the health care cost containment successes of the private sector, they neglect to mention that their budget cuts will only allow Medicare costs to grow at a rate of less than five percent per person, while private health care costs are projected to grow at a rate of seven percent per person. Those are exactly the figures. That is exactly the information.

Mr. President, that means that even if the Medicare Program, which cares for the sickest and the frailest members of our society—the same members, I might add, Mr. President, who have been systematically excluded by the insurance companies from coverage because of preexisting conditions—even if Medicare can capture all of the efficiencies of the private sector, there still would not be enough money to cover the costs of this program.

Mr. President, Minnesotan providers have already suffered from inadequate payments for Medicare. For example, Minnesota's HMOs are currently offered inadequate payments for the Medicare population. As a result, many of our HMOs have declined to participate in the Medicare Program on a capitated basis. Minnesota, compared to California, compared to New York, compared to Florida, sometimes only receives half of the reimbursement per person.

Mr. President, what I am saying is that we, in Minnesota, have kept the inefficiencies out of the system. We have already cut the fat. If these payments come to Minnesota, capitated at a fixed amount way under the cost of providing care to beneficiaries under a voucher-type scenario, seniors will be forced either to pay more out of pocket—and we are not talking about a high-income population when we talk about the elderly in Minnesota or in our country—or they will have to go without coverage.

Mr. President, beyond the impact of Medicare cuts felt by seniors and the disabled communi-ty, we will all pay the costs of Medicare indirectly. We will pay it in one of two ways: Either as children or grandchildren, we will have to help pay the costs of our elderly parents or grandparents.

Many families are already under a tremendous amount of economic pressure. The bottom seventy-percent of the population has been losing ground economically over the last fifteen years. I think it is rather naive to believe that families will have a lot of extra income to pay this additional cost.

Or, when the hospitals, clinics, and doctors are in a position to do so, and I do not blame them for this, they will just shift the costs. It is like Jell-O. Put your finger in one part of the Jell-O and it just shifts. What they will do, since the Medicare reimbursement will be significantly under the cost of providing care —that is already the case in Minnesota—these cuts will not work in my state, I tell members now. This slash-and-burn approach will not work in Minnesota. It will not only hurt Medicare beneficiaries. It will also hurt care givers and providers and, in addition, those care givers and providers in the metro area, if they can, will shift the cost of private health insurance. Then the premiums will go up, then the employers will have a difficult time carrying insurance, and more will be dropped from coverage.

This is crazy public policy that some people are advocating around here.

Mr. President, Medicare Dependent Hospitals, which have a Medicare load of sixty-percent or more have significantly lower overall margins than other hospitals, and will face two choices: Either those hospitals will close down or they will have to reduce services.

Minnesota has four Medicare-dependent hospitals in the urban areas, and we have forty of those Medicare dependent hospitals in the rural areas. In addition, forty-three percent of Minnesota's hospitals currently lose money on

Medicare patients. If the proposed Medicare cuts are enacted, sixty-seven percent of Minnesota's hospitals would lose money on Medicare patients.

Small, isolated rural hospitals require a stable funding source in order to provide care . I will tell you right now, in many of our smaller communities, in many of our greater Minnesota communities, in many of the communities in rural America, what is going to happen is that those hospitals with a Medicare patient mix of sometimes up to eighty percent are simply not going to be able to make it. And when those clinics and hospitals close, that means not just Medicare recipients but other citizens as well do not receive the care that they need.

Medicare has come to symbolize this nation's commitment to health and financial security for our elderly citizens and their families. It is a successful program that has played a central role in improving both access to and quality of health care services, not only for our country's elderly and disabled, but for all of us. We are talking about our parents and our grandparents.

Mr. President, I will, as we go to the thirtieth anniversary of Medicare, vigorously oppose all efforts or any effort to dismantle a Medicare system in order to give a tax cut that will disproportionately benefit those people who need it the least.

Let me repeat that. I will resist any effort to dismantle the Medicare Program in this country in order to give tax cuts to those citizens who, in fact, least need the financial assistance.

Thirty years ago, Medicare was part of a Democratic vision for a better America. Mr. President, today it still is. I come from a state that has made an enormous contribution to our nation. I come from a state that has made a contribution through a great Senator and a great Vice President, Hubert Humphrey—Hubert Humphrey and Walter Mondale and Don Fraser—and Minnesota

had a lot to do with the beginning of the Medicare Program and with support for this program, which has made such a positive difference in the lives of people, our senior citizens around this country. I intend to fight hard to make sure that we keep this as a high quality program.

My mother and father depended on this program. They are no longer alive, but for them, if not for Medicare it would have been financial disaster. So I do not intend to see this program dismantled—not on my watch as a Senator from Minnesota. And the more we get into this debate, the more people in Minnesota and all across this country are going to say: Senators, whether you are Democrats or Republicans, this is unacceptable and unconscionable. Do not be cutting Medicare, do not be cutting Medicare and quality of services for elderly people in our country, all for the sake of tax cuts for wealthy people in our country. There is no standard of fairness to that.

PRIVITIZATION OF SOCIAL SECURITY
June 10, 1998

Mr. President, I also, if I could, want to take just a few minutes to speak about Social Security, about its future, and about a campaign under way to trade it in for a privatized system like the one we have in Chile.

President Clinton has called for a nationwide debate on Social Security for the balance of this year, to be followed by a White House conference in December and legislative action early next year. I think it is time—perhaps well past time—for the defenders of Social Security to speak up and be heard.

As far as I am concerned, Social Security is one of America's proudest accomplishments of the twentieth century. It has given retirement security to Americans of all ages and has rescued millions of seniors from the scourge of poverty. Everyone says they want to protect and preserve this remarkably efficient and effective program which is so beloved by the American people. But you would never know it, judging from the direction the debate is taking.

The premise of the debate is that Social Security is on the verge of bankruptcy and must be transformed in order to survive. I strongly disagree. Social Security is not in crisis. It is not broke. It is not facing bankruptcy. It may need some modest adjustments, but the greatest dangers facing Social Security today are the many misguided proposals to "fix" it.

You can hardly open a newspaper these days without reading about the impending collapse of Social Security. This is nonsense. Social Security is now taking in 101 billion dollars more each year than it pays out in benefits.

In April, the Social Security trustees reported that the trust funds will be able to cover benefits for the next thirty-four years, until the year 2032. After that, without any changes to the system, it will still be able to pay out seventy to seventy-five percent of the promised benefits, virtually indefinitely without any change whatever in the system. There is no reason why Social Security should come to an abrupt end in 2032 or any time thereafter.

Some would seize upon this projected funding imbalance decades from now as an excuse to undermine the program. They want to replace Social Security with a privatized system in which retirement security depends solely on success in playing the financial markets. But why would we want to get rid of a program that has worked so well? Why should we want to "end Social Security as we know it?" In fact, that's what I think some of these proposals should be called—"ending Social Security as we know it."

If we really want to protect and preserve Social Security, we should be guided by two principles. First, we should focus all of our energies on the real problem, which is a possible imbalance in the trust funds after the year 2032. Second, under no circumstances should we allow funding for Social Security to be squandered on the fees, commissions, and overhead of Wall Street middlemen.

There are a number of ways to go about this. Several prominent economists have come forward with detailed reform packages that would guarantee long-term balance of the trust funds. Other proposals will be coming out soon. These are relatively minor adjustments to the current system. They are not radical surgery.

Privatization, on the other hand, is radical surgery. And it doesn't even solve the problem. In fact, it actually takes away money from the trust funds.

How could that be? The answer is so-called "transition costs." They are really going to be a huge problem. Right now, over eighty percent of payroll taxes are used to pay benefits for current retirees. Under a privatized system, those payroll taxes would be diverted into individual retirement accounts. But younger workers would still have to pay payroll taxes to fund benefits for current retirees. In effect, they would be paying twice. There is no way of doing that without increasing taxes, cutting benefits, or depleting the trust funds.

Here is an idea: Instead of paying unnecessary transition costs, what if we used that money to restore the trust funds? The same goes for the more modest steps toward privatization now being discussed in Congress. Some members have proposed diverting one, two, or three percent of the 12.4-percent payroll tax into new individual accounts. Others would use a budget surplus to do the same thing. Instead of setting up private accounts, we could just as easily use that money to shore up the trust funds.

That is the problem we are supposed to be fixing, isn't it? It's hard to explain how you are saving the trust funds when you're taking money out instead of putting money in.

The important thing, Mr. President, is to stay focused. As our guiding principle, we should insist that any legislation purporting to save Social Security actually live up to its billing. It should reserve for the trust funds any new savings or revenues. We shouldn't let some speculative shortfall, thirty-four years from now, be used as an excuse to force through a very different—and, I would add, a very radical—agenda.

Why are we getting sidetracked with individual accounts and privatization schemes that don't actually solve the problem? The reason is simple—money. Wall Street money, and lots of it. Mutual fund companies, stock brokerages, life insurance companies and banks are all salivating at the prospect of 130 million potential new customers coming their way. Privatization of Social Security could bring them untold billions of dollars in extra fees and commissions. That is why they have invested millions of dollars in a massive public relations campaign promoting privatization, and they are doing a heck of a good job of it. That is one reason why they have contributed so heavily to congressional and presidential campaigns. The heavy hitters, the big givers, they are heavily involved in this campaign.

Let me read from a story in the *Washington Post* on September 30, 1996. The headline says, "Wall Street's Quiet Message: Privatize Social Security."

It reads:

Wall Street is putting its weight behind the movement in Washington to privatize Social Security. . . . Lobbyists for Wall Street are trying to stay behind the scenes as they argue for privatization because they and their firms so obviously stand to profit by the changes they are promoting, according to financial industry executives. Representatives of mutual funds, brokerages, life insurance companies, and banks are involved in a lobby-ing effort to have the government let Wall Street manage a slice of Social Security's money . . . Representatives of investment firms have begun lobbying Capitol Hill and the White House to advance their agenda, according to financial service industry executives. . . .Wall Street officials want to avoid or at least deflect accusations that they are seeking to transform Social Security to line their own purses.

And, I might add, their own purposes.

There has been some very good reporting in the *Post*, in the *Wall Street Journal,* and elsewhere on exactly who is paying how much money to whom.

It is absolutely unbelievable the way in which these Wall Street interests have hijacked this debate. It is time for those of us who want to protect this system to stand up and begin to speak out and fight back against these very radical efforts to privatize a social insurance program that has been such a huge success, not just for senior citizens, but for our parents and our grandparents.

I think it would be a tragedy if we stood by and let the trust funds be squandered by Wall Street—and squandered on Wall Street. In Chile, where they privatized Social Security in 1981, an estimated nineteen percent of worker contributions gets skimmed off the top by pension companies. That's nineteen percent skimmed off the top by the middlemen.

Social Security in our country, by contrast, has administrative costs of less than one percent with no fees, no commissions. One percent administrative costs, no fees, no commissions, not going to the big Wall Street interests. And now we have these efforts to privatize the system and turn over a large part of the surplus to Wall Street? Unbelievable.

Champions of privatization like to brag about higher returns on the stock market as compared to Social Security. I think those claims are exaggerated. But even if they were true, you don't need individual accounts managed by Wall Street campaign contributors to capture the higher yields. You would get the same average returns if Social Security did the investing itself. And that way, seniors would still be guaranteed a monthly benefit indexed for inflation.

I'm not saying we should do that, necessarily. Stock markets go down as well as up. With all the financial turmoil in Asia and Russia right now, we might want to think twice about betting the future of the trust funds on go-go emerging markets. But whatever we do, we should insist that the trust fund money not be siphoned off to Wall Street middlemen.

I want to say that again to my colleagues. We might want to think twice about betting the future of the trust funds on go-go emerging markets. But whatever we do, we should insist that this trust fund money not be siphoned off to the Wall Street middlemen, which is actually what the privatization proposals do.

Our immediate focus should be on fixing the problem at hand—a projected shortfall in the trust funds thirty-four years in the future. We should not be diverting resources to half-baked schemes that would only make the problem worse.

We should not let Wall Street campaign contributors push through a "reform plan" that would only give them a slice of the trust funds. Privatization is a phony solution to a phony crisis.

Social Security has been phenomenally successful for over a half a century—sixty years. It ensures millions of Americans against disability, death of a spouse, and destitution in their old age. Compared to private retirement plans, it is a very good deal. And it is the most successful antipoverty program America has ever devised.

It is simple. You reach the age of sixty-two or sixty-five, you get older, you are no longer working, your earnings decline. There was a time when prob-

ably half of the poverty population in our country were the elderly. That was a national disgrace. That is no longer the case. This is a very successful program.

While all of us should be saving more, the fact is that there will always be millions and millions of Americans who depend solely on Social Security for their retirement security. In fact, as fewer and fewer Americans have employer-provided pensions and as businesses are rapidly shifting from defined benefit plans to defined contribution, we need Social Security now more than ever. This is no time to "end Social Security as we know it."

We now have proposals, privatization schemes, to "end Social Security as we know it." That is what this is all about. I am amazed that we have not had more discussion about how to modify and support Social Security as opposed to the privatization schemes that dismantle Social Security.

I will give some of my colleagues credit. They have been able to take, thirty-four years in the future, a potential shortfall and reduce it to an agenda that dismantles the Social Security system as we know it.

We need to have a major discussion and debate over this. In the coming weeks and months, I plan to be talking at great length about how we can correct the projected shortfall thirty-four years from now without ending Social Security as we know it. Right now, friends of Social Security are generating a number of proposals that do not amount to radical surgery. Those ideas deserve to be heard. Advocates for the privatization plan favored by Wall Street should not have a monopoly over this debate. If we have a fully informed discussion and all options are really on the table, I am very confident that the American people will support a progressive solution that does not end Social Security as we know it.

I yield the floor.

6

RACE

> "One young white girl, age nine, went out in her block and, with chalk, wrote on a sidewalk about what is happening in our country: 'Without justice there can be no peace.' Her neighbor, an African-American black girl, age nine, could not read what was on the sidewalk. That tells us so much about our country and how much we still have to do."
> ~Senator Paul Wellstone, May 6, 1992

Senator Paul Wellstone's graduate dissertation was entitled, "Black Militants in the Ghetto: Why They Believe in Violence." It was an eighty-four page description and analysis of poor African-Americans in Durham, North Carolina, based upon interviews regarding their views toward the police and government. The dissertation ultimately concluded that African-Americans resort to violence because the government does not to address their concerns. They are given no other choice. Those same conclusions are echoed by Senator Wellstone twenty years later as he responds to the riots in Los Angeles, California, after a jury acquitted four white police officers in the beating of Rodney King.

In other speeches related to race and inequality, Senator Wellstone speaks about the shared interests of rural whites and urban African-Americans. These commonalities were illustrated by Senator Robert F. Kennedy during his tours of the rural south and urban north in 1966 and 1968. Indeed, during Senator Wellstone's speech entitled the "urban crisis" he also speaks about the same issues in rural America.

RODNEY KING INCIDENT: A BETRAYAL OF JUSTICE

April 30, 1992

Madam President, I am saddened and shocked by the verdict in the Rodney King case. As I watched the verdict being read in the courtroom and the aftermath on the streets, I kept thinking what a huge step backwards this verdict represents for race relations and civil rights. African-Americans are angry. All Americans are angry. And this anger is legitimate. This verdict represents a betrayal of justice. We need to right the wrong that has been done.

When we all saw the videotape of Los Angeles policemen beating Rodney King last year, we were shocked. An unarmed African-American civilian being clubbed and beaten by four policemen as others looked on. What is happening to America, twenty-five years after the civil rights revolution? Many in the African-American community are saying that the only thing different this time was that the beating was captured on tape and the perpetrators could not escape justice.

So America assured itself that a public, televised trial would bring justice to Mr. King and to the African-American community. Political leaders urged patience and confidence in the judicial system. They said this case would expose police brutality. They said this case would make white America more aware of the problems people of color face every day on the streets of their communities. They said let the system work.

Well, now what do we say? This verdict is a travesty. Not just because four policemen whom the whole world saw brutally beat an unarmed man walked free. No, that is only part of the problem. The verdict is a travesty because of what it says to the members of the African-American community and other communities of color. It says that even when there is videotaped evidence of brutality, it is very difficult to get justice. It says that despite twenty-five years of changes in civil rights, we have not come very far at all. It says that for all the progress in legislation and court rulings, yesterday we took a giant step backwards.

But we cannot let the outrage and indignation about the verdict lead to more violence. Violence begets violence begets violence. It is not the answer. It will not bring justice. As angry and as upset as people are, beating and murdering innocent people and burning community buildings will not redress grievances. There has to be a better way.

Nobody wants to defend violence, and I will not. But no one should be comfortable with the violence of homelessness, with the violence of joblessness, with the violence of hunger.

I have been talking today with members of the African-American community in my state of Minnesota. Like Americans everywhere, they are outraged about what has happened. They are agonizing about what to do and how to respond in a constructive way. What I am hearing them say is that we must redress this injustice.

What we need to do is to demand action by federal officials. Policing in the community requires

sensitivity, respect, fairness, and justice. I urge the Justice Department to expedite its review of this case for violations of the civil rights laws. The American people deserve an accounting of what happened in Los Angeles. I urge that the department prosecute violations to the fullest extent of the law. I urge President Bush to make sure that such a review is completed as quickly and comprehensively as he said he would this morning.

I also urge him to treat the case with the gravity and respect it deserves and to retract his statement that the justice system works. I would also urge the president to provide the leadership on civil rights that has been lacking in recent years.

I will be offering the mayors of both Minneapolis and St. Paul as well as members of the African-American communities of both cities any assistance they need at the federal level.

And, finally, I ask that all Americans come together over this incident and work to bridge our differences and solve our problems. We cannot afford as a nation, as a people, to continue to tear ourselves apart. We must stand together to demand justice and equality.

THE URBAN CRISIS AND THE HEALING OF AMERICA
May 6, 1992

I thank Senator Kennedy from Massachusetts for his statement. I am proud to serve in the Senate with him because I think he has been a giant in this whole struggle for civil rights and human rights and opportunities for all our citizens. It was an eloquent statement, and I think it was very important. I certainly wish to be included as an original cosponsor of his proposal.

Mr. President, let me follow up on the statement of the Senator from Massachusetts with one Minnesota story, and a report on a meeting I went to today that I think is relevant and should be reported on the floor.

Minnesota's story, phoned to me here from my office in Minnesota: One young white girl, age nine, went out in her block and, with chalk, wrote on a sidewalk about what is happening in our country: "Without justice there can be no peace." Her neighbor, an African-American black girl, age nine, could not read what was on the sidewalk. That tells us so much about our country and how much we still have to do.

Mr. President, I want to report to you on a meeting I attended today on M Street here in Washington, D.C., at the Metropolitan AME Church, which, interestingly enough, the great black abolitionist Frederick Douglass actually attended. This was a gathering that Mayor Kelly hosted. Reverend Jesse Jackson brought people together from around the country. And the interesting thing is that the focus was in two areas.

Number one, the focus was on voter registration, on people, young people especially, exerting their political rights on behalf of their economic rights.

And number two, a very positive focus, was really on the kinds of things Senator Kennedy was talking about. The focus was on jobs; it was on education; it was on opportunity; and it was on investing in our own communities.

Mr. President, I have to tell you I am committed one way or another to bringing back the whole question of whether or not we are going to waive the budget agreement, not spend more as a nation but at least redirect some of our resources into our own communities. I think it is time we understand that part of the definition of real national security is going to be the security of local communities where there are jobs, where there is housing, where there is education and where there is opportunity.

There are some people from Rushford, Minnesota, here today, and I have to tell you that these economic issues are also real, compelling rural issues. The fact that poor people and people who are struggling in rural areas might be more hidden does not make the poverty any less real. I want to just make it clear. We have much to do in our country by way of investment in rural America, as well.

A final point, Mr. President, because I promised that I would be brief. The interesting thing about this gathering today at the Metropolitan A.M.E. Church was there was a focus on a call to action. The mayors' march on May 16, is going to be so important, and will be followed up by events on June 19, which will be a national day of protest, with massive efforts on voter registration, massive focus on these domestic issues, saying to people in our country, especially the people that live in the cities that do not have the hope: There are alternatives.

Saint Augustine said: Hope has two lovely daughters: Anger and Courage. The anger at what is wrong, and the courage to know that we can change it.

I think that is what we need in our country today—the politics of courage, the politics of caring, and the politics of investment in our communities and in our people.

BLACK HISTORY MONTH
February 26, 2001

Mr. President, I rise today to speak on behalf of this year's Black History Month theme, "Creating and Defining the African American Community: Family, Church, Politics, and Culture." I would like to note that while we take time in February to recall the contributions, accomplishments, and services that our fellow citizens have rendered, it is important to remember that the contributions of African-Americans to America happen every day in every walk of life.

Moreover, in our review of these vital contributions, we are called upon to acknowledge the courage, talent, determination, leadership, and vision of those men, women, and children who made an impact in the face of incredible obstacles.

This year's theme, I believe, is fundamental not only in defining the African-American community, but the American community at large. The struggle for a better America begins with each individual and his or her call to civic duty. The historical context of building a better America begins with gaining a deeper understanding of our history and how our social environment has been shaped.

The civil rights movement helped our nation, and particularly our government, recognize that universal participation and rights are enjoined upon all citizens, regardless of the color of their skin. One of the many lessons that can be gleaned from this movement is that it is our duty as Americans to embrace the diverse elements of our society so that future generations can see themselves in our nation's past and realize that they have a role to play in seizing the future's countless opportunities.

In acknowledging the various elements of the African-American community of Family, Church, Politics, and Culture, I would like to acknowledge a few of the outstanding contributions of African-Americans in the state of Minnesota. Their efforts have helped shape the social, economic and political landscape of that vibrant community as well as the community at large.

Just recently, the United States Postal Service issued a stamp in its Postal Service's Black Heritage commemorative series. This stamp commemorates the life and accomplishments of one of the great leaders of the civil rights movement, Mr. Roy Wilkins, who grew up in Saint Paul and attended the University of Minnesota.

In 1931 he was appointed assistant executive secretary of the National Association for the Advancement of Colored People, NAACP, the largest civil rights organization in the U.S. From 1934 to 1949 he was editor of *The Crisis*, the official magazine of the NAACP. Wilkins served as a consultant to the War Department on black employment during World War II. After the war he continued his service to the NAACP; he was executive secretary from 1955 to 1965 and executive director from 1965 until his retirement in 1977. He played a major role in the preparation of Brown versus Board of Education of Topeka, 1954, and was one of the organizers of the March on Washington in 1963. It is only fitting that the legacy of a man of such integrity, vision, and deep conviction is given tribute through this special recognition. His leadership and dedication to the civil rights cause is exemplary.

I am proud to honor the religious community not only for their spiritual guidance of the African-American community, but also for their unwavering efforts to improve the quality of life in our cities and state. The Coalition of Black Churches in Minneapolis and the St. Paul ministerial Alliance truly have made a difference in the community with their outreach on behalf of their congregations and community, through their experience and sacrifice, through their political will with their legislative agendas, and most importantly, through their leadership and exemplary behavior. They are not simply preaching the meaning of values, family, and community service, they are also showing us.

In the arena of politics, Ms. Neva Walker became the first African-American woman to be elected to the Minnesota Legislature just last fall. Given the dispiriting level of civic participation in our society today, I truly am appreciative of the vision and leadership that Representative Walker brings to her constituents and our state. I am honored to know and work with Representative Walker. As the first African-American woman legislator in our state I know she will make important changes, provide needed leadership, and introduce legislation that will greatly help many people.

Our community also is extremely privileged to have an organization with the capacity and outreach of African-American Family Services. For twenty-five years, this organization has reached out to the community to provide culturally specific services and programs ranging from providing critical services in clinical health, family preservation, domestic violence, and adolescent violence prevention and anger management. In addition, this organization provides its clients and the community with a resource center, which includes a resource library and a technical assistance center, which creates training programs to educate human resource professionals on enhancing service delivery to African-American clients.

A tribute to some of the heroes of the community would not be complete without a mention of two men who brought so much joy to the fans of the Minnesota Twins. Mr. Kirby Puckett and Mr. Dave Winfield, who were both inducted into Major League Baseball's Hall of Fame, provided Twins fans in Minnesota and around the country with some spectacular plays which will forever be in our memories.

Aside from their outstanding professional accomplishments, both players continue to be exemplary role models and community leaders.

Let us take this opportunity to re-dedicate and re-invigorate ourselves, as Americans, to the cause of working together to create a society which not only understands the concept of unity in diversity, but lives it; which not only preaches economic justice, but implements it; that not only espouses equality of opportunity, but ensures it.

7

MAINTAINING PUBLIC ASSISTANCE

> "Mr. President, I do not particularly care about words like 'entitlement.' But I do think as a nation we are a community, and up until the passage of this legislation, if signed into law, we as a nation said, as a community we will make sure there is a floor beneath which no child can fall in America. Now we have eliminated that floor. We are now saying as a Senate that there will no longer be any floor beneath which no child can fall. And you call that reform?"
> ~Senator Paul Wellstone, August 1, 1996

During then-Governor Bill Clinton's 1992 presidential campaign, one of his biggest applause lines related to his promise to "end welfare as we know it." The pledge was premised upon the idea that the public assistance programs were fundamentally flawed. It was argued that the programs created by President Franklin Delano Roosevelt during the Great Depression and President Lyndon Johnson during the 1960s as part of his Great Society created dependence rather than a path toward independence. He also fought tirelessly to maintain funding for basic public assistance, such as the school lunch program and WIC program, which provided nutritional supplements and food for women with infants and children.

While acknowledging that the public assistance programs were not perfect, Senator Wellstone was often the only senator to speak against these "reforms." He believed that many of the measures being proposed were punitive, and often based on stereotypes rather than reality. He argued that the people most hurt would be the millions of children who lived in poverty, and he argued that forcing a single-mother to work a minimum wage job with no health care or day care undermined society rather than strengthened it.

IN OPPOSITION TO THE "PERSONAL RESPONSIBILITY AND WORK OPPORTUNITY RECONCILLIATION ACT OF 1996"

August 1, 1996

Mr. President, I do want to talk about this piece of legislation. I have heard some discussion about doing good. Let me start out with what is a very important framework to me as a Senator from Minnesota. It is a question. Will this legislation, if passed, signed into law by the President, create more poverty and more hunger among children in America? And if the answer to that question is yes, then my vote is no.

Mr. President, we were discussing welfare reform several years ago, and we said that we should move from welfare to work, that that would include job training, education training, making sure the jobs were available that single parents—mostly mothers—could support their children on, and a commitment to child care.

Just about every single scholar in the United States of America has said that this is what reform is all about. You have to invest some additional resources. Then, in the long run, not only are the mothers and children better off, but we are all better off. That is real welfare reform. Slashing close to sixty billion dollars in low-income assistance is not reform, colleagues. It is punitive, it is harsh, and it is extreme.

Mr. President, we have been focusing in this Congress on the budget deficit. I think, today, what we see in the U.S. Senate is a spiritual deficit because, Mr. President, I know some of my colleagues do not want to look at this. They push their gaze away from unpleasant facts and an unpleasant reality. Sometimes people do not want to know what they do not want to know.

Mr. President, the evidence is irrefutable and irreducible: This legislation, once enacted into law, will create more poverty and hunger among children in America. That is not reform.

Mr. President, we have here about twenty-eight billion dollars of cuts in nutrition assistance. I believe when the President spoke yesterday he was trying to say that does not have anything to do with reform, and he intends to fix that next Congress. But I worry about what will happen now. Mr. President, seventy percent of the citizens that will be affected by these cuts in food nutrition programs are children, fifty percent of the families have incomes of under $6,300 a year. Our incomes are $130,000 a year.

Mr. President, there will be a three-billion-dollar cut over the next six years in food assistance, nutrition assistance, even for families who pay over fifty percent of their monthly income for housing costs. So now we put families in our country—poor families, poor children—in the situation of "eat or heat," but they do not get both. At the same time, my colleagues keep wanting to cut low-income energy assistance programs. This is goodness? This is goodness?

Mr. President, I was involved in the anti-hunger struggles in the South. I saw it in North Carolina, and I remind my colleagues, maybe they want to go back and look at the exposés, look at the Field Foundation report, look at the CBS report, "Hunger USA." Where are the national media? Why are we not seeing documentaries right now about poverty in America?

Mr. President, the Food Stamp Program, which we dramatically expanded in the late 1960s and early 1970s, with Richard Nixon, a Republican, leading the way, has been the most effective and important safety-net practice in this country. As a result of expanding that program, we dramatically reduce hunger and malnutrition among children in America.

Now we are turning the clock back, and some of my colleagues are calling this reform. Mr. President, how did it get to be reform, to cut by twenty percent food nutrition assistance for a poor, eighty-year-old woman? How dare you call it reform. That is not reform. How did it get to be reform to slash nutrition programs that are so important in making sure that children have an adequate diet? How dare you call it reform. That is not reform. How did it get to be reform to essentially eliminate all of the assistance for legal immigrants, people who pay taxes and work? How dare you call that reform. That has not a thing to do with reform.

The Urban Institute came out with a report several weeks ago. Isabel Sawhill, one of the very best, said this legislation will impoverish an additional 1.1 million children. We have had these analyses before. The Office of Management and Budget had a similar analysis. So did the Department of Health and Human Services. How dare you call a piece of legislation that will lead to more poverty among children in America reform?

Marian Wright Edelman of the Children's Defense Fund is right: To call this piece of legislation reform is like calling catsup a vegetable. Except this time it is more serious, because many more children, many more elderly, many more children with disabilities will be affected.

Mr. President, the evidence is really irreducible and irrefutable. Bob Greenstein, who has won the MacArthur Genius Award for his work, crunched the numbers about what it means in personal terms, real terms for the most vulnerable citizens in America, but my colleagues are too worried about polls. They are too worried about the politics of it, and they turn their gaze away from all this.

Mr. President, I do not particularly care about words like "entitlement." But I do think as a nation we are a community, and up until the passage of this legislation, if signed into law, we as a nation said, as a community we will make sure there is a floor beneath which no child can fall in America. Now we have eliminated that floor. We are now saying as a Senate that there will no longer be any floor beneath which no child can fall. And you call that reform?

Mr. President, we had a proposal out here on the floor of the Senate that said, if you are going to cut people off from work, if you are going to cut people off from welfare, at least require the states to provide vouchers. The CBO tells us we do not have the money for the job training slots, and people will not necessarily find work, and then you will cut the adult off work. So we added an amendment that said, "For God's sake, at least make sure there are vouchers for Pampers, for health care, for food for the children." That amendment was rejected.

So we have no requirement that at the very minimum, even if you are going to cut a parent off of welfare, at least make sure the law of the land says that every state from Mississippi to Missouri to Minnesota to California to Georgia, that at least there will be vouchers for Pampers, for food, for medical assistance, and you vote "no" and you say there will be no vouchers. And you call that reform?

Mr. President, in the Senate, I introduced an amendment, and it was accepted. It said in all too many cases, too many of these women have been victims of domestic violence, they have been battered, and welfare is the only alternative for too many women to a very abusive and dangerous situation at home. So every state will be required to have services for these women and not force people off the rolls if, in fact, there needs to be additional support.

It took Monica Seles two years to play tennis again after she was attacked. Imagine what it would be like to be beaten up over and over again. That amendment was knocked out in the conference—no national requirement, no protection. Maybe it will be done in the states and maybe it won't.

Mr. President, I had a safety valve amendment. It was defeated. Senator Kerry from Massachusetts had another one which was watered down, but important. It was knocked out in conference committee. It said, why don't we at least look at what we have done, and if in fact there is more poverty and hunger, then we will take corrective action in two years. That was knocked out in conference committee. You call that reform?

Mr. President, let me be crystal clear. You focus on work, you focus on job training, you focus on education, you focus on making sure that families can make a transition from welfare to work, and that is great. Eliminating services for legal immigrants, draconian cuts in food nutrition programs for children and the elderly, deep cuts in assistance for children with disabilities—none of this has anything to do with reform. This is done in the name of deficit reduction.

When I had an amendment on the floor that dealt with all of the breaks that go to some of the oil companies, or tobacco companies, or pharmaceutical companies, that was defeated. When we had a budget that called for twelve billion dollars more than the Pentagon wanted and we tried to eliminate that, that was defeated. But now when it comes to poor children in America, who clearly are invisible here in Washington, D.C.—at least in the Congress—faceless and voiceless, how generous we are with their suffering. And you dare to call that reform? You dare to say that, in the name of children, when you are passing a piece of legislation that every single study says will increase poverty and hunger among children. Vote for it for political reasons, but you can't get away with calling it reform. It is reverse reform. It is reformatory, it is punitive, it is harsh, it is extreme. It targets the most vulnerable citizens in America—poor children.

Mr. President, in this insurance reform bill we are going to be dealing with, late last night someone inserted a two-year monopoly patent extension for an anti-arthritis drug, a special interest gift to one drug company because then you don't have the generic drugs. Late last night, someone put this into the insurance reform bill. There you go. There is some welfare for a pharmaceutical company. But they are the heavy hitters. They have the lobbyists. They are well-connected. We do just fine by them. But for these poor children, who very few members of the Senate even know, we are all too generous with their suffering.

Mr. President, I had an amendment that was passed by a 99-to-0 vote that said the Senate shall not take any action that shall create more hunger or homelessness among children. Now we are slashing twenty-eight billion dollars in food nutrition programs with the harshest effect being on children in America. Can my colleagues reconcile that for me? I would love to debate someone on this. I doubt whether there will be debate on it because the evidence is clear.

Mr. President, President Clinton said yesterday that he will sign the bill, and he said that he will work hard, I presume next Congress, to correct what he thinks is wrong. He pointed out that these draconian cuts in food nutrition programs and in assistance to legal immigrants are wrong, they have nothing to do with reform. He is absolutely right.

Personally, it is difficult for me to say, well, with the exception of these draconian cuts in food assistance programs for children and the elderly, with the exception of these draconian cuts for children with disabilities, and draconian cuts for legal immigrants, this is a pretty good bill otherwise. I can't make that argument. But I will work with the president because, clearly, this is going to pass, and, quite clearly, corrective action is going to have to be taken next Congress.

But, for myself, Mr. President, I am a senator from the great state of Minnesota. As Senator Hubert Humphrey said, the test case for a society or government is how we treat people in the twilight of their lives—the elderly; how we treat people at the dawn of their lives—the children; and how we treat people in the shadow of their lives—the poor, and those that are struggling with disabilities. We have failed that test miserably with this piece of legislation.

Mr. President, I come from a state that I think leads the nation in its commitment to children and its commitment to fairness and its commitment to opportunity. As a senator from Minnesota that is up for reelection this year, there can be one zillion attack ads—and there already have been many, and there will be many more—and I will not vote for legislation that impoverishes more children in America. That is not the right thing to do. That is not a Minnesota vote.

Mr. President, in my next term as a U.S. senator from Minnesota, I am going to embark on a poverty tour in our country. I am going to bring television with me, and I am going to bring media with me, and I am going to visit these children. I am going to visit some of these poor, elderly people. I am going to visit these families. I am going to visit these legal immigrants. I am going to have my nation focus its attention, and I am going to have my colleagues, Republicans and Democrats alike, focus their attention on these vulnerable citizens.

And, if in fact we see the harshness, the additional poverty, and the additional malnutrition, which is exactly what is going to happen, I am going to bring all those pictures and all of those voices and all of those faces and all of those children and all of those elderly people back to the floor of the U.S. Senate, and we will correct the terrible mistake we are making in this legislation.

Mr. President, I yield the floor.

WHAT IS HAPPENING WITH WELFARE REFORM?
February 9, 1998

Madam President, there were two articles today, one article in the *New York Times*, a front-page story: "Pessimism Retains Grip on Region Shaped by War on Poverty," Booneville, Kentucky, eastern Kentucky, Appalachia. At the same time, there was also an editorial in the *Minnesota Star Tribune*. I ask unanimous consent that both the *New York Times* piece and this editorial be printed in the *Record*.

* * *

Madam President, I just want to read one part of the editorial today in the *Star Tribune*:

> But since Congress passed the Personal Responsibility and Work Opportunity Act, better known as welfare reform, that self-regulated feature has vanished. States can kick families off assistance for many reasons—failing to find work, breaking administrative rules, or simply exhausting their benefits "clock," a time as short as eighteen months in some states.

The context for this piece was that seven Midwestern welfare administrators have banded together, and they want us to ask questions about what is happening with the welfare bill in the country.

I just want to say to colleagues that we would be making a mistake if we assumed that two million fewer families on welfare meant also that we had two million fewer families that were poor in America. What the *New York Times* front page article points to—and I had a chance to visit Letcher County, Kentucky, this summer—what this editorial speaks to, I think, is a really important question.

I am going to have an amendment that I am going to offer on the first bill that is appropriate which essentially says this: We cannot automatically equate reduction in caseload with reduction in poverty, and what we need to know as responsible policymakers is what is happening with these families.

When I say "these families," I am really talking about, in the main, women, and children. I know that in my travels around the country—and I do no damage to the truth, I don't think I exaggerate at all—I met too many families where, as it turns out, three- and four-year-olds were home alone. The single parent is working now, but the child care has not been worked out. Or it is a very ad hoc child care arrangement, hardly what any of us would like for our own children, not really good developmental child care.

In addition, too many first and second graders, I said before on the floor of the Senate, are now going home alone because their single parent, the mother, is working, but there is nobody there to take care of them when they are home. First and second graders are going home sometimes in some very dangerous neighborhoods.

It is also true, Madam President, that wherever I travel, when I am told in any given state we have reduced the welfare rolls by X number of families, the question I have is, where are they? What kind of jobs do these mothers now have? Do they pay a living wage? Where are the children? Is [there] decent child care? And the interesting thing is that hardly anywhere in the country do we have the data. I can't get answers to those questions.

So, the amendment that I am going to have on the floor of the Senate soon will essentially call on states to provide to Health and Human Services data, let's say, every six months as to how many families are actually reaching economic self-sufficiency.

I am not trying to bias the conclusion one way or the other, but since, depending on the state, three years from now or two years from now or a year and a half from now or four years from now, there is a drop-dead date certain where all these children—women and children—will be removed from any assistance, we ought to know what is happening. That is all I am saying to colleagues, let's have the data, let's make sure we know what is happening to those families. That will be an amendment I will bring to the floor soon.

The second amendment I want to mention today is, I think, very much within the same context and, I think, important. Around the country, as I travel, I cannot believe how many women who are in a community college, who are on the path to economic self-sufficiency in school, are now being told that they have to go to work. It may be a $5.50-an-hour job, but they are essentially told they can no longer be in school.

Madam President, I would argue that this is very shortsighted. This is very shortsighted. As a matter of fact, if these women can complete their two years in the community college or even get a four-year degree, they and their families will be much better off.

So the second amendment I am going to offer will essentially call for a student exemption. It will say, let's let these welfare mothers pursue and complete their education. They and their families will be much better off. I hope that the community colleges and the universities will speak up for these families because they know what is happening. This is, I think, a profound mistake.

THE STATE OF AMERICA'S CHILDREN
March 28, 1995

Mr. President, today, the Children's Defense Fund, a wonderful organization—and thank God there is such an organization with a strong voice for children—has issued a report, "The State of America's Children."

I would, for my state of Minnesota, like to release some statistics from this report on the floor of the Senate and then I would like to talk about what these statistics mean in personal terms for my state and for the politics of the country for this Congress.

Minnesota's children at risk—this report was issued today by the Children's Defense Fund: 60,615 children lacked health insurance in the years 1989 to 1991—over 60,000 children lacking health insurance; 27,462 reported cases of child abuse and neglect, 1992—27,462 reported cases; 116 young men died by violence, 1991; forty-eight children were killed by guns, 1992.

Only 71.4 percent of two-year-olds were fully immunized, 1990—thirty percent of children not fully immunized. This is my state of Minnesota and, in my humble opinion, that is the greatest state in the country; thirty-five percent of fourth-grade public school students lacked basic reading proficiency, 1992.

Those are Minnesota's children at risk.

Mr. President, on the back of this report released today by the Children's Defense Fund, there are the following statistics, which I have read on the floor of the Senate before, but this is a new report, new data:

Every day in America, three children die from child abuse.

Every day in America, fifteen children die from guns.

Every day in America, twenty-seven children—a class roomful—die from poverty.

Every day in America, ninety-five babies die before their first birthday.

Every day in America, 564 babies are born to women who had late or no prenatal care.

Every day in America, 788 babies are born at low birth weight, less than five pounds eight ounces.

Every day in America, 1,340 teenagers give birth.

Every day in America, 2,217 teenagers drop out of school—each day.

Every day in America, 2,350 children are in adult jails.

Every day in America, 2,699 infants are born into poverty.

Every day in America, 3,356 babies are born to unmarried women.

Every day in America, 8,189 children are reported abused or neglected.

Every day in America, 100,000 children are homeless.

Every day in America 135,000 children bring guns to school.

Every day in America, 1.2 million latchkey children come home to a house in which there is a gun.

Mr. President, I would like to, from this Children's Defense Fund report that came out today on the state of America's children, talk about what this means with Minnesota children at risk.

A nation that would rather send someone else's child to prison for $15,496 a year, or to an orphanage for over $36,000 a year, then invest in $300,000 worth of immunization and $100,000 worth of prenatal care to give a child a healthy start, $1,800 to give that child a summer job to learn a work ethic, lacks both family values and common and economic sense.

Mr. President, let me just add that as long as we are going to be talking about a budget deficit and addressing that budget deficit, I think it is time that we also address a spiritual deficit in our nation. I have brought an amendment to the floor of the U.S. Senate four times which has been defeated. I will bring it back on the floor this week, especially with the rescissions bill over here.

I commend Senator Hatfield, and others, for their fine work in at least restoring some of the cuts for some programs that are so important. I know that I met with citizens back in Minnesota about cuts to the Low Energy Assistance Program. In my state of Minnesota, over 100,000 households, 300,000 individuals, I say to my colleagues, thirty percent elderly, members of household, forty percent child, over fifty percent someone working; this was a grant of about $350 that enabled somebody to get over a tough time, with forty percent using it only one year. People were terrified. I will thank Senator Hatfield and others for not zeroing out that program.

As I look at these cuts that are before us, Mr. President, I would like to raise some questions not about the budget deficit but about the spiritual deficit. Minnesota children at risk. I will have this amendment on the floor and I will ask one more time for my colleagues to go on record that we will not pass any legislation, take any action that would increase the number of hungry or homeless children in America. That amendment has failed in four separate votes, though the support for the amendment is going up; the last time it received forty-seven votes.

Mr. President, I want to ask the following question: Who decides that we are going to cut child nutrition programs but not subsidies for oil companies? Who decides that we are going to cut the Headstart Program but not subsidies for insurance companies? Who decides that we are going to cut child care programs but not tobacco company subsidies? Who decides, Mr. President, that we are going to cut educational programs for children, but not military contractors?

Mr. President, some people are very generous with the suffering of others. And it is time that we understand that we should not be making budget cuts based on the path of least political resistance, making cuts that affect citizens with the least amount of clout that are not the heavy hitters and do not have the lobbyists.

There needs to be a standard of fairness. I will insist on that during this debate. Mr. President, if you will allow me fifteen seconds for a conclusion, over and over again on the floor of the U.S. Senate, I will, if you will, shout it from the mountain top. There will not be any real national security for our nation until we invest in the health and the skills and the intellect and the character of our children. That is what this debate is about.

FUNDING THE SCHOOL LUNCH PROGRAM

July 9, 1997

Mr. President, just as a courtesy to my colleagues, let me say that I am not offering a new amendment. This is an amendment that I introduced yesterday morning. I wanted to take advantage of this time to speak about this amendment.

This amendment would authorize the Secretary of Defense to transfer five million dol-

lars out of the 265-billion-dollar Pentagon budget—some 2.6 billion dollars more than the president himself asked for—to the Secretary of Agriculture, to be used for outreach and startup grants for the school breakfast program.

Mr. President, this amendment involves a very small amount of money. While it involves a small amount of money—at least given the kind of money we are dealing with here—it actually speaks to a very large question. I think the question has to do with what our priorities are.

I think it is a distorted priority to provide the Pentagon with 2.6 billion dollars more than it originally asked for. For the third year in a row— these are one of the few times I can remember in my adult life that the Congress actually wants to provide the Pentagon with more money than the Pentagon has actually asked for. At the same time, when it comes to some really vitally important programs that dramatically affect children's lives, we don't make the investment.

By way of background: In the welfare bill that passed last Congress, five million dollars was eliminated from a critically important program, which was a program that on the one hand provided states and school districts with the information they needed—call it an outreach program—about how they could set up a breakfast program, and on the other hand, it provided some badly needed funding for some of the poorer school districts to actually, for example, purchase refrigerators in order to have milk.

It is difficult to understand how this could have been cut, especially given the heralded success of the school breakfast program. Some things I guess we do not know enough about, but we do know that a nutritious breakfast really is important in enabling a child to learn. We also know that if a child is not able to learn, as I said yesterday, when he or she becomes an adult they may very well not be able to earn. This is a small amount of money that makes a huge difference.

So this amendment says that out of a 265-billion-dollar Pentagon budget, some 2.6 billion dollars more than the Pentagon asked for, can't we authorize the Secretary of Defense to be able to transfer five million dollars—five million dollars—for school breakfasts? For what I would call catalyst money that gets necessary information out to the states and school districts and some needed assistance by way of refrigerators and resources to enable them to expand the school breakfast program.

Mr. President, I want to point out by way of context that there are still some 27,000 schools that do not have school breakfast programs available. There are some eight million vulnerable, low-income children, therefore, who are not able to participate. Too many of those children go to school without having had a nutritious breakfast.

This may seem abstract to many of us in the Senate, but it is a very concrete and a very important issue.

This amendment has the support of FRAC, the Food Research Action Center, which has a longstanding history of working on childhood hunger and nutrition issues. It has the support of the Elementary School Principals Association, the American School Food Services, and Bread for the World.

Mr. President, I might point out that these organizations have a tremendous amount of credibility for all of us who care about hunger and malnutrition. These are organizations that have been down in the trenches for years working on these issues. I don't think anybody can quarrel with the values and ethics of Bread for the World and the work that they have done, much of it very rooted in the religious community, and the American School Food Services. These are food service workers. These are the people who know

what it means when they can't provide a nutritious breakfast to low-income students.

This is a special endorsement for me because my mother was a food service worker.

What the Elementary School Principals Association is saying by endorsing this amendment is simply this: If a child hasn't had a nutritious breakfast, how is that child going to be able to learn?

Mr. President, let me talk a little bit about the extent of hunger and the scope of the problem. This is from the Food Research Action Committee.

Approximately four million American children under the age of twelve go hungry, and approximately 9.6 million are in risk of hunger. According to estimates based on the results of the most comprehensive study ever done on childhood hunger in the United States—this was the community childhood hunger education project—based on the results of over 5,000 surveys of families with incomes below 185 percent of poverty, applied to the best available national data, FRAC estimates that of the approximately 13.6 million children under age twelve in the United States, twenty-nine percent live in families that must cope with hunger or the risk of hunger during some part of one or more months in the previous year.

Let me just raise a question with colleagues before we have this vote. I just think that this goes to the heart of what we are about. This goes to the heart of priorities.

I, as a senator from Minnesota, tire of the symbolic politics. We have had the conferences on early childhood development. The books and the reports, the magazines, the TV documentaries have come out.

We know—let me repeat this—we know that in order for children to do well, it is important that they have a nutritious breakfast. We know that when children are hungry, they don't do well in school. We know, as parents and grandparents, that we want to make sure that our children and our grandchildren start school after having a nutritious breakfast. And we also know, based on clear evidence, that sometimes we don't know what we don't want to know—that there is a significant amount of children who still go to bed hungry or still wake up in the morning hungry and go to school hungry.

Why can't the U.S. Senate make this small investment in this program which was so important in enabling states and school districts to expand the school breakfast program?

Mr. President, I am going to bring this amendment to the floor of the Senate over and over and over again starting with this defense authorization bill.

Let me just read. I am assuming that my colleagues are interested in this information, and I am assuming that we want to address the problem. Let me just talk a little bit about this relationship between hunger and nutrition and learning.

Under-nutrition increases the risk of illness and its severity. Under-nutrition has a negative effect on a child's ability to learn. Iron deficiency anemia is a specific kind of under-nutrition and is one of the most prevalent under-nutritional problems in the United States especially among children. Even mild cases lead to shortened attention span, irritability, fatigue and decreased ability to concentrate. Hunger leads to nervousness, irritability, disinterest in the learning situation, and an inability to concentrate. Hunger disrupts the learning process—one developmental step is lost, and it is difficult to move on to the next one.

A United States Department of Agriculture study of the lunch and breakfast programs demonstrated that these programs make nutritional improvements in children's diets.

I could go on and on, but—I see my colleague from Arizona in the Chamber—I will try to summarize. Let me just make it clear that the data is out there. And over and over again, in report after report after report, we see clearly that malnourished children are not going to do well in school, and we know that eight million low-income children are not able to participate because there is no School Breakfast Program.

We had a five-million-dollar USDA outreach program that enabled school districts to get started, provided them with badly needed information, provided them with refrigerators if they needed that, and we eliminated it. And at the same time we have a Pentagon budget that is 2.6 billion dollars more than the Pentagon asked.

We all say we care about children. We are all referring to these studies that say children have to do well in school, we are talking about the importance of good nutrition, and here we have an opportunity to make a difference.

So, Mr. President, I want to over and over again come to the floor with amendments that speak to this question. One more time, just in terms of looking at the endorsements for this amendment, we have endorsements from FRAC, which is Food Research and Action Center—FRAC has been as involved in children's nutritional issues as any organization I know—the Elementary School Principals Association—they are saying to us, colleagues, at least make sure that children are able to have a nutritious breakfast. I think the elementary school principals know something about learning and something about children at this young age—American School Food Services and Bread for the World.

I hope we will have strong support for this amendment.

I point out by way of conclusion that if you look at participation in the School Breakfast Program from 1976 to 1996 —and remember, once upon a time, I say to my colleagues, we used to think this program was only for rural areas, for students with long bus rides, students who were not going to be able to eat at home. Now what we find is the reality that in many of these families there are split shifts, different shifts, both parents working, and all too often these kids in urban areas and suburbs come to school and they really have not had a nutritious breakfast.

We saw a good increase in participation in the School Breakfast Program from 1976 to 1996, but now what has happened as a result of eliminating this small five-million-dollar outreach program is there is tremendous concern from USDA all the way to the different child advocacy organizations that the participation is going to begin to decline.

So here is an opportunity, colleagues, to invest a small amount of money in the basic idea that each child ought to have the same opportunity to reach his or her full potential. This is an opportunity for all of us to come through for these vulnerable children, understanding full well—and I know my colleague from Arizona is out here, but I say to him and this really is my conclusion—understanding full well that, indeed, there is a linkage to reform and to the work that he and others are doing on trying to get the money out of politics. There are a number of us who are absolutely convinced we have to act on this agenda. That is to say these children and these families are not the heavy hitters; they are not the big players; they are not the givers; they do not have the big lobbyists; they all too often are faceless and voiceless, and that it is profoundly wrong. I hope to get 100 votes for this amendment.

I yield the floor.

SENATOR JOHN MCCAIN OF ARIZONA: Before I call up my amendment, I wish to respond to my friend from Minnesota for just a moment on his amendment. I preface my remarks by saying I know of no more passionate or com-passionate member of this body than the senator from Minnesota, nor do I believe that there is anyone in this body who articulates as well as he the plight of those who, as he pointed out, may be underrepresented here in this body in our deliberations. I have grown and developed over the years a great respect and even affection for the senator from Minnesota because of my admiration for his incredible commitment to serving those who may not always have a voice.

But I say to the senator from Minnesota that this amendment, like many others, is what I call the Willie Sutton syndrome. When the famous bank robber was once asked why he robbed banks, he said, "Because that's where the money is." And time after time, I see amendments that are worthwhile and at times, as the senator from Minnesota just articulated, compelling, but they come out of funds that are earmarked for national defense. In my view, that is not an appropriate way to spend defense money.

I would also quickly point out that this is not the first time it has happened. There are literally billions of dollars now that we spend out of defense appropriations and authorization that have absolutely nothing to do with defending this nation's vital national security interests, again because of the Willie Sutton syndrome. Although I admire and appreciate the amendment of the senator from Minnesota, I would oppose it, not because of its urgency but because of its inappropriate placement on a defense appropriations bill. And I would also like to work with the senator from Minnesota when the Labor-HHS appropriations bill comes to the floor to see if we cannot provide that funding, which the senator from Minnesota appropriately points out is not a great deal of money given the large amounts of money we deal with and also considering the importance and urgency of the issue.

Mr. President, I ask unanimous consent—

SENATOR WELLSTONE: Will the senator yield at this moment?

SENATOR MCCAIN: I would be glad to yield to the senator from Minnesota for a comment.

SENATOR WELLSTONE: I thank my colleague. The respect is mutual.

I just wanted to say—it was going to be a question, but I can just make a comment instead—as a matter of history, the School Lunch Program was created by the Congress fifty years ago, and I quote, "As a measure of national security to safeguard the health and well-being of the nation's children." It was a direct response to the fact that many of the young men who were drafted in World War II were rejected due to conditions arising from nutritional deficiencies. So there is, in fact, a direct linkage to national defense.

It is, in fact, very much a national security issue to make sure that children have full nutrition and that we do not end up with men and women later on who have not been able to learn, not been able to earn and may, in fact, not even be healthy enough to qualify to serve our nation.

So it is an interesting history, and I just wanted my colleague to know that this program is very much connected to national security.

My second point is I too look forward to working with my colleague in the future. But I hope to win on this amendment now. This is simply a matter of saying, look, we have a budget that is 2.6 billion dollars over what the Pentagon asked. There have been plenty of studies which have pointed out excesses in the defense budget. Can we not at least authorize the Secretary of Defense to transfer this five million dollars.

And then, finally, I say to all my colleagues that I think there is going to come a point in time where people cannot—and I know the Senator from Arizona is not trying to do this—but people cannot say, well, we shouldn't vote for this now; we can't vote for this now; we won't vote for this now; there will be a more appropriate place; there will be a more appropriate time. And I find that when it comes to all these issues that have to do with how can we refurbish and renew and restore our national vow of equal opportunity for every child, the vote always gets put off. It always gets put in parenthesis. So I absolutely take what my friend from Arizona said in good faith. I look forward to working with him. But I do think that on this bill, on this amendment, this is the time to vote for such a small step for a good many very vulnerable children in our country.

I thank my colleague for his graciousness.

8

EDUCATION

> "We doom children to unequal lives in our public school system because we do not make the commitment to public schools in the United States of America."
>
> ~Senator Paul Wellstone, October 1, 1991

Senator Wellstone spoke often about caring for and nurturing children, as well as decrying the large class sizes and lack of funding for special education, head start, and teacher salaries. In his book, *Conscience of a Liberal*, Senator Wellstone states:

> When historians write about American politics over the past several decades, the ultimate indictment will be of the ways in which we have abandoned children and devalued the work of the adults who take care of children.

This passion and commitment to children is reflected in Senator Wellstone's speeches about education. His empathy is also reflected in his opposition to high-stakes testing, which was and is often promoted as "reform."

As someone with a minor learning disability, which caused him to have difficulty with standardized tests, Senator Wellstone was keenly aware of the stress that such tests caused students. He also believed that in the absence of any funding either to pay for the testing or address the underlying causes of a child's poor performance on a test, it was merely setting the school and children up for failure.

EDUCATION IN AMERICA
October 1, 1991

"We have a school in East St. Louis named for Dr. King," she says. "The school is full of sewer water and the doors are locked with chains. Every student in that school is black. It is like a terrible joke on history." A fourteen-year-old girl, East St. Louis, and I quote from Jonathan Kozal's fine book, *Savage Inequalities: Children in America's Schools.*

Letter to the editor, *Minnesota Star Tribune*, by a father of a six-year-old, excited that his daughter was going to a fine elementary school: "But imagine my dismay on bringing my daughter to the first day of first grade and finding that there was a total of thirty-six students in the class?" The school had to let go a first grade teacher.

At the Minnesota State Fair, Mr. President, I met a young woman. I said, "I'm Paul Wellstone." She introduced herself. I said, "What do you do?"

She said, "I'm a teacher." She said it really beaming; she was so proud.

I said, "What level do you teach at?"

She said elementary school.

I said to her, "Well, I was a college teacher, and if I had to do it over again, I would have taught in elementary school. It is so important what happens at that level."

By this time there were about fifty people around us and then, Mr. President, I made a mistake. I said, "What school do you teach at?"

And she looked at me, very awkward, very painful expression, and she said, "I do not have a job."

The classes are overcrowded. We know what we need to do. We have a young woman who wants to be an elementary schoolteacher, and we do not make the commitment.

The president of the United States visited Deal Junior High School in Washington, D.C. It is a fine school. Every politician is for the children. It has become the functional equivalent of kissing babies. It is a good photo opportunity to go to a really fine school.

But, Mr. President, what about the children in Anacostia? The president says what we need is not more resources but more results.

So that what we do in this administration proposal is we help one-half of one percent of the schoolchildren in this country. What about the rest of the schoolchildren?

Talk about choice, which includes private schools, which will, I think, Mr. President, further segregate education by both race and economic bracket, what about the children that we consign to schools that they would never go to if they had a choice?

Mr. President, we doom children to unequal lives in our public school system because we do not make the commitment to public schools in the United States of America.

We send all too many children to schools that no president and no politician and no CEO would ever send their children to. That is the reality of public education in the United States of America in all too many communities.

And then, Mr. President, we are told we need yet another report, and then another report, and then another report. We harp on the complexity of the matter to the point where that has become the ultimate simplification. We know what works.

We know that the first educational program is to make sure that every woman expecting a child has a diet rich in vitamins, minerals, and protein, and we do not fully fund the Women Infant Children Program. We know that for children to do well by the time they are in elementary school, they have to during those magic years—and every one of us as a parent knows this—have a warm, nurturing and supportive environment.

We do not fully fund the Head Start Program. The administration says we do not have money to do that. We know that if you want to have a good elementary school education, you need a ratio of one teacher to fifteen students so that teacher can give those students the nurturing and the encouragement and the intellectual stimulation that those students deserve.

We certainly know that something has gone wrong in our country when college students will tell us that they sell plasma at the beginning of the semester to buy textbooks because they cannot afford their education, and the community college teachers tell us that their students are too exhausted to learn.

I have to tell you something today, Mr. President, on the floor of the U.S. Senate. There have been enough reports, there has been enough rhetoric, and this administration's education program amounts to nothing more than what I would call a stone soup philosophy: Boil the water with the stone, and at the end you get no new nutrient, no new flavor, no new commitment to children.

We will only do well as a country when we finally understand that the real national security for America will be when we invest in the health and the skills and the intellect and the character of our children. That is the commitment we will make in the U.S. Senate; that is the commitment that has to be made in the House of Representatives.

I simply will not be silent when I see this administration offering up an educational program that is cynical. It is a sham. It has no bearing to the concerns and circumstances of the lives of so many children in this country.

It is time for us to draw the line in the Senate, and it is time for us to make a commitment to children in this country, a commitment where the rhetoric is backed up by a commitment of resources.

EDUCATING CHILDREN

February 6, 2001

Mr. President, I had a chance to speak before the National School Board Association yesterday. Sometimes it is only when you speak that you realize how strong your conviction is on an issue. I have come to the floor of the Senate to make an appeal to all senators, starting with Democrats.

The President, in his inaugural speech, talked about leaving no child behind. And the President, in his education proposal, also spoke about leaving no child behind. I think that is a wonderful value and a wonderful vision for our country. That, by the way, is the mission of the wonderful organization called the Children's Defense Fund headed by Marian Wright Edelman.

If we look at the arithmetic of the president's tax cut he is proposing this week for the country, and if we are to stay true to the theme of accountability—the president in his education proposal called for accountability—I would like to hold the administration accountable on the floor of the Senate, and with amendments and with debate, in what I think is going to be a historic debate.

The non-social Security surplus—putting the Social Security trust fund aside—is 3.1 trillion dollars. President Bush calls for 1.6 trillion dollars in tax cuts. The argument is: There is 1.5 trillion dollars left. What is the problem?

The problem is, first of all, when you look at the 1.6 trillion dollars and when you look at the 3.1-trillion-dollar surplus, it is not really that, because we all know the Medicare trust fund money will be kept separate, and now all of a sudden 3.1 trillion dollars in surplus becomes 2.6 trillion dollars. When you add to that the tax extenders—the tax credits that we all know will be extended—and the payments that will go to farmers and other groups of citizens in our country, we are now down to two trillion dollars. And when you understand that there will be Social Security trust fund solvency issues, which, if we do not deal with those issues, will mean that either benefits are cut or the age eligibility goes up, it may be less than two trillion dollars. That is two trillion dollars.

On the other side of the equation, the 1.6 trillion dollars in tax cuts—once you now understand that we will no longer be paying down part of the debt, and interest payments go up—becomes two trillion dollars—two trillion dollars and two trillion dollars—two trillion dollars in tax cuts, only really two trillion dollars in surplus; and there will be no resources for our investment to leave no child behind. There will be no resources.

So the only thing you have is a proposal, A, with vouchers, which I think is a nonstarter and I think ultimately will be discarded. Then what you have is telling states and school districts: You do tests every year, starting at age eight—third grade—all the way up to eighth grade. But we are setting the schools and the children and our teachers up for failure because we are not providing any of the resources to make sure that all of those children will not be left behind and will have an opportunity to achieve.

Fanny Lou Hamer is a great civil rights leader from the state of Mississippi. She once uttered the immortal words: I'm sick and tired of being sick and tired.

I am sick and tired of symbolic politics with children's lives. Where in this budget, where in the arithmetic of the tax cuts and the surplus, will there be the investment to make sure that no child is left behind?

Two percent of all the children who could benefit from Early Head Start, two years of age and under, benefit today. That is all we have funded.

With only fifty-percent of Head Start, only ten-percent for good child care for low-income families, much less middle-income families, when are we going to fully fund the IDEA program, which we made a commitment to school districts and states to do? Not in this budget. Not in this budget.

I say to senators and, in particular, since the majority leader is on the floor, to Democrats, it is extremely important that we have a civil debate, but it should be a passionate debate. We ought not to believe that in the call for bipartisanship, we should not as senators speak up for the values and the people we represent. On present course, the best we are going to get is a decade; if we fold and if we do not challenge the tax cut proposals and the plan of this administration, the best we will get is not one dollar for investment in children, in education, in health care, in prescription drug costs; and the worst we will get is deficits going up again.

I would like to, as a Democratic senator from Minnesota, make three suggestions:

A, we should hold the president and this administration accountable for the words, "leave no child behind." I take that seriously. I don't let anybody get away with saying my goal and my value and my vision is to leave no child behind, when I see only a pittance, if that, of investment in the health and skills and intellect and character of our children so we leave no child behind.

B, Democrats ought to be able to present a set of tax cuts which do not provide the vast majority of the benefits to the top one or five percent of the population. A lot of what President Bush is unfolding this week doesn't add up. You have the waitress, the single parent, making $23,000 a year with two children. She is not helped, because the tax cuts are not refundable. These tax cuts overwhelmingly go to the most affluent and powerful citizens. We should be able to present a clear alternative.

Finally, I would be willing to debate anybody, anywhere, anytime, anyplace over tax cuts that go to the very wealthy versus prescription drug costs for elderly people. You don't do that on the cheap. I would be willing to debate anybody on tax cuts that go to wealthy, high-income citizens versus expanding health care coverage for the forty-four million people who have no health insurance at all. I would be willing to debate anybody over tax cuts going primarily to wealthy people versus doing more for children, so when they come to kindergarten they really are ready to learn.

If we can't stand for these values and can't have this debate, then what in the world do we stand for? One more time, I summarize: The 3.1 trillion dollars becomes about 2.6, 2.7 trillion dollars right away because we are not going to touch the Medicare trust fund money, nor should we. Then we all know we are going to extend the tax credits. So all of a sudden it is about two trillion dollars. And the 1.6 trillion dollars in tax cuts automatically, once we understand we now have to pay the interest that we wouldn't have paid if we were paying down the debt, goes to two trillion dollars.

Where is going to be the investment in the children? Where is going to be the investment in education? Where is going to be the investment so that we make sure no child is left behind? When are we going to do something about the fact that we have the highest percentage of poor children among all the western European and all the advanced economies in the world? When are we going to do something about the fact that single elderly women also are among the poorest citizens in our country? Where is going to be the investment?

You don't proclaim the goal of leaving no child behind and then expect to do this on a tin- cup budget. That is all we are getting from this president and his priorities. It is time for debate on the floor of the Senate about the priorities of our country.

I yield the floor.

VOTING AGAINST
NO CHILD LEFT BEHIND
December 18, 2001

First of all, I thank my colleagues for their fine work.

Second, it is a little frustrating for me. There are many provisions in this bill that I had a chance to work on and to write. I am proud of it. But I have to say to the senator and especially my conservative friends that this is a stunning unfunded mandate. You are taking the essence of grassroots political culture and school districts and telling every school district and every school to test every child in grades three, four, five, six, and seven—not just Title I but every child in every school.

I have heard discussions about national priorities. This bill now makes education a national priority. But the only thing we have done is have a federal mandate that every child will be tested every year, but we don't have a federal mandate that every child will have the same opportunity to

do well in these tests. If they do not do well, they will need additional help.

Colleagues, just because there is money for the administration of the tests doesn't mean this isn't one gigantic unfunded mandate.

Look at this in the context of recession, hard times, and the cutbacks in state budgets and cutbacks in education. Look at this in the context of our now adding a whole new requirement and telling every district they have to test, having high stakes and holding the schools accountable.

My colleague from New Hampshire said: Senator Wellstone, you are talking about the IDEA program, but that is not really ESEA, and that is separate from Title I.

That is not what I hear in Minnesota.

I thank Senator Harkin for championing this cause. What I hear at the local level is if we had given Minnesota the two billion dollars they would have gotten if we made it mandatory on a glidepath for full funding over the next ten years, and forty-five million dollars this year, I was told we would put fifty percent of it into children with special needs. But then we could have additional dollars for other programs. Right now, the federal government has not lived up to its promise. We are now taking our own money that we could be using for after-school, for technology, for textbooks, for teacher recruitment, and we have to spend that money; whereas, we would have that additional money available if you would just provide the funding for IDEA. You can't separate funding for IDEA from any of the other educational programs.

This is not just about the children who have a constitutional right to have the best education. That is Senator Harkin's, and it is his soul. He has made that happen.

This is also about all the other children and support for educational programs at the local level. Title I money has gone up. But in the context of economic hard times and all the additional families and children who are becoming barely eligible, I will tell you something. I know that some senators do not like to hear this. We are in profound disagreement on this.

I think in our states we are going to hear from school board members and teachers, and we are going to hear from the educational community. They are going to say to us: What did you do to us? You gave us the tests, and then you gave us hardly anything that you said you would give us when it came to IDEA. You didn't provide the resources. You made this a giant unfunded mandate. You say you are going to hold our schools accountable, but by the same token, you haven't been accountable because you have not lived up to your promise.

They are right. I think there is going to be a real negative reaction from a lot of States. In my State of Minnesota, we have hard economic times. We are cutting back on education. We are laying off teachers.

I have two children who teach in our public schools. I have been to a school about every two weeks for the last eleven years. I believe I know this issue well. We are seeing all of these cutbacks. Minnesota is going to say: Why didn't you live up to your promise? You have given the tests and all this rhetoric about how it is a national priority, and I don't believe the Bush administration is going to make this a commitment next year. I do not know that you do.

Frankly, they now have this education bill. This was our leverage, which was to say we can't realize this goal of leaving no child behind—not on a tin-cup budget—not unless you make this

commitment. And there will be no education reform bill because it can't be reformed unless we live up to our commitment of providing the resources. And we have not.

I was in a school yesterday—the Phalen Lake School. I loved being there. It is on the east side of St. Paul. I don't think one of the students comes from a family with an income of over $15,000, or maybe $10,000 a year. It is just a rainbow of children with all kinds of culture and history. They are low-income children in the inner city.

Do you know why I went. They raised money to help the children in Afghanistan. The president asked them to do so. They are all beautiful. I loved being there. But do you want to know something. I know what those children need because there are teachers who tell me what they need. They need the resources for more good teachers and to retain those teachers. They need to come to kindergarten ready to learn without being so far behind .

Where is our commitment to affordable child care? We have two trillion dollars in tax cuts, and thirty-five billion dollars or forty billion dollars in the energy bill as tax cuts for producers. Where is the commitment to developmental child care from this Congress?

I know what they need. They need more after-school programs. They need a lot more Title I money—not just thirty-three percent or thirty-four percent of these children but many more children, and more help for reading and smaller class size. They need all of that. We could have provided them a lot more, and we didn't.

I will vote no.

9

THE ENVIRONMENT

> "Mr. President, I believe as a Senator from Minnesota that we have reached a point where unduly delaying action on reducing greenhouse gas emissions is foolhardy and it is tantamount to betrayal of our future generations. We know what this is going to do. The consequences can be catastrophic for our country and for the world, and I believe that the President and the United States of America have to do better in addressing this challenge."
>
> ~Senator Paul Wellstone, October 22, 1997

In 1969, Senator Gaylord Nelson of Wisconsin had an idea to raise awareness about environmental issues. For the past ten years, he had become frustrated by the lack of interest of his senate colleagues about the environment. While traveling from Berkeley after an environmental speech, he read an article about anti-war teach-in. It occurred to Senator Nelson that holding "teach-ins" might similarly help raise awareness of environmental issues.

In December, Senator Nelson selected a twenty-five-year-old named Denis Hayes as national coordinator. Hayes was the former student body president at Stanford, and had intended to go to Harvard Law School. Hayes, postponed those plans, and with the help of thousands of volunteers and the leadership of Senator Nelson, the first inaugural Earth Day occurred a year later on April 22, 1970.

Senator Nelson's work is often credited for creating momentum for the establishment of the Environmental Protection Agency as well as the passage of laws that eventually became known as the Clean Water Act. In his writings and speeches, Senator Wellstone embraced the same sense of activism and justice advanced by Senator Nelson. Indeed, Senator Wellstone was one of the first senators to call for the United States to sign an international treaty related to global warming and agree to specific benchmarks for carbon reduction.

A GLOBAL WARMING CHALLENGE
October 22, 1997

Mr. President, I would like to comment on what is a challenge unique in human history that we face as a nation, and I am talking about global warming. It is unique because we have to make important decisions without a visible crisis staring us in the face.

In the 1970s, we had the long gas lines, we had two oil price shocks, the taking of hostages by a revolutionary mob in Iran, and that spurred our nation to reduce its reliance on oil. And in the 1960s and the 1970s we had the dark clouds of particulates and the smog that smothered urban areas which moved us to clean up the air. Today, we are faced with a potentially greater threat, but it is not a visible threat. We are talking about something that is going to happen, something that is going to affect our children and their children, and the question is what are we going to do? It is a challenge for my state of Minnesota. It is a challenge for our country. It is a challenge for the whole human race. It is also a challenge about leadership. I am talking about the problem of global warming, the problem of climate change.

In 1992, for the Earth summit, President Bush made a commitment to return greenhouse gases to 1990 levels by the year 2000, and we have not lived up to that commitment. We have not honored that commitment. I believe the president, in 1993, made a similar commitment that we would reduce our greenhouse gases to the 1990 level by the year 2000.

I believe that the president's announcement today will fall far short of meeting this challenge—but I certainly want to say to the president and to the White House that I appreciate their efforts to try to move this process forward as we move toward a very important international gathering in Kyoto.

For more than a decade, the scientific community has investigated the issue. Initially, its reports called for more research, better modeling techniques, more data. But in December 1995, the Intergovernmental Panel on Climate Change, composed of more than 2,000 scientists from more than 100 countries, concluded that there was a discernible human impact on global climate.

In June, more than 2,000 U.S. scientists, including Nobel laureates, signed the Scientists' Statement on Global Disruption, which reads in part that the accumulation of greenhouse gases commits the Earth irreversibly to further global climate change and consequent ecological, economic and social disruption.

Mr. President, I believe as a senator from Minnesota that we have reached a point where unduly delaying action on reducing greenhouse gas emissions is foolhardy and it is tantamount to betrayal of our future generations. We know what this is going

to do. The consequences can be catastrophic for our country and for the world, and I believe that the president and the United States of America have to do better in addressing this challenge.

What has saddened me about this debate is that I believe we should be below 1990 levels certainly before the year 2010. I believe our country should make a commitment to meeting these kind of targets. I think the evidence shows that as opposed to being on the defensive, we should be proactive, and the very bridge the president talks about building to the next century is going to be a bridge that combines a sustainable environment with sustainable energy with a sustainable economy.

I think the country that is the most clean country is going to be the country with an economy powered by clean technologies, industries, and businesses. It is going to be a country run with an emphasis on energy efficiency and with a renewable energy policy. It is going to be a country which will generate far more jobs in the renewable energy and clean technology sectors, which are labor intensive, small business intensive and community building sectors.

We have an opportunity as we move into the next millennium to really create a new marriage between our environment and our economy. We are all but strangers and guests on this land, as the Catholic bishops have said. We have to take action now. What the president is calling for is not likely to be enough to address this challenge and the task before us. We can do better as a nation. We can be more respectful of our environment while still growing our economy.

In the Red River Valley, the people of North Dakota and people of Minnesota went through a living hell this past winter and spring. We don't want the floods in the Red River Valley to be five-year occurrences. And there will be other catastrophic consequences from global warming. For my state it could be agricultural devastation; for my state it could be deforestation and lower lake levels in the Boundary Waters, an area that we love, a crown jewel wilderness area in northern Minnesota.

The more important point, however, is that not only for ourselves but for our children and grandchildren we need to take much stronger action. We have to stand up to some of the powerful forces that are saying no to a meaningful treaty. We have to lay out a proactive, positive agenda which makes it crystal clear that energy efficiency and renewable energy and clean technologies will create many more small businesses and many more jobs for our country.

This marriage between our economy and our environment would respect the environment, respect the economy, and would give us an energy policy that is much more productive and positive, while helping us to build and sustain our communities and our country.

I am disappointed in the position the president seems to have taken on targets and timetables for climate change action. I hope as we move forward toward an international treaty, our country will take a stronger negotiating position. We need to be the leaders of the world in meeting what I think is perhaps the most profound environmental challenge which we have ever faced.

ENVIRONMENTAL JUSTICE
February 9, 1998

Madam President, I want to move on and talk about a related topic, in fact, very related, and this is a discussion that is urgent and long overdue. It has to do with the bill, S. 270, that would result in the dumping of low-level radioactive waste in a small, poor, majority Latino community in rural west Texas. I want to stop that from happening,

not only in Sierra Blanca, but in poor minority communities all over this country.

The best way to get this conversation going, which is a conversation about environmental justice, is to make sure that the story of Sierra Blanca gets told, and it is an incredible story.

Last week, several of the people who have been telling that story for several years were here in Washington. Father Ralph Solis, who is the parish priest for Sierra Blanca, led a delegation of Texans who told us of the anger and the anguish of the people of Sierra Blanca. It is not just the people of Sierra Blanca who are organizing. Citizens from all over Texas, from cities and towns through which radioactive waste will be passing on its way to Sierra Blanca, are all demanding that their voices be heard.

The newspaper columnist Molly Ivins has written that, "This is community action and local organizing at its very best." I couldn't agree more.

Let me tell you something about Sierra Blanca. It is a small town in one of the poorest areas of Texas. The average income of the people who live there is less than $8,000 a year, and thirty-nine percent of them live below the poverty line. Over sixty-six percent of the residents are Mexican American, and many speak only Spanish. It is a town that already has one of the largest sewage sludge projects in the world. Every week, 250 tons of partially treated sludge are brought to Sierra Blanca.

So why has Sierra Blanca been targeted with both a sewage sludge project and a radioactive dump? I am firmly convinced the issue here is one of environmental justice. The tragedy of Sierra Blanca is part of the larger and very disturbing pattern across the country. In far too many instances, poor people of color simply don't have the political clout to keep the pollution out of their communities. Studies by the United Church of Christ's Commission for Racial Justice, for example, found that race was the single best predictor of the location of commercial hazardous waste facilities, and Texas was second only to California in the number of such facilities located in communities with above-average percentage of minorities. I don't think that is a coincidence.

Let me be clear about one thing, Mr. President. Sierra Blanca is not being singled out because its residents are unusually fond of waste. In April 1992, the Texas Waste Authority commissioned a telephone poll of surrounding communities, areas where the poorest residents don't even have telephones, and they found that sixty-four percent of the people oppose the dump.

But you don't need a poll to tell you that. Just show up at any town meeting or any licensing hearing. Local residents are often angry and emotional about their community being turned into a radioactive dump. And they have every right to be.

Let us be clear about one other thing as well. Science does not explain the selection of Sierra Blanca, either. In the early 1980s, the Texas Waste Authority screened the entire state to find the most scientifically appropriate site. Their engineering consultants, Dames & Moore, concluded that the Sierra Blanca site was unsuitable for a nuclear dump because of its complex geology. But, lo and behold, that was the site that was chosen.

You will hear again and again from colleagues on the other side that this sitting decision is a purely local matter. It is not. The most obvious reason is that it is up to the Congress to ratify this Compact between Texas, Maine, and Vermont. Without the Compact, it is unlikely there will be a dump. Without the upfront payments from the other states, where is the construction money going to come from? And by the Texas Waste Authority's own projections, the dump will not be economically viable if Maine and Vermont do not sign up in advance. Texas does not generate enough waste.

There are other reasons why this debate rises above the purely local level. If the Texas Compact passes the Senate, it is entirely possible that Sierra Blanca will become the low-level radioactive waste dump for the entire country. Backers of the Compact say that that is not their plan. They say no other states besides Maine and Vermont will ship waste to Texas. If that is the case, then I propose a solution. And I am hoping there will be support for this.

Let the Senate agree to an amendment I want to offer, which is just like the Doggett amendment that passed the House, limiting the Compact to Maine and Vermont. Now, it seems to me, if the argument is being made that the only waste that is going to come to Texas is from Maine and Vermont, then let us just pass that amendment. And let us be clear about it. Then the debate is over.

But we cannot shirk our responsibilities by pretending that this is nothing more than a state or local affair. The Sierra Blanca dump is unlikely to be built if the Senate rejects this Compact. But if the Senate approves this Compact, Sierra Blanca may become the nation's premier dump site for low-level radioactive waste. It is that simple.

The Senate vote will largely determine whether or not a grave injustice is inflicted on a community that deserves no such thing. It would be easy for all of us to turn our backs and just ignore this issue. But there is no way for the Senate to wash its hands of this business. For good or ill, we bear moral responsibility for what happens to the people of Sierra Blanca. This is a wrong that richly deserves to be righted. And we have the power to do just that.

Mr. President, again, let me just make it clear that this is an issue of environmental justice. It is a David versus Goliath fight. There are lots of big guns in here that are pushing for this waste dump site. But we have one thing on our side. My colleagues have said, "Rest assured, this will only be waste from Maine and Vermont that will go to Texas." I say, if that is the case, please support the Doggett amendment. It has already passed the House of Representatives. Then we can go forward.

I will have one other amendment which just says that if we approve the Compact, but it turns out that it can be proven that this has a discriminatory effect on a community of color or low-income people, then they have the right to go to court. If those amendments pass, then this Compact will pass the floor of the Senate.

Mr. President, I do believe that the people of Sierra Blanca and hundreds of minority communities just like them from around the country have not been given their due. But we can make the system work. I am firmly convinced of that. Sometimes justice needs a second chance. Sometimes it needs a little push. And over the next few weeks, I think we are going to give justice a second chance on the floor of the U.S. Senate.

I am hoping that these amendments will be accepted. I believe that would be the right thing to do. I think there should be strong bipartisan sup-port for that. If that does not happen, then I am prepared to use all of the hours on the floor of the U.S. Senate that I have at my disposal as a senator—and I will use those many hours—to talk about environmental justice in this country.

Over and over and over again, we essentially take this waste and we dump it, right on the heads of low-income people. Over and over and over again, we look to the communities of color, we look to poor communities, we look to the communities that are not the heavy hitters, that are not well connected, and this is where we put it.

This happens all across the country. I can bring to the floor of the Senate study after study after study that show that. I can marshal the evidence. I am hoping that we will agree that this Compact will be something we can pass, if we make it clear that the waste can only come from Maine and Vermont. If not, I think for the first time on the floor of the U.S. Senate we will have a really—maybe not the first time—but we will certainly have a very thorough and important debate, I think, about environmental justice.

10

HUMAN RIGHTS ABUSES IN CHINA

> "Some say that we cannot influence what goes on in China, that the country is too proud, too large, and that changes take too long. I disagree. . . . As Americans, it is our duty and in our interest to make the extra effort required to promote freedom and democracy in China, and to bring it into compliance with international standards on human rights."
> ~Senator Paul Wellstone, October 28, 1997

Senator Wellstone used his position to bring attention to human rights abuses throughout the world, but the vast majority of his speeches on this issue related to China. Regardless of the economic opportunities that could be generated by increased trade with China, as well as China's strategic military position in the Asian peninsula, Senator Wellstone's criticism was unflinching. He called upon China to release political dissidents. He opposed the normalization of trade or "free trade" with China. He even publicly opposed China's bid to host the 2008 summer Olympics and admonished his fellow senators for not joining his opposition.

IN OPPOSITION TO MOST FAVORED NATION TREATMENT TO THE PRODUCTS OF THE PEOPLE'S REPUBLIC OF CHINA CONFERENCE REPORT

February 25, 1992

Mr. President, I rise in support of the conference report on this important legislation to impose conditions on continued most-favored-nation status for China. I supported the majority leader's earlier legislation to require the president to terminate MFN status for China 180 days after enactment unless China had fulfilled various criteria in the areas of human rights, trade, weapons proliferation, and forced labor.

Congressional votes on this issue in the Senate last July and in the House last November sent powerful signals to the government of China on the broad bipartisan consensus on this issue developed during the last year. Today we can send an even more powerful signal by passing this legislation and putting the Chinese government on notice: the United States will not tolerate persistent, egregious human rights abuses by its trading partners.

I remain deeply troubled by the administration's willingness to overlook China's major violations of internationally recognized standards of human rights and its failure to observe the international nonproliferation regimes. I believe the administration's policy of maintaining cordial relations with the government of China is unwise, and joined twenty of my Senate colleagues in a recent letter urging the president to reject Chinese Premier Li Peng's request for a meeting in New York three weeks ago.

Almost three years after the brutal massacre in Tiananmen Square in June 1989, with continued repression against supporters of the democracy movement in China and in occupied Tibet, Congress must finally act decisively to demonstrate that unrelenting repression of basic human rights will not be condoned among our trading partners.

This conference report would prohibit a one-year renewal of MFN status in June of this year unless the president certifies that China has accounted for and released its citizens detained, accused or sentenced due to activities related to the Tiananmen Square massacre. The original Senate version would have also conditioned MFN renewal on several provisions regarding arms control, human rights, trade, the status of Hong Kong, and suspension of China's forced sterilization program. Many of these provisions were weakened at the urging of the administration to require simply that the president certify to the Congress that China is making "overall significant progress" in each area.

The provisions requiring presidential certification of progress toward, for example, ending religious persecution in China and Tibet, halting intimidation of Chinese students in the United States, allowing human rights groups to monitor trials and prisons, removing unfair trade barriers to United States goods, protecting United States copyrights and intellectual property, adhering to international arms control regimes, and reforming other areas are thus not as strong as I had hoped. The destabilizing effect of the arms sales, including: First, the sale of nuclear-capable M-11 missiles, and their mobile launchers, to Pakistan; second, the sale of technology to Algeria which could be used to develop nuclear-grade materials; and third, China's provision to Iraq of materials used in the production of nerve gas and missile fuel, all fly in the face of China's claims regarding nonproliferation.

While I am disappointed we were not able to maintain the tougher sanctions in the House-Senate conference committee, I am hopeful that these changes will provide a veto-proof majority for this legislation. I will support the conference report, and urge my colleagues on the appropriate committees of jurisdiction to continue to monitor closely enforcement of its provisions by the Bush administration, over whose stubborn objections the measure will hopefully be enacted.

I know that for many farmers who could be affected by a slow-down in grain exports to China, especially those from farm states like Minnesota, legislation to suspend MFN status to China remains a two-edged sword. China is a major United States agricultural export market, although its rank fluctuates widely from year to year. For example, in 1986, it ranked sixtieth; the next year, it ranked seventeenth. According to the Congressional Research Service [CRS], in 1989 China was the eighth largest foreign market for United States agricultural exports, purchasing more than 1.4 billion dollars' worth of products. In 1990, China ranked eleventh among United States foreign agricultural markets, importing about 800 million dollars' worth of agricultural products. China has participated in both the Export Enhancement Program and the Targeted Assistance Program in recent years. While it has been eligible to participate in U.S. export credit guarantee programs (GSM-102 and GSM-103), it has not yet done so.

But I believe it is wrong to assume that American farmers oppose automatically conditioning MFN status on human rights and other reforms. Conditioning trade benefits on basic human rights is important to American farmers, in spite of the potential short-term burdens those conditions may impose. I urge my colleagues not to sell farmers short on their support of human rights worldwide.

Agricultural trade with China must remain a serious factor as we seek to develop a coherent trade policy, and as we link United States trade policy to overall foreign and human rights policy. I know the burdens that China could impose upon United States—including Minnesota—wheat farmers by retaliating against our refusal to condone China's appalling record on human rights, labor rights, unfair trade practices, and arms exports. The worst-case scenario, which assumes a complete cutoff by China of wheat imports from the United States, would likely entail negative economic consequences for our state. I am hopeful that such a scenario can be avoided.

Let me reiterate my position. I do not favor using food as a weapon, and I do not favor grain embargoes as a general tool of foreign policy. Declining to extend MFN status to China, however, is neither of those. MFN status is a benefit that can and should be revoked if circumstances warrant. China's longstanding abuses warrant such a revocation. I am hopeful that the measures required by this conference report will result in positive movement on the part of China, not unjustified retaliation.

More than a year after the Bush administration renewed MFN status to China claiming that the policy would promote human rights, the State Department's own recently published Country Reports on Human Rights Practices for 1991 observes that "China's human rights practices remained repressive, falling far short of internationally accepted norms." Unwarranted detention, indiscriminate sentencing, and brutal torture of members of China's pro-democracy movement and others continues unabated. In addition, China continues to refuse to participate as a full and responsible party in international efforts to control the proliferation of sophisticated military technology and weapons, including biological, nuclear and chemical technologies. The United States must finally insist

upon real changes in these practices before again renewing MFN status to China.

In this exceptional case, where the government of China has consistently ignored international calls for reform, I believe that we should use legitimate trade-policy tools to prompt significant reforms in human rights, unfair trade practices, and weapons proliferation. I urge my colleagues to underscore the importance of upholding internationally recognized standards on these issues by supporting this conference report. I urge my colleagues to signal to the Chinese leadership that MFN is a benefit they can no longer take for granted. I urge my colleagues to vote not only for this conference report, but to vote to over-ride the president's anticipated veto should it come to the Senate floor.

Retention of preferential trade advantages under MFN status is critically important to the Chinese government. The United States should insist on real and substantial reforms in these areas before renewing unrestricted MFN status. If the U.S. Congress must lead the way on this issue over the objections of President Bush, as it has on so many others, so be it. A foreign policy which fosters peace, democracy, respect for human rights and fair trade must continue to be our goal.

UNITED STATES—CHINA SUPPORT
October 28, 1997

Mr. President, I rise to address the direction of our country's relationship with China. Right now, the Clinton administration is busy with the state visit of Chinese President Jiang Zemin. A state visit is the highest, most formal diplomatic event hosted by the United States. The champagne will flow, and flattering toasts will be made.

I disagree with this red-carpet treatment, Mr. President. There is no question that United States-Chinese relations are crucial and important for both countries. It is wrong, however, for the United States to host a state visit for President Jiang Zemin until we see significant progress made on human rights in China. Instead of a ceremonial visit, we should be holding a working visit with the Chinese leadership, focusing on the critical issues that exist between our two nation, like human rights, weapons proliferation, and trade.

China continues to wage a war against individual freedoms and human rights. Hundreds, and perhaps thousands, of dissidents and advocates of political reform were detained just last year. They included human rights and pro-democracy activists, and members of religious groups. Many have been sentenced to long prison terms where they have been beaten, tortured, and denied medical care.

Scores of Roman Catholics and Protestants were arrested. A crack-down in Tibet was carried out during the "Strike Hard" campaign. Authorities ordered the closure of monasteries in Tibet and banned the Dalai Lama's image. At one monastery which was closed, over ninety monks and novices were detained or disappeared.

Harry Wu, a man of extraordinary courage and character, has documented China's extensive forced labor system. His research has identified more than 1,100 labor camps across China, many of which produce products for export to dozens of countries around the world, including the United States.

Because he criticized his government, Harry Wu was also imprisoned in these camps. For nineteen years in twelve different forced labor camps across China, Harry was forced to mine coal, manufacture chemicals and build roads. He survived beatings, torture, and starvation. He witnessed the death of many of his fellow prisoners from brutality, disease, starvation, and suicide.

According to Amnesty International, throughout China, mass summary executions continue to be carried out. At least 6,000 death sentences and 3,500 executions were officially recorded last year. The real figures are believed to be much higher.

Our own State Department reported that in 1996: "All public dissent against the party and government was effectively silenced by intimidation, exile, the imposition of prison terms, administration detention, or house arrest. No dissidents were known to be active at year's end."

Mr. President, that is a chilling, deeply disturbing statement. It cuts to the core values of our nation. And it was made by our own government, and this administration. Yet, this week, the administration will welcome President Jiang with pomp and circumstance. These actions indicate that, where China is concerned, what we have is not a policy of constructive engagement, but one of unconditional engagement.

Let us put some names and human faces to the statistics and generalities we have all heard with regards to China.

In May 1996, Wang Hui was detained. She was the wife of a jailed labor activist. While detained, she was denied water and other liquids. She tried to kill herself by hanging. According to Human Rights Watch, after being cut down by police, she was punished with severe beating.

Ngawang Choephel is a Fulbright Scholar from Middlebury College. He studied music, and returned to his homeland to document the ancient music and culture of Tibet. It is disappearing under the heel of the Chinese government. As a result of his work, he was convicted in February, and sentenced to eighteen years imprisonment for espionage. His crime—sending videotapes of ethnic Tibetan music and dancing out of China.

Last year, Wang Dan was sentenced to eleven years in prison on charges of conspiring to subvert the Chinese government. Prior to sentencing, Wang had already been held seventeen months in incommunicado detention. His crime: He was a leader of the Tiananmen movement.

Two years ago, Beijing sentenced Wei Jingsheng to fourteen more years of incarceration for the crime of peacefully advocating democracy and political reform. Wei had been arrested and sentenced after he wrote wall posters on the Democracy Wall outside Beijing. They argued for true democracy and denounced Deng Xiaoping.

I have read Mr. Wei's work and his letter from prison. I can't tell you how impressed and moved I was by them. As a political scientist, I seldom, if ever, have read such an eloquent and intelligent espousal of democracy and human rights. Making the letters all the more remarkable is the fact that they were written while Wei was in prison or labor camps, mostly in solitary confinement. He has been jailed for all but six months of the last eighteen years.

Wei Jingshen is not only China's most prominent dissident and prisoner of conscience, but ranks with the greatest fighters for democracy and human rights of this century. He brings to mind Martin Luther King, Nelson Mandela, and, of course, Alexander Solzhenitsyn. I was honored to join many of my colleagues in nominating Wei for the Nobel Peace Prize.

Last week, Mr. Wei's sister came to the United States to tell the administration that he is dying in jail, and that this summit may be his last chance of emerging from detention alive. It is urgent that the Chinese government release Wei and that he be given the medical care that he desperately needs, but has been denied.

By agreeing to this state visit without any significant concessions on human rights, like the release of Wei Jingsheng, the Clinton administration squandered its strongest source of leverage with Beijing.

This is not to say that all dialog between the United States and China or that working level visits

are wrong. Instead, I believe that the symbolism of a state level visit is inappropriate given our strong disagreement with China over its human rights record. That is why I cosponsored a resolution with senators Feingold and Helms to urge the president to downgrade this event from a state visit to working visit.

The Chinese have said they do not welcome American advice on what they view as a "purely internal affair." Welcome or not, President Clinton must insist that China's leaders take specific actions on human rights.

Indeed, I believe strongly that the administration has a moral duty to press a range of issues with the Chinese government that it may not welcome, but that are of enormous importance to the Chinese people, and the United States.

Specifically, I call on President Clinton to demand:

The immediate and unconditional release of Wei Jingsheng, Wang Dan, and other prisoners of conscience held in jails in China and Tibet.

Improvement in the conditions under which political, religious, and labor dissidents are detained in China and Tibet. This includes providing prisoners with adequate medical care and allowing international humanitarian agencies access to detention facilities.

Significant progress in improving the overall human rights conditions in China and Tibet. The Chinese government must take concrete steps to increase freedom of speech, freedom of religion, and freedom of association, in order to comply with the Universal Declaration of Human Rights, which it signed in 1948.

Some say that we cannot influence what goes on in China, that the country is too proud, too large, and that changes take too long. I disagree. For years we have pressured the Chinese on human rights, and to let up now is tantamount to defeat for the cause of human justice. Dissidents who have been freed and come to the United States have thanked advocates for keeping them alive, by keeping the pressure on, and focusing attention on their plight.

As Americans, it is our duty and in our interest to make the extra effort required to promote freedom and democracy in China, and to bring it into compliance with international standards on human rights.

Mr. President, I yield the floor.

BEIJING'S BID FOR THE OLYMPICS
July 12, 2001

The International Olympic Committee is going to announce tomorrow which country will host the 2008 summer games. The competition is fierce. Toronto and Paris are serious contenders. Yet it seems likely that Beijing will get the prize.

I will speak briefly about this decision because I think there should be some discussion on the Senate floor and the implications. I believe China's authoritarian and oppressive government should not be granted the privilege of hosting the 2008 games. The current government in Beijing does not deserve the international legitimacy and the spotlight that this honor bestows. Its chronic failure to respect human rights violates the fundamental spirit of the Games, and I think it should disqualify Beijing.

Many of my colleagues argue that human rights should never be a consideration in determining our trade relations with other countries. I don't agree. I do think a government's record on human rights should not be ignored with respect to choosing the site for the Olympics which confers enormous prestige on the host government and which is intended to celebrate human dignity and achievement.

I have a sense-of-the-Senate amendment because the feeling was it would be inappropriate to do it on an appropriations bill. I do not believe doing it that way gets the support that it deserves. I know there are senators who argue that to say the Olympics should not be in China is to politicize this question. If we are silent about this and Beijing hosts the Olympics, we are making a political statement. The political statement we are making is [that] their violation of human rights does not matter.

Either way, it is a political statement. I prefer to speak out for human rights. The Olympics are first and foremost about sports and the joy of athletic competition, but human rights and dignity are also central to the Olympic ideal. The Olympic charter makes clear "respect for universal fundamental ethical principles" are central to the Olympic ideal.

Look at the State Department report. China's government record has worsened as it committed "numerous serious abuses" from raiding home churches, imprisoning Tibetan monks and nuns, locking up Internet entrepreneurs, silencing democracy activists, and cracking down on Falun Gong."

The Chinese government continues to hold a number of American scholars on suspicious charges of spying. Dr. Gao Zhan has not been allowed to contact her husband, her five-year-old child, both American citizens, or her lawyer or the State Department.

This doesn't matter? Moreover, hundreds of thousands of people languish in jails and prison camps merely because they dared to practice their Christian or Buddhist or Islamic faith. These are the facts. Respected international human rights organizations have documented hundreds of thousands of cases of arbitrary imprisonment, torture, house arrest, or death at the hands of the government. That is a fact.

What they have done, the brutal crackdown on the Falun Gong is unbelievable. This is a harmless Buddhist sect. According to international media reports, approximately 50,000 of these practitioners have been arrested and detained, more than 5,000 have been sentenced to labor camps without a trial, and hundreds have received prison sentences after sham trials, show trials. Detainees have often been tortured and scores of practitioners of this faith have died in government custody. These are facts. This is the empirical evidence.

Millions of others have been persecuted for so-called crimes such as, if you are ready, advocating for political pluralism and the ideals of democracy. Hundreds continue to languish in jail under a "counterrevolutionary" law which the government repealed three years ago. Some of them are survivors of the Tiananmen Square massacre.

While China signed the International Covenant on Civil and Political Rights—I remember the Clinton administration has made such a big deal of this—the Chinese government has not ratified it. Instead, it stepped up its repression of individuals seeking to exercise the very rights the covenant is designed to protect. And we do not speak out about this.

We make the argument, to grant this country the honor of hosting the Olympics, we should not raise questions about this because to raise questions would be to make a political statement about the Olympics. Isn't it also making a political statement about the Olympics not to raise questions, to legitimize and validate this repression?

Chinese courts have sentenced members of the Chinese Democracy Party, an open opposition party, to terms of eleven, twelve, and thirteen years for "conspiring to subvert state power." This is a fact.

Charges against these political activists—do you know what they are? They included this: They organized a party—wound up in prison. They received funds from abroad promoting independent trade unions—they wound up in prison. They used e-mails to distribute materials abroad—they wound up in prison. And they gave interviews to foreign reporters—they wound up in prison.

Here is where the Olympics is going to go. Without a word from our government? Without a word from the Senate?

Chinese officials have also ruthlessly suppressed dissent from ethnic minorities, including Xinjiang and Tibet. According to a report by Amnesty International, the Chinese government has reportedly committed gross violations, including widespread use of torture to exact confessions, lengthy prison sentences, and numerous executions. Are we not going to speak up about a government that tortures its citizens and that executes its citizens for no other reason than they have had the courage to speak up for democracy or to try to practice their religion?

In an apparent attempt to stop the flow of information overseas about this crackdown, Chinese security officials continue to detain a prominent businesswoman, Ms. Rebiya Kadeer, in the Province of Xinjiang. Her husband is a U.S. resident who broadcasts on Radio Free Asia and the Voice of America, championing the cause of people. She was arrested by the Chinese security forces on her way to meet with members of a visiting Congressional staff delegation.

For years, the same Ms. Kadeer has been praised by the Chinese government for her efforts to promote economic development, including a project to help women own their own businesses. She has also been praised in the *Wall Street Journal* for her business savvy. She owned a department store in a provincial capital, as well as a profitable trading company. But now she has been put out of business, charged with—here is the charge, Mr. President—"illegally offering state secrets across the border," and sentenced to eight years of hard labor. Her son and her secretary were also detained and sent to a labor camp.

Given this horrendous record, I do not believe China should be rewarded for this sort of repression. I am not a cold war warrior. I am not trying to resurrect the cold war. My father was born in Odessa, Ukraine. Then, to stay ahead of czarist Russia, he was a Jewish immigrant. They moved to Habarovsk in the Far East, Siberia, and then Harbin, and lived in Pakeen, lived in China, and he came to the United States of America at age seventeen, in 1914. I am an internationalist.

I look forward to the day that Beijing hosts the Olympic games. The Chinese people are some of the most extraordinary, talented, and resourceful people on the planet. I do not for a moment want to bash or overgeneralize. I dream of a day when I can come to the Senate floor and I can cel-

ebrate the idea of China hosting the Olympic games. But not now. Not with the persecution, not with the torture, not with the murder of innocent citizens, not with the political oppression, not with the religious persecution, not with what they have done to the country of Tibet, the people of Tibet.

I believe strongly China's authoritarian, repressive government should not be granted the privilege of hosting the 2008 games. It does not deserve the international legitimacy and spotlight that this honor bestows. Instead, this government's chronic failure to respect human rights, I believe, violates the fundamental spirit of the Olympic games and should disqualify Beijing.

This is perhaps my morning for tilting at windmills because I believe the international committee will probably give China the Olympic Games, but sometimes it is important just to make that statement on the floor of the Senate. I believe others should speak out as well.

11

BOSNIA

> "How can we turn our gaze away from what is happening? Ethnic cleansing, rape camps, the systematic slaughter of people? I just do not feel like we have spoken up. I think the standard that historians are going to use to measure us is who spoke up and who did not."
> ~Senator Paul Wellstone, March 5, 1993

In light of his opposition to military action in Iraq, Senator Wellstone is often viewed as a pacifist. His advocacy for military intervention in Bosnia, however, dispels such simple stereotypes. Senator Wellstone recognized that there was a time and place to deploy troops to maintain a peace and break a cycle of violence.

As the Cold War ended, Yugoslavia began the process of breaking up into smaller nation-states: Bosnia and Herzegovina, Croatia, Slovenia, Macedonia, Serbia and Montenegro. Bosnia and Herzegovina were the most ethnically diverse. Although a coalition government was initially formed in 1991 that included each ethnicity, conflicts immediately arose about the future of Bosnia and Herzegovina. Soon there was widespread armed conflict among Bosnians, Serbs, and Croats, including rape and ethnic cleansing.

The Dayton Peace Accords, signed on December 14, 1995, carved Bosnia into two autonomous and ethnically based entities, separated by a demilitarized zone. It created a temporary peace, enforced by United Nations peacekeeping troops, although tensions remain.

Senator Wellstone was one of the first United States Senators to argue in favor of both diplomatic and military intervention in Bosnia. His speeches on the subject were eloquent and personal. He often referred to his father's heritage as a Jewish immigrant, in the context of the United States' duty to actively stop genocide wherever it occurs in the world.

WHAT WILL HISTORY SAY?
March 5, 1993

Madam President, Tony Lewis said:

When starving Muslims in the Cerska area came out of their villages to collect the few relief bundles that had fallen anywhere near them, Serbs shelled them.

Serbian forces used the airdrops as a cover for a major offensive against the Cerska enclave. They overran it, and according to reports from the area, killed hundreds of civilians. A United Nations official called it a "massacre."

We have in Minnesota a torture center. It is probably very well known around the country. I wish there was no need for it. And we have men and women who came from other countries to this center so they can try to recover and rebuild their lives from the torture that they have experienced.

I met with a woman who is a psychiatrist who just came back from Serbia. She spent time with women who have been raped in the rape camps.

I do not know quite what to say on the floor of the U.S. Senate today—I once read from a book called *The Abandonment of the Jews*—except to say this. I speak first as a U.S. senator from Minnesota. I speak second of all as an American Jew.

I sometimes wonder whether or not we have learned anything in the world in the last forty years. I think there comes a time when silence is betrayal, and I think we have had too much silence in the U.S. Congress over this issue.

I told my wife, Sheila, the other day: I do not want to be self-righteous about it. I have been part of that silence.

A long time ago, I called for some kind of military action, arguing that between doing nothing and protracted ground warfare there surely were other military options. But yet and still, I really worry that historians are going to write about me and others, and that what they are going to say is: They were too busy; they had campaign reform to work on, health care reform to work on, budgets to work on.

How can we turn our gaze away from what is happening? Ethnic cleansing, rape camps, the systematic slaughter of people? I just do not feel like we have spoken up. I think the standard that historians are going to use to measure us is who spoke up and who did not.

I hope that committees in the U.S. Senate will start hearings, and I hope that here on the floor of the Senate and the floor of the House of Representatives, representatives and senators will come to the floor and speak about what it is they believe should be done. I must tell you, I am not proud. I am not proud of the European countries, and I am not proud right now of our very timid response.

I think we have turned our gaze away from a slaughter, from a slaughter of people, from ethnic cleansing, from the murder of people, from the rape camps. I do not think we can be silent any longer. I do not believe we can turn our backs on this any longer. And I believe there has to be some kind of strong international response.

Madam President, I hope next week I will have more to say, more to say in specifics. But, like many senators, I am going home this weekend, back to Minnesota. And I just did not want to leave this week without saying something about this.

LIFTING THE ARMS EMBARGO ON BOSNIA AND HERZEGOVINA
May 12, 1994

Mr. President, today we consider legislation to end the United States arms embargo on Bosnia. As many of my colleagues know, I have for over two years operated within a very interventionist framework on Bosnia. I have persistently argued that brutal Serb aggression has been intolerable, and that we must do what we can to stop it in a much more forceful way than we have so far.

When the Senate voted in January on this issue, I supported the view that the U.N.-sponsored international arms embargo against the Bosnian Muslims should be lifted. I continue to believe that. Today we must choose between two alternative men of reaching that goal.

My trip to the former Yugoslavia a few months ago underscored for me the proportions of the crisis, and the need for more forceful intervention by United States and our NATO allies. It confirmed what I had believed for many months with respect to the role of the U.N. forces there: that they have been struggling under a mandate that is much too limited. I know they have been subjected to much criticism, some of it justified. They have been in a very difficult position for a very long time.

During my trip, I talked with United Nations troops throughout the region, who have been doing a tough job with relatively few resources and too little political support for their difficult mission. If we are to expect the U.N. forces there to do its job better, they need a tougher, broader mandate to enable them to respond more quickly and more forcefully to Serb aggression and harassment.

I saw the results of the war, talked with refugees about the devastating impact of the war on their families, their homes, their lives, and their futures. And I returned to the United States more convinced than ever that the United States must take a firmer stance toward Serbian aggression.

And we have in recent months begun to take a firmer stand, shamed into it by the marketplace bombing of Sarajevo and the continued bombardment of innocent civilian populations in and around Gorazde. The continued threat of NATO air strikes to protect the Muslim enclaves, which are authorized by Congress in the Mitchell amendment, must be real and immediate.

The senseless slaughter of innocent non-combatants, and the persistent ethnic cleansing campaigns, must be stopped by forceful NATO and U.N. action. We cannot continue to allow the U.N. and Bosnian Muslim forces to bear the brunt of persistent Serb harassment and attack.

To do this, I believe we must lift the embargo now. If possible, we should do it with the assent of the international community, in full recognition of the implications of that action.

That has not always been my position. For many months, I opposed lifting the arms embargo. But I returned from my sobering trip last December convinced that the embargo policy is no longer sustainable. We must send a strong signal of our willingness to at least allow the Bosnian Muslims to defend themselves.

The Mitchell amendment does that. It is the one of the two alternative approaches that I believe makes the most strategic sense, and that poses the greater likelihood of success in our efforts to protect civilian populations there.

For months, the administration has pressed our Western allies unsuccessfully to lift the arms embargo against the Bosnian Muslims. Today we read in the papers that the dispute over how to handle Bosnia between the United States and France is rising to new heights. Those tensions will continue to grow, and frankly do not look as though they can be resolved very easily at the Security Council.

But if our high-minded commitment to a new world order in which the United Nations helps to act as a guarantor of rights and freedoms around the world is to mean anything at all, we must give the Security Council another, final chance to reconsider its opposition to lifting the arms embargo.

The Mitchell amendment requires the president to seek immediately the agreement of our allies to terminate the embargo. I urge him to do that with all the diplomatic and political force that can be mustered, as soon as possible.

If the Security Council vetoes such an effort, or if the president refuses to pursue it vigorously at the United Nations, then I think we must pursue the immediate lifting of the embargo if circumstances continue to deteriorate there, and allow the Bosnian Muslims to defend themselves against Serb aggression. That is why I requested that a firm deadline be included in the amendment, to guarantee that the administration's consultations with Congress to lift the embargo proceed as quickly as possible if the United Nations refuses to go along.

I must say honestly, while I intend to vote for the Mitchell amendment today, I am at the end of my rope on this question. If the international community is unwilling to act to lift the embargo, and is unwilling to intervene more forcefully by military and other means to protect humanitarian aid delivery and noncombatant populations in the enclaves, then we must act to lift the embargo, and provide certain limited and defense military materiel, in the form of the heavy artillery and mortars which they lack, to the Bosnian Muslims. It is unjust and immoral to allow them to continue to be pounded by Serb attacks without adequate means of protecting themselves.

This military assistance is limited to the provision of appropriate arms that would allow the Bosnian Muslims to defend themselve. It does not urge, nor would it authorize, the dispatch of U.S. military advisors or other troops to the region. Even in the face of the continuing horrible tragedy there, that would be a serious mistake.

The Mitchell amendment does require that any intervention by U.S. ground troops be explicitly authorized by Congress; that is a key provision. It also requires the president to clearly define in law the goals and purposes of any such military action, the rules of engagement, the respective roles of U.S. and U.N. forces, and the plan for disengagement of Western forces there.

I will vote to approve the Mitchell amendment, and against the Dole amendment, for the reasons I've described. I know that colleagues on both sides of this debate all share the same goal: to stop the killing and stabilize the situation in Bosnia so that a more just peace can be sought under the auspices of the international community. I believe the Mitchell amendment best meets that goal, and does so in a way that satisfies our international commitments. I urge my colleagues to join me in supporting the Mitchell amendment.

BOSNIA
July 14, 1995

Mr. President, I want to take a few moments to take the floor. I do not know quite how to do this. I may not do it very well. I do not know whether my words will accomplish anything. But sometimes, you know, you just feel like you should speak on the floor of the Senate. That is what comes with the honor of being a U.S. Senator.

Mr. President, on the front page of the *Washington Post* today—this just needs to be recognized on the floor of the Senate—there is a headline, "For Ousted Bosnians, a Trail of Tears."

Under that headline, "Serbs Force Thousands of Muslims in Harrowing Journey."

Then there is a picture of older men, women, and children, a Bosnian woman wheeling what I gather would be, Mr. President, her elderly father in a wheelbarrow. And the first paragraph reads, "Bedraggled, hungry and scared, thousands of Bosnian Muslims flooded into a swelling makeshift refugee camp with little food, water or medicine today after a harrowing journey into Muslim-held territory from the fallen town of Srebrenica, now occupied by Bosnian Serbs reveling in their victory."

Mr. President, another article in the *Washington Post* is headlined, "Serbs Start Expelling Muslim Civilians From Seized U.N. Conclave," with pictures of women and children herded into refugee camps.

Mr. President, these pictures send chills down my spine. I am the son of a Jewish immigrant born in Odessa in the Ukraine who lived in Siberia in Russia. I am an American Jew, and these pictures send chills down my spine, along with the reports that the Serbs are taking all young men, boys sixteen years of age, away from their families. I do not know where they are taking them to. But they are taking them away to find out whether they are guilty of "war crimes."

Mr. President, I do not know exactly what it is the international community should do. But I am convinced the international community has to do something.

Mr. President, it is as if the world has not learned anything in the last half a century. We really are talking about genocide of people.

I will not talk about the position a number of senators took several years ago in calling for action. I took such a position. Normally, I do not talk about intervention, international military intervention, but several years ago several of us came to the floor and said it had to happen. That is beside the point.

Mr. President, I was thinking about this this morning, and I was talking to my wife, Sheila. We have been debating the regulatory reform bill, and it is extremely important. I have been involved in the debate about the rescissions bill. All of us care about our work, and all of us give everything we have, whether we agree or disagree. The presiding officer and I, who are good friends, are good examples; we do not agree on all issues. But I am trying to figure out, for God sake, what in the world is the world going to do? What is the civilized international community going to do? We see people just expelled, expunged, young men taken away from families to see whether they are "guilty of war crimes." Elderly and children, one-year-olds put on trains—to go where? What is going to happen to these people?

Sometimes, in the history of humankind, silence is betrayal. I do not think we can be silent about it. I wish to God I knew exactly what the international community could do. The fact that there are no good choices does not mean we still should not choose some course of action. I do not mean any easy fix, Mr. President. I do not mean something where we essentially turn our gaze away from the rape and torture and murder of innocent people.

So, Mr. President, I just wanted to take a few minutes to speak to these pictures. If my father, Leon, was alive—he is no longer alive—he would say that there exists on the part of humankind an enormous capacity for good but also, unfortunately, an enormous capacity for evil. It is that parallelism that makes it all so complicated.

I assume that next week in this chamber we will be talking about what is now happening in the former Yugoslavia. I do not know what the focus of the debate will be. I know there are several resolutions, but I think it has to be more than resolutions and amendments. The international community cannot turn its gaze away from this. This is genocide. We should have learned some lessons over the last half a century. I do not think we can go about our normal business just because it is long distance, somewhere away. These are all of God's children.

President Clinton's Planned Deployment of Ground Troops to Bosnia
December 13, 1995

Mr. President, four years of mass executions, mass rape, mass murders, brutal ethnic cleansing, sieges against civilians, terror campaigns, atrocities, and genocide not seen in Europe since the end of World War II—one-quarter-million people dead, three million people in the region refugees, and if we were to think about this in terms of our population, that would be the equivalent of 170 million American refugees.

The people of Bosnia deserve relief from years of armed conflict, relief from displacement, relief from malnutrition and hunger, relief from winters without heat or electricity, relief from war crimes and, yes, relief from the indifference of the rest of the world.

I traveled to the former Yugoslavia by myself two years ago. I went with my legislative assistant, Colin McGinnis. I visited with people in the refugee camps, and I saw enough pain and enough misery to last me for a lifetime. The Dayton agreement is the best and perhaps it is the last chance for peace in the region. That is why I intend to support it.

While I am speaking on the floor, I would like to express my thanks and my love to the family of three American diplomats killed in Bosnia while serving the cause of peace.

Our proper constitutional role as senators and representatives is to not give broad grants of authority to any president. I have talked to experts outside the Congress, had many briefings from people in the administration, met with people in the former Yugoslavia, and I have tried to the best of my ability to make the best decision for my country and for the world that I live in. I believe it is our responsibility to make sure the objectives are limited. I believe it is our responsibility to insist on as much clarity as possible.

There are several reserve units going from Minnesota, and, as a senator, I owe those families. It is my responsibility to make sure that everything is done that can be done to preserve their safety and the safety of all of our soldiers who are there—not to go to war, as I listen to the senator from Oklahoma, but are there to secure a peace.

Do I have concerns? You bet I have concerns. I do not think the arms control provisions of this agreement are very strong. I worry about the international police provisions; I think they are weak. I believe that there should have been, in the Dayton agreement, really a clear understanding—we keep talking about this one-year time agreement—that the Europeans are a part of the transition and that they assume the responsibility for peacekeeping so that when we leave after a year or thereabouts, in fact the presence of NATO is there.

Because it is not clear to me that we will be able to accomplish our objectives in that period of time.

Do I worry? You bet I worry. I have been up at night trying to decide what the right decision would be. I worry about the land mines. I have had briefings from our military, and there are reasons for all of us to worry. Our soldiers are trained, they have been doing the training in Germany, but I worry about that. I worry about depending on Milosevic. I think Milosevic is a war criminal. And when I hear Milosevic has made this commitment and that commitment, it makes me nervous.

I wonder what the meaning is when General Mladic says he has not agreed to this agreement. Does he go to the hills with his soldiers? I worry about that as well.

This has been a difficult decision for me, but in the end I really believe that we are doing the right thing as a nation. In the end, I think the alternative to no peacekeeping force there—and there will be no peacekeeping force and there will be no agreement if we are not a part of that force—will be a living hell. The alternative, I say to my colleagues, will be a living hell: More genocide, more rape, more murder, more mass executions in Bosnia. And it could be a war that spreads to Central Europe.

We are there to do the right thing. I believe that. I believe that for our children. I believe that for my children.

In the end, I stand on the side of hope, hope for an end to this conflict, hope for an end to its attendant horrors, hope for a better world that we live in, hope for the peoples of that region, hope for an end to the bitter ethnic divisions, hope for an end to the religious hatred.

I believe that we, therefore, in casting this vote in supporting our soldiers and in supporting this peacekeeping mission—I believe we cast the right vote. That is why I will vote for the Dole-McCain resolution, and that is why I am in opposition to the Inhofe-Hutchison resolution.

Mr. President, on the day before the formal signing of the Paris Peace Agreement on Bosnia, we are gathered here for a historic debate. I want to share with my colleagues my views on the deployment of United States peacekeepers to Bosnia to participate in the NATO peacekeeping mission there.

Designed to help put an end to the violence that has cost so many lives and so much suffering over the last four years, it offers real hope for peace. After much thought, I have come to a simple conclusion. With U.S. participation in the NATO peace effort, there is a real chance for a durable peace that could break the brutal cycle of violence there. Without our participation, we face an almost certain resumption of the fighting, and possibly a wider Balkan war.

This war has taken a horrible toll, not only on the people of the region, but also on the conscience of people everywhere who have watched it unfold in all its horror on their TV screens, and struggled to figure out a way to help end it.

For four years the people of Bosnia have suffered some of the worst atrocities in Europe: mass executions, mass rapes, brutal ethnic cleansing, sieges against innocent civilian populations, and terror campaigns. Atrocities we have not seen since the end of World War II.

So far, the war there has left a quarter of a million dead, and nearly three million people from the region refugees, expelled from their homes and villages in brutal campaigns of ethnic cleansing.

Three million refugees. Think of that. If such a war were fought here in the United States, by population share that would be equal to about 170 million American refugees.

The people of Bosnia deserve immediate relief from the years of armed conflict, displacement, malnutrition and hunger, winters without heat or electricity, war crimes, and at times indifference by the rest of the world. The Dayton agreement offers a promise of such relief. I visited the Balkans two years ago. I met many people there, including many refugees who had been expelled from their homes, and who had lost loved ones and friends. I know the trials and horror they have experienced.

Even in the face of these horrors, the president's decision to send United States troops to Bosnia is one of the most difficult foreign policy choices our country has confronted since the end of the cold war. The risks of the deployment, though I think they have been greatly reduced by the administration's careful planning, are real. From the millions of landmines left over from the war, to irregular forces, to weather, to other hazards, this mission is not without its dangers.

But while many of us have had differing views about the proper United States role in Bosnia over the past four years, and some of us had pressed for tougher action against the Serbs for many months, there is one thing that is becoming more and more clear. The Dayton agreement is the best, and perhaps the last, chance for peace in the region. That's why I intend to support it.

Full and effective implementation of this agreement offers the best hope to stop this brutal war, and to give the parties a chance to recover, and to rebuild their cities, to rebuild their nations. After months of fruitful negotiations led by the United States, and with the Europeans providing the bulk of peacekeeping forces to help monitor the agreement, I believe it would be a mistake for the U.S. Congress to sound an uncertain, quavering trumpet now regarding our commitment to peace in the region.

Through tough-minded, tenacious diplomacy, President Clinton's envoy Richard Holbrooke worked for many months to help the warring parties craft an agreement that could bring an end to the bloodshed. He deserves our praise, and our thanks—as do those three American diplomats killed in Bosnia while serving the cause of peace.

President Clinton observed in his recent speech that the United States can't be the world's policeman, but we can become involved in circumstances such as this, where we have a compelling national interest in maintaining the peace, where we have a chance to be effective, and where we have a clear duty to help.

Over the course of the last few weeks, I have talked with the president and with his chief foreign policy advisors, including Secretary of State Christopher and Secretary of Defense Perry, and pressed them to ensure our mission was clear, limited, and governed by strict rule of engagement that would allow our troops to protect themselves in any circumstances. The Dayton Agreement provides for sweeping NATO rules of engagement that will allow U.S. forces to use all appropriate force to protect themselves. In the last two weeks, I have been urging administration officials to clarify the limited, narrow goals of the mission; how they intend to measure progress toward those goals, and the limits they will impose on U.S. troop activity in the region. I believe they have made real progress in clarifying each of these areas.

This is our proper role in Congress: to press administration officials to clarify key points of their plan, ensure that objectives are limited and attainable, that an exit strategy is clearly laid out, and that planning for a post-U.S. presence upon withdrawal, composed presumably of Europeans, is moving forward. I believe that we have done that, pressing those responsible in the administration to close some gaps in their thinking that will serve our troops well in the long run.

I have thought long and hard about this deployment and, in addition to my discussions with the president and his senior advisors, have consulted extensively with those whom I represent in Minnesota, administration officials at the working level in the Pentagon, the State Department, and elsewhere. I have talked with outside regional experts, and others. I've talked with Minnesota military personnel who are being deployed to Europe. There are several reserve units from Minnesota whose members are being deployed to Europe, and I am aware of my direct and profound responsibilities to them and to their families—and to the families of all our troops—to ensure that everything possible is done to preserve their safety.

The Dayton Agreement, especially its key military annexes, were clearly designed with these concerns in mind. And it has garnered broad support. It has the support of the Russians, of the U.N. Security Council, NATO, the European Union, and the Organization for Security and Cooperation in Europe, each of whom will play a key role in its implementation. It is truly a multilateral effort, of which the administration should be proud.

But even though we played a key role in the development of this agreement among the parties, let us not forget one critical thing; this is their agreement, not ours. It was developed by the parties, not imposed by outsiders. They have asked other nations, including the United States, to help secure the future of that agreement.

And they have assured us, NATO, and the U.N. Security Council that they will respect its terms, and take steps to protect our peacekeeping forces. Over twenty-five nations have responded to the call to help secure this peace. As the last remaining superpower, we have an obligation to join them. If the current ceasefire holds, and the peace agreement is signed tomorrow in Paris and begins to be implemented on schedule in the next few weeks, we have a duty, I believe, to help.

I think it would be irresponsible to sit aside and allow the horrors that have taken place in Bosnia to continue. Our great hope is that this peace agreement might finally secure a lasting peace; we must not abandon that hope now by cutting off funds for our troops, or by refusing to grant at least conditional support for the mission.

I have decided to support this peacekeeping deployment, even though I am fully aware of the potential risks and problems with it. For example, I believe the arms control and international police provisions of the Dayton Agreement are weak, and must be strengthened. And they are being strengthened and fleshed out, by NATO planners and through proposals offered last weekend at the London Implementing Conference. In the end, how they are implemented will make the big difference, and we in Congress must monitor this carefully. The reporting requirements of the Dole-McCain resolution will help ensure that Congress is kept informed on a formal, timely basis of developments in key areas of the accord's implementation, in both its military and civilian aspects.

Likewise, I remain somewhat concerned that the very broad NATO rules of engagement leave considerable room for interpretation on the part of NATO field commanders there about how to react when faced with violent civil disturbances, hostage situations, harassment by irregular forces, or other similar situations. I know they do so to provide flexibility to our commanders in the field, but this is another area which must be mon-

itored carefully. Supervising the separation of forces, maintained by the parties, is one thing. But serving as local police forces is quite another. While I know the Dayton Agreement prohibits the latter, we must be careful to ensure that the potential for any mission creep is strictly limited.

We have heard a lot of heartfelt debate today, and expressions of concern about the potential for an extended, open-ended deployment. To those who are worried that Bosnia could turn out to be a quagmire, I can only say I have consulted as broadly as I could, weighted the risks as responsibly as I could, and I do not believe that is going to happen. I believe the administration has built into its implementation plans sufficient safeguards to avoid this problem, including strict limits on the areas where our troops will be, and on their mission. If I did believe this was a real risk, I would fiercely oppose this deployment. Let there be no mistake. This will be a NATO operation, with clear lines of command and rules of engagement, run by an American general. The mission is not open-ended. Our troops will be heavily armed, with the power and authority to respond to any potential threats as forcefully as necessary.

Of course, there are some concerns that can never be fully met. For example, I have doubts about the sincerity of Serb President Milosevic, and about his ability to deliver on his promises. I have even less confidence in the Bosnian Serbs. I am frankly alarmed that General Mladic has not been willing to support the agreement, that Serb civilians in the Sarajevo suburbs have been so vocal in opposing it, and that the Bosnians have resisted cutting their ties with radical states like Iran. But those doubts should not deter us from at least supporting this attempt at peace; they simply offer reasons for caution.

I have raised some of these concerns explicitly with the president and his advisors. I have asked tough questions of administration officials about how they intend to make good on United States commitments to lead an effort to provide arms and training to the Bosnian government while serving as neutral peacekeepers. While I have in the past supported lifting the arms embargo against the Bosnians, I believe that with this agreement there is a real chance to stabilize the situation through arms control, rather than primarily through building up the opposing armies.

That's where our emphasis should be now. Demilitarization on all sides, not remilitarization, is the appropriate course to follow to establish a military balance between the Serbs and the Muslim-Croat Federation. Once a full NATO balance-of-forces assessment is complete, the report required by the Dole resolution is submitted to Congress, and the arms build-down begins in earnest, I am hopeful that full compliance with the arms control provisions of the peace agreement will go a long way toward equalizing the forces. And if it does not complete the task, there will be plenty of moderate Muslim nations willing to help arm, equip, and train the Bosnians to better defend themselves, as necessary.

I have also raised questions about the criteria that will be applied by NATO to measure progress toward its goals, and about the timetable for the eventual withdrawal of U.S. forces. Administration officials have provided me with all the information they could on these questions. While many of us would like to know that our troops will come home by next Christmas, I do not think the administration can realistically provide firm assurances that that will happen, and I think that it would be foolish to demand them as a condition for our support, since it could place our troops in great jeopardy if they are pulled our prematurely.

I do know the president intends to have us get in, complete our mission, and get out, as swiftly as possible, and that General Shalikashvili has indicated that one year is more than sufficient time to accomplish the limited military goals of the mission. Completing our mission should be our primary goal, not meeting some arbitrary timetable that may be driven more by domestic politics than by the situation on the ground in Bosnia.

Whether one year is also sufficient time to secure other, broader goals, including return of refugees, free and fair elections, and rebuilding of war-torn Bosnia, is unlikely. I know of almost no one who believes it is possible in that timeframe. But at least this year-long respite can end the violence, and start them on the road toward peace. I hope that we will be able to work out an agreement with out allies that will provide for a much smaller, residual force that could stay there longer, if needed, to monitor compliance with the accord. Composed largely of NATO troops from Europe, this force could begin to shoulder primary responsibility for the mission after nine to ten months. I have urged the administration to explore this more vigorously because I think it is key to our exit strategy in the region. I would have preferred that it be built into this resolution. But I am satisfied that the administration has taken seriously this concern and will take steps to explore it with our allies.

On these and many other questions, administration officials have been very forthcoming. Where they were unable to provide clear answers, for example on the planned composition of a follow-on force if such a force were necessary after U.S. withdrawal, they outlined for me the state of their current thinking. Frankly, there is still much work to be done by NATO, the U.N. Security Council, and others over the course of the next few weeks and months to nail down answers to some of these key questions. But overall, I am satisfied that this deployment has been carefully planned and will be executed ably by our military forces. It is the responsible thing to do, the right thing to do. And that's why I intend to support it.

Many Americans remain skeptical of U.S. participation in this peacekeeping effort. I continue to believe it is critical that the president have the support of the American people and their representatives in Congress before moving forward. And I think that as this process has moved forward, and the president and his advisors have made clear the limited, narrow nature of the NATO mission, more Americans are being persuaded that this peacekeeping effort is the right thing to do.

Whatever we decide today, the president has already started sending U.S. troops to serve as advance support for the U.S. mission there. We must support the troops, and their families here in the United States, in every way we can. This resolution expresses clearly our support for their efforts.

Mr. President, this has been a difficult decision for me. But in the end I stand on the side of hope—hope for an end to the conflict and its attendant horrors, hope for a better future for the peoples of that region, hope for an end to the bitter ethnic and religious hatreds that have engulfed the region. It is a hope tempered by realism, though, about the road that lies ahead, and the potential pitfalls of this agreement.

Finally, let me say this. Over the last few weeks, some have asked me why I would be willing to consider supporting this peacekeeping deployment, when I opposed our going to war in the Persian Gulf. There [are] a host of major differences between the two situations, not least of which is that our troops were being sent to the Persian Gulf to go to war; in Bosnia, they are going to secure a peace. They have been invited by the parties in Bosnia to secure a peace agreement, under firm security assurances provided by the parties. I opposed the war in the gulf, among other reasons, because—like Chairman of the Joint Chiefs of Staff Colin Powell—I believed the tough U.N.-imposed sanctions ought to have been given more time to bite. In Bosnia, I do not believe that are realistic alternatives to this peacekeeping deployment that have gone untried.

This may be the opportunity that is needed, Mr. President, to break the cycle of violence in the lands of the former Yugoslavia by helping to keep the sides apart for a year in order to give them some time to begin putting their lives back together. Hopefully a year of peace will bring about something more lasting. It is my hope for the future of the peoples of that region that has led to me to conclude that we should support the president's action. I urge my colleagues to join me in support of this resolution.

12

NOMINATIONS AND CONFIRMATIONS

> "I am in a state which is a civil rights state. I am from a state which is a human rights state which passed an ordinance that said there shall be no discrimination against people, not only by race but sexual orientation, for housing, employment—across the board. Therefore, I vote the tradition of my state; I vote my own life's work "no" to this nomination." ~Senator Paul Wellstone, January 31, 2001

The United States Constitution, Article 2, Section 2, grants the United States Senate the power to "advise and consent":

The President shall have Power, by and with the Advice and Consent of the Senate, to make Treaties, provided two thirds of the Senators present concur; and he shall nominate, and by and with the Advice and Consent of the Senate, shall appoint Ambassadors, other public Ministers and Consuls, Judges of the supreme Court, and all other Officers of the United States, whose Appointments are not herein otherwise provided for, and which shall be established by Law: but the Congress may by Law vest the Appointment of such inferior Officers, as they think proper, in the President alone, in the Courts of Law, or in the Heads of Departments.

Thus, the president of the United States must nominate and seek confirmation of his or her appointments to the United States Supreme Court, federal judges, Cabinet-Level officers, and other high-ranking officials.

Senator Wellstone did not oppose every appointment, but, at times, he would not consent to the nominee's confirmation. His opposition was always rooted in a fundamental belief that he

could not compromise, and his speeches offered a glimpse into Senator Wellstone's beliefs about the Constitution and the proper role of government.

THE NOMINATION OF JUDGE CLARENCE THOMAS

September 30, 1991

Mr. President, the decision as to whether or not to confirm Clarence Thomas to be the 106th Supreme Court Justice in the United States of America is as important a decision as I will make in the U.S. Senate.

Mr. President, let me talk about this with a sense of history, perhaps as a former political science teacher or professor. At the Constitutional Convention, it was very clear that there would be two branches of government, the executive and the legislative branches of government.

The debate that took place had to do with how the judicial branch of government would be created. The decision that was made was that the executive branch and the legislative branch were to be coequal partners in making this decision. And the reason that everybody understood that this was such an important decision has to do with the very distinctive and critical power that the Supreme Court has, which is the power of judicial review. That really is the power of validation; that is the power to declare constitutional or unconstitutional the laws of the land.

It was also understood, Mr. President, at that Constitutional Convention—and I think all of us in the country need to understand this—that the Supreme Court remains the one institution that can really protect all of us against any usurpation of power that might take place by the legislative branch, or might take place by the executive branch; that the Supreme Court of the United States of America is, in fact, the one branch of the government which is the guardian of first amendment rights, which by the way are the rules that we agree to live by in a democracy; and that the Supreme Court of the United States of America is the only institution where every citizen, every citizen, regardless of income, has absolutely equal constitutional standing.

It is also important, Mr. President, to understand that a Supreme Court Justice is not elected, that a Supreme Court Justice can serve for decades, and that the consequences of the decisions rendered by a Supreme Court Justice have momentous consequences for the lives of people.

It was with this sense of history and this sense of understanding of the Constitution, Mr. President, that I have asked myself the question: What does the advise and consent function mean? What is necessary for all of us as senators to be able to carry out that responsibility?

I said to people back in Minnesota that I had made no decision. I said that I wanted to wait until after the Judiciary Committee had a full hearing, and I wanted, Mr. President, that process to be a searching process.

Questions needed to be asked and questions needed to be answered. And it was important to understand Clarence Thomas's philosophy, the kind of framework that he works within, the kind of values that would undergird decisions that he would render.

Important questions needed to be asked about his position about the scope of privacy, about separation of church and state, about first amendment issues, about what constitutes cruel and unjust punishment. All these questions needed to be asked. It needed to be a searching process. And these questions needed to be answered.

I was attracted to Clarence Thomas in one respect before these Judiciary Committee hearings took place. I read just about everything that he wrote. I tried to follow his speeches. Clarence Thomas gave an interview in 1989 in which he said, "It is important that we stick by our principles. That really is important to me, that we don't yield on our principles."

I was attracted to that kind of philosophy. But something happened during the judiciary hearing process. What happened was that Clarence Thomas came in and he said, "The articles that I have written and the speeches that I have given, these were just creatures of the moment; ignore that." He said, "I am stripped like a runner, I am an empty vessel, I have no particular policy preferences."

Mr. President, I am now put in a position as a U.S. senator where I cannot confirm someone who says they have no views. I cannot give my advice and consent to someone who says that he is an empty vessel. I cannot carry out my constitutional responsibility to do well for people in my state and do well as a U.S. senator and do well for the people in this country unless I have an understanding of what the nominee stands for.

This has really been a difficult decision for me to make. I have really struggled with this. I have agonized over this question. I wanted us to have a full hearing process. I wanted it to be a searching process. I wanted to find out what would be the philosophy that would undergird the decision of Clarence Thomas.

The questions have not been answered. Mr. President, I would say to you that as a U.S. senator, I am going to be consistent in my standard. I am going to say to any administration, whether that administration is Democrat or whether that administration is Republican, it is simply unacceptable to send a nominee here to the U.S. Senate, coached or whatever, with the basic idea that a nominee just simply does not tell us where that nominee stands on the critical constitutional questions of our time. I will not support such a nominee. I will not support such a nominee. I do not think, as U.S. senators, we can carry out our constitutional responsibility unless we know the views of such a nominee.

So I wish today on the floor of the U.S. Senate to say to the people of my state, Minnesota, and to say to the people of the country, I have tried to search and search about this question. I believe this is a thoughtful decision I have made. I know it is a terribly important decision. And the conclusion I have reached is I cannot give my advice and consent to someone who refuses to explain his basic philosophy on the critical constitutional issues of our time. I will not discharge my responsibility as a U.S. senator by voting yes. Therefore I will note no.

NOMINATION OF ALAN GREENSPAN, OF NEW YORK, TO BE CHAIRMAN OF THE BOARD OF GOVERNORS OF THE FEDERAL RESERVE SYSTEM
June 20, 1996

I thank the Chair. I am going to actually pick up on some points that have been made by my colleague from New York, for whom I have deep respect, and by my colleague from Iowa. First of all, let me thank Senator Harkin from Iowa for doing something very important as a senator. He has insisted that at least we have a debate about economic policy, that we have a debate about monetary policy, that we not just go forward and confirm someone to be chairman of the Federal Reserve Board without any discussion or debate. I do not think this debate is at all personal. I think each and every one of us has gone out of our way to say that we hold the chairman in high personal regard. But this is a debate about economic policy. My colleague has taken a lot of criticism for insisting that there be a debate. That is all he has ever asked for. I thank him for doing that.

My colleague from North Dakota earlier made an important point, which is, it used to be, back in the 1870s, 1880s, 1890s, and the early part of this century, that there was an important debate about monetary policy. It was not conspiratorial, it was important, because people know that real interest rates and monetary policy can make or break communities' lives. They can make or break families' lives. They have a huge impact, a huge impact on small business people, a huge impact on farmers, a huge impact on whether people can afford to buy a home, a huge impact on whether or not people can afford to take out a loan for their son or their daughter to go on to higher education.

This is a fundamentally important debate we are having. It is not hate; it is debate. I think it is an extremely important question that my colleague has been raising.

When I listen to this discussion, I have to smile, because I do think to a certain extent some of my colleagues, either by accident or by design, are being a bit ahistorical.

Let me also, teacher to teacher, professor to professor, respond to a little bit of what Senator Moynihan said. He never, of course, leaves out a historical analysis, and people in good faith can reach very different conclusions, but I would like to go back to the 1946 Employment Act in our country which called for the Federal Reserve Board to be a part of this and to keep inflation down, but also with the mandate of achieving maximum employment. That was an important piece of legislation.

There was a classic book written called *Congress Makes a Law*, by Stephen K. Bailey, all about the Murray-Wagner Act that finally passed in 1946. Full employment, the idea that people should be able to find work, decent wages under civilized working conditions, was the number one issue for the country. The Depression was fresh in everybody's memory, and World War II, in fact, pumped up the economy, and people found it to be a pleasant experience to be able to work. Women were in the work force. Men and women of color were also finding jobs. So after the war was over, the No. 1 challenge for our country was, how do you have an economy that generates jobs for people that are living-wage jobs? That is what it was all about.

I smile when I hear some of the analyses by some economists—not by all—that, as a matter of fact, what we have here is a situation of full employment, because the unemployment rate is 5.6 percent. Therefore, we have full employment.

People in Minnesota and around the country have to just be scratching their heads and wondering what is going on here. Ten blocks from here, why do we not go out and ask people whether or not they think we have full employment. Just ask them. This does not measure sub-employment, it does not measure the one million discouraged workers, it does not measure people who are working part time because they cannot work full time.

Do you know what else it does not measure? It does not measure all the people who have jobs but not jobs they can count on. It does not measure all the working poor people, who work fifty-

two weeks a year, forty-hours-plus a week, and still make only poverty-level wages.

So, when we hear all these macro figures about how we cannot afford to have unemployment below 5.5 percent, otherwise we will set off this inflationary cycle, this is the old "Phillips curve" argument. It has been discredited over and over again. It is not the experience in our own country. We have had no evidence that we are about to see a cycle of inflation.

What we have instead is a policy that works great for bondholders, great for Wall Street, but does not work well for families in our country. Every time we are about to have a real recovery and every time small businesses are about to have a break or every time farmers are about to have a break or every time homeowners are about to have a break or every time some of the businesses in our country which are interest-sensitive businesses are about to have a break and every time we are about to generate more jobs that people can count on, we have this policy, which I think is outdated and which I think, in fact, helps some folks at the top but puts a squeeze on the vast majority of people in this country. That is what this debate is all about.

When we get to this policy of maintaining and insisting that two-percent growth is all we can do as a nation, that we have to always cool down the economy, that we have to have price stability, the question that needs to be asked on the floor of the Senate is the question people ask in cafes in our country: Who exactly is deciding? Who exactly is benefiting? And who is being asked to sacrifice? Who decides that we can only afford economic growth of two percent a year? Who decides that interest rates will be kept at this high level and not reduced? And whose farm goes under the auctioneer's hammer? Who goes without a job? Who goes without a job that pays a decent wage? Who goes without a job working under civilized working conditions? Who is not able to pay for higher education for their children? That is what it is all about.

I suggest to my colleagues that this argument that we now have about full employment—my God, just tour the cities. Go to Hartford. Go to Minneapolis. I heard statistics about my state. Yes, the official unemployment level is down, but that does not measure sub-employment. I will repeat that. Not the discouraged workers, not people who are part-time workers, and not people who are working but working at jobs they cannot count on—that is what this is all about: living-wage jobs. I can tell you that a much too significant percentage of the population all across this country, including Minnesota, is struggling to make ends meet.

This effort to always cool the economy down, fight this bogeyman of inflation and insist on this stringent monetary policy has made it very difficult for families to do well. That is what this debate is all about.

My colleague from New York talked about the piece that he read today in the *Washington Post* about discouraged employers. It is interesting to hear about discouraged employers, but I suggest to colleagues, Democrats and Republicans alike, that is only one piece of the story. That is true.

I meet with businesses owners in Minnesota who say the same thing. I meet with small businesses owners and a good many of them say to me, "Paul, we are not worried about the minimum wage raise, but do you know what? We are technology companies and we cannot find skilled workers."

That is true. That is one piece of it. But I also suggest to my colleagues, it is only one small piece of it. The other piece has to do with this effort to keep economic growth down, to argue we can only afford two-percent-a-year growth in our economy, to constantly, therefore, make this an economy where we have a recovery but a recovery where people are not able to find the jobs at decent wages.

* * *

Mr. President, my colleague essentially made what was my second point. One had to do with the Employment Act of 1946 and what is the mandate of the Federal Reserve Board and how this monetary policy has, in fact, made it impossible for our country to achieve what should be the No. 1 domestic priority, which is an economy that produces jobs that people can count on, jobs at decent wages, living-wage jobs under civilized working conditions where men and women can support their families.

This is the trade-off. Some people are very generous with other people's suffering. It is great for bondholders, great for Wall Street. It is not great for Main Street. It is not great for wage earners. It is not great for farmers. It is not great for small business people. It is not great for homeowners. It is not great for people trying to afford a higher education for their children. And the second point is precisely this: there is a rather significant correlation between the tight monetary policy and the lopsided economy we have. That is what we have right now. We ought to be focusing on how we can raise the standard of living of middle-class and working families in our country.

I suggest to you one of the reasons we have not been able to do that, one of the reasons that the bottom sixty percent has been standing still and even losing ground over the past twenty years-plus is because of this monetary policy. It is time we debate it and, I must say, that I believe that this policy has been profoundly mistaken with very harsh consequences for the vast majority of working people in this country.

Mortimer Zuckerman, in an editorial in *U.S. News & World Report*, wrote:

> Alan Greenspan's "dear money" leadership has caused the Fed to exert a monetary choke hold on one of the weakest economic recoveries

since World War II at the cost of billions of dollars in lost output and tens of thousands of uncreated jobs.

That is the point I was trying to make.

The renowned economist, James Galbraith, criticizes Greenspan this way:

He is pathologically adverse to full employment, pathologically overanxious about inflation. His policies are the reasons, for the most part, that unemployment has stayed high and that wages have not raised in the past decade, and he's determined to keep things that way.

Again, that is my point about this whole issue of good jobs and good wages.

Finally, Felix Rohatyn writes:

Every major American social and economic problem requires stronger economic growth for its solution. This includes improvements in public education, as well as increasing private capital investment and savings, balancing the budget and maintaining a social safety net, improving the economic conditions in our big cities and reducing racial policies as a result.

This, again, is tied in to the whole question of monetary policy. Thomas Palley, of the *New School for Social Research*, writes:

Greenspan's "soft landing" has been perfect for Wall Street, keeping the lid on wages while keeping consumer demand strong enough to earn massive profits.

Mr. President, I think Felix Rohatyn is right on the mark. I maintain that this debate is not about one person. This is a debate about monetary policy that should be a front-burner issue in the United States of America. This is policy that can make or break people's lives; that can make or break small businesses; can make or break farmers, I say to my colleague from North Dakota; can make or break middle-class families; can make or break working people.

The key to decent jobs at decent wages, the key to investment in our cities, the key to economic opportunities, the key to improving the standard of living for the vast majority of people in this country is a combination of a number of different things. I suggest that one critical piece is monetary policy.

I believe that Chairman Greenspan's policies have, again, been profoundly mistaken and I think have had serious consequences for the vast majority of people in this country. I would rather stand for Main Street interests, I would rather be on the side of small business people, I would rather be on the side of working families,

I would rather be on the side of middle-income Americans, I would rather be on the side of growing this economy, I would rather be on the side of jobs with decent wages, I would rather be on the side of economic fairness, I would rather be on the side of economic opportunity and, for those reasons, I will vote "no."

The Nomination of John Ashcroft
January 31, 2001

Mr. President, I have voted for any number of the president's nominees to serve in our Cabinet, even though I am 100-percent sure I am going to be in disagreement with them on some of the really major public policy questions that face our country.

It is very rare that a Cabinet nominee is defeated by the Senate. It does not happen very often. There is a presumption that the president should be allowed to choose his or her people to serve in the Cabinet. In addition, I do know Senator Ashcroft. I respect his religious convictions. I have had personal interaction with him, which I have enjoyed. And if he is confirmed, I will wish him the very best because he will be attorney general for our country.

But there is also a set of other questions that are important to me as a senator from Minnesota. To be the attorney general, and to head the Justice Department, is to be the lawyer for all the people in the country.

I had a great man who worked for me here who passed away from cancer this last year, Mike Epstein. When I first met Mike, he said to me: I have been in Washington for thirty years, but I still believe in changing the world. I hope we can work together.

He came to the Justice Department and worked with Bobby Kennedy, dealing with enforcement of the Civil Rights Act; the Justice Department, dealing with enforcement of the Voting Rights Act.

Colleagues, in Minnesota, when we were celebrating the life of Dr. Martin Luther King, Jr., I was speaking at a gathering. I didn't expect the reaction. I remember a book Dr. King wrote called *Where Do We Go from Here: Chaos or Community?* I had this cadence where I said: We have a long ways to go. And in the cadence, I said: We have a long ways to go when people of color are pulled along the side of the road on their way to vote because they are people of color.

I could not believe the reaction of the African-American community, the Latino community, the Southeast Asian community, and the Native American community. They know that what happened in Florida was wrong. Something went wrong there. And they are very mindful of voting rights, the hate-crimes legislation, the Violence Against Women Act, the Church Arson Act.

The attorney general is the person who advises the president on judicial appointments, whether it be to a federal district court, the court of appeals, or the U.S. Supreme Court. I do not honestly believe John Ashcroft is the right person to be attorney general for our country.

Some of my colleagues on the other side of the aisle—I just heard this as I came in, getting ready to speak—have labeled disagreement with this choice and questions that have been raised— I am going to raise civil rights questions; this is my background; this is my life—as a personal attack on John Ashcroft. I don't see it that way.

In fact, I said to John on the telephone: I never will savage you. I don't believe in it. I hate it. Some of my colleagues have spoken on the floor with a considerable amount of eloquence about that.

But my baptism to politics was the civil rights movement. I learned from men and women of color—many of them young, and many of them old, and hardly any of them famous, though they should be famous—about the importance of civil rights and human rights. This is the framework I bring to the Senate. This is why I am going to vote no.

I don't agree with some of the positions Senator Ashcroft took as a senator, but that is not the basis of my vote.

Some of his views on abortion, to make abortion a crime even in the case of rape and incest, are extreme and harsh. I once said in a TV debate that John Ashcroft gives me cognitive dissonance because I like him as a person and I don't understand how a person whom I like can hold, sometimes, such harsh views. I don't agree with his position on abortion. I don't agree with some of his other positions.

It is not his voting record. Without trying to be self-righteous on the floor of the Senate or melodramatic, I have spent hardly any time with groups or organizations except at the beginning when people came by and I said: Please give me everything to read and let me think this through myself.

I am troubled by the statements made by John Ashcroft and his role in blatantly distorting the record of Judge White. I am going to say "blatantly distorting the record" because I think that is what happened. The evidence is compelling. We heard from Judge White about that as well. To call him a pro-criminal judge on the basis of the decisions he had rendered—I don't want to say it was "extraordinary"—crossed a line. I have a right as a senator to say, if John Ashcroft, as attorney general, with the key position he would be playing in terms of judges and the federal judiciary, is going to use the same standard and the same methodology he used to oppose Justice White, then a lot of justices, a lot of men and women who could serve our country in the federal judiciary, will never make it. That is one of the reasons I oppose this nomination.

The question was put to John Ashcroft in the committee about his opposition to Jim Hormel: Did he oppose Jim Hormel because he was gay? Senator Ashcroft stated that "the totality of circumstances suggested that Mr. Hormel would not make a good ambassador." What made up that totality? Senator Ashcroft didn't attend Mr. Hormel's hearings. He refused to meet with Mr. Hormel. He never returned any of Mr. Hormel's calls. And in the hearing, John Ashcroft suggested or stated that Mr. Hormel "recruited him" to the University of Chicago School of Law. But Mr. Hormel says: I don't ever recall recruiting anybody for the University of Chicago. And he can't remember a single conversation with John Ashcroft over the past thirty-some years.

John Ashcroft also told us, in the battle over the nomination, that Mr. Hormel, by simply being an openly gay man who is also a civic leader, has "been a leader in promoting a lifestyle, and the kind of leadership he has exhibited there is likely to be offensive to individuals in the setting in which he is assigned," suggesting that Luxembourg, as a Catholic nation, would find it difficult to receive him.

The evidence is that Luxembourg openly embraced him. He was a great ambassador. It is also a questionable assumption because it is a Catholic country, that Catholics would not embrace a person, would not judge a person by the content of his character.

I want to be clear that, as a senator, as I think about who should head the Justice Department and who should be the attorney general and I think about my own life, when I was teaching, I used to insist that students answer the following question: Why do you think about politics the way you think about politics? Then I never graded their answer. I just wanted them to think about what really shaped their viewpoint. I have been thinking a lot about that in relation to this debate. There are sets of facts and different versions of truth and all the rest.

What shapes my viewpoint? I am a product of the civil rights movement. I am not a hero like John Lewis, but I helped. Men and women in the civil rights movement were my teachers. This is a civil rights vote. This is a human rights vote.

I know that John and his supporters will say: Judge us by what is in our heart. For people across the country, people of color, people who have a different sexual orientation, they judge you by your actions. They judge you by what you have said. And I believe the Justice Department has to be all about justice. I don't think John Ashcroft is the right person to head this Justice Department.

It is not any one thing. I will be honest. I will admit a bias. I don't have a great feeling for Bob Jones University. As long as we are talking about race, they banned dating between students of different races and continue to have a policy that states that gay alumni—yes, former students—should be arrested for trespassing when they step foot on the grounds of their alma mater. I don't have a good feeling for this school. I am speaking within the civil rights and human rights framework. I don't know why John Ashcroft accepted an honorary degree. I don't know why you would want to honor such a school. I don't know why you wouldn't want to renounce all of those policies.

It is just one piece of evidence, and I know John has made it clear that he disagrees with some of what the school is about.

I don't understand the interview with *Southern Partisan* magazine. I find it to be bizarre. This is a magazine which goes out of its way not to promote racial reconciliation or healing but just the opposite. I don't understand John Ashcroft's animus toward Ron White or toward Jim Hormel. If it wasn't that, then it probably was some form of political opportunism. I certainly don't understand the association with *Southern Partisan* magazine and not even being willing to renounce this magazine or acknowledge his error in doing the interview at the recent hearings.

I don't know why he refused to sign the pledge that his office would not discriminate in its employment practices based on sexual orientation. It is his first amendment right. The point is, we are talking about somebody to head up the Justice Department.

I consider this to be a civil rights vote and a human rights vote. That is why I am voting no. Despite what John Ashcroft said during the hearings about his limited role in the state of Missouri on any number of legal cases dealing with civil rights and human rights, I will discuss his role in opposing what was a voluntary desegregation order. I will highlight the testimony of one who knows John Ashcroft's record in this area best, Bill Taylor. I will highlight Bill Taylor's testimony because I consider him to be a giant. I am proud to say he is one of my teachers. He is a real hero. He is one of those who joined Thurgood Marshall's team in the years just after the Brown decision to work for full implementation of Brown v. Board of Education.

Over two decades, he served as the lead counsel for a class of parents and students in the St. Louis case. During the most active part of that time, John Ashcroft was attorney general and governor of Missouri. Listen to the words of Bill Taylor in his testimony before the Judiciary Committee:

> I have thought seriously since this nomination about whether Mr. Ashcroft's conduct in the St. Louis case was simply that of a lawyer vigorously defending the interests of the state or whether some of his actions went over the line of strong advocacy and reflect on his qualifications to serve as attorney general of the United States. My conclusion is that the latter is the case. I believe that in his tenure as attorney general, Mr. Ashcroft used the court system to delay and obstruct the development and implementation of a desegregation settlement that was agreed to by all major parties except the state.

In so doing, he sought to prevent measures that were a major step toward racial reconciliation in an area where there has been much conflict, and to thwart a remedy that ultimately proved to be a very important vehicle for educational progress. John Ashcroft massively resisted this desegregation effort.

I think the most troubling aspect of the Missouri school desegregation issue, to me, is that John Ashcroft consistently used his fervent opposition to the federal judge's desegregation order as a political issue in the campaign.

I want to be real clear about it because I am not going to get into any pitched, acrimonious battle with anyone here on the floor of the Senate. But the fact that I talk about his resistance to this voluntary desegregation case is that I am so troubled by the ways in which he went after Justice White; the fact that I talk about Bob Jones University and *Southern Partisan* magazine is not because I am interested in any personal attack. I already said I don't understand how it is that a person I like so much personally can hold such harsh views. But he is the lawyer for all the people of the United States of America if he is attorney general. He will head up the Justice Department. This is the Voting Rights Act. This is the Civil Rights Act. This is the Violence Against Women Act. This is all about whether or not you can have a man or a woman—in this particular case a man—who will head the Justice Department and will lead our country down the path of racial reconciliation.

We have a huge divide in the United State of America on the central question of race. We have a question before us as to whether or not we have a man who can lead the Justice Department for justice for all people and who will be a leader when it comes to basic human rights questions. He is not the right choice.

I thank the Judiciary Committee, Democrats and Republicans alike, for the way in which they conducted the hearings.

I say to John Ashcroft, whom I am sure is viewing this debate and listening to all of us, that if confirmed, again, I wish him the very best. He will be the attorney general for all of us in our country. But I also would like to say, to me, this is, in my 10.5 years in the Senate, as close as I can remember coming to a basic civil rights vote, a basic human rights vote, and I cannot support John Ashcroft to be attorney general and to head the Justice Department; not on the basis of everything I believe in about civil rights and human rights; not on the basis of the younger years of my life; not on the basis of being a United States senator from the State of Minnesota who had Senator Hubert Humphrey, who gave one of the greatest civil rights speeches ever at the 1948 Democratic Party Convention.

I am in a state which is a civil rights state. I am from a state which is a human rights state which passed an ordinance that said there shall be no discrimination against people, not only by race but sexual orientation, for housing, employment—across the board. Therefore, I vote the tradition of my state; I vote my own life's work "no" to this nomination.

13

FREEDOM OF SPEECH

> "But, to me, the real soul of the flag, going beyond the physical presence of the flag, is the freedom that the flag stands for. I don't think we should give up on that freedom. I don't think we should amend the first amendment to the Constitution. I think it would be a profound mistake. I say that out of respect for those who disagree with me in the Senate. I say it out of respect for those in the veterans community who disagree with me."
> ~Senator Paul Wellstone, March 28, 2000

Senator Paul Wellstone's biggest asset was his ability to speak passionately about the issues that he cared about. It was a gift that he used to organize people, both as a college professor working with the rural poor and as a candidate for public office. He used his speaking ability to organize and protest. He also broadly defended First Amendment protections of the freedom of speech. His support of First Amendment rights encompassed virtually all forms of speech, including flag burning, even though Senator Wellstone had never and would never burn a flag.

FLAG DESECRETION
CONSTITUTIONAL AMENDMENT
March 28, 2000

Mr. President, I come to the floor not the first time to announce my opposition to this proposed constitutional amendment, giving power to the Congress and the states to prohibit physical desecration of the flag of the United States.

I wish to speak about this a little bit more personally because I think all of us come to our point based upon real-life experience. My father was a Jewish immigrant born in the Ukraine and who

fled persecution from Russia. My mother's family came from the Ukraine as well. As a first generation American on my father's side, I revere the flag, and I am fiercely patriotic. I love to see the flag flying over the Capitol. I love to recite the Pledge of Allegiance to the flag. I think it is a beautiful, powerful symbol of American democracy.

What I learned from my parents more than anything else, and from my own family experience as the son of a Jewish immigrant who fled czarist Russia, is that my father came to the United States because of the freedom—the freedom we have as American citizens to express our views openly, without fear of punishment.

I am deeply impressed with the sincerity of those who, including Senator Hatch, favor this constitutional amendment. I am impressed with the sacrifice and patriotism of those veterans who support this constitutional amendment. I think in the veterans community there certainly are differences of opinion. I do not question their sincerity or commitment at all.

It is with a great deal of respect for those with whom I disagree, including some members of the American Legion, that I oppose this amendment. I oppose it because, to me, it is ultimately the freedom that matters the most. To me, the soul of the flag, as opposed to the physical part of the flag, is the freedom that it stands for, the freedom that my parents talked about with me, the freedom that all of us have to speak up. I do not want to amend the Bill of Rights for the first time in its 209 years of existence. I don't want to amend the First Amendment, the founding principle of freedom of speech from which all other freedoms follow.

I want to very briefly read from some of what our justices have had to say because I think they say it with more eloquence than I could. In Texas v. Johnson, an opinion written by Justice Brennan, joined by Justices Marshall, Blackmun, Scalia, and Kennedy—and I note this is a diverse group of judges we are talking about—they said:

> If there is a bedrock principle underlying the First Amendment, it is that the government may not prohibit the expression of an idea simply because society finds the idea itself offensive or disagreeable. . . . The way to preserve the flag's special role is not to punish those who feel differently about these matters. It is to persuade them that they are wrong. . . . We do not consecrate the flag by punishing its desecration, for in doing so we dilute the freedom that this cherished emblem represents.

If freedom of speech means anything, I think it means protecting all speech, even that speech which outrages us. I have no use for those who desecrate the flag. Speech that enjoys widespread support doesn't need any protection. As the great Justice Oliver Wendell Holmes pointed out, freedom of speech is not needed for popular speech, but instead it is for the thought that we hate, the expression threatened with censorship or punishment.

I quote from General Powell's letter. He has been quoted several times, but it is too eloquent to pass up:

> We are rightfully outraged when anyone attacks or desecrates our flag. Few Americans do

such things and when they do they are subject to the rightful condemnation of their fellow citizens. They may be destroying a piece of cloth, but they do no damage to our system of freedom which tolerates such desecration. . . . I would not amend that great shield of democracy to hammer a few miscreants. The flag will still be flying proudly long after they have slunk away.

Our late and dear friend and colleague, Senator Chafee, who was a highly decorated soldier in two wars wrote:

> We cannot mandate respect and pride in the flag. In fact, in my view, taking steps to require citizens to respect the flag sullies its significance and its symbolism.

Finally, my colleague from Wisconsin mentioned Senator Glenn, another real American hero. Senator Glenn said:

> Without a doubt, the most important of those values, rights and principles is individual liberty: the liberty to worship, to think, to express ourselves freely, openly and completely, no matter how out of step these views may be with the opinions of the majority.

That is the first part of my presentation—just to say that I love this flag. I think when you have the family background I have, you are fiercely patriotic. I love this country. My mother and father are no longer alive, but I still think they know I am a senator. They weren't alive when I was elected. It would mean everything in the world to them. But, to me, the real soul of the flag, going beyond the physical presence of the flag, is the freedom that the flag stands for. I don't think we should give up on that freedom. I don't think we should amend the first amendment to the Constitution. I think it would be a profound mistake. I say that out of respect for those who disagree with me in the Senate. I say it out of respect for those in the veterans community who disagree with me.

14

FARMERS AND RURAL AMERICA

"Everywhere the family farmers look, whether it be on the input side, or to whom they sell, you have monopolies. We have to, as senators, be willing to be on the side of family farmers and take on these monopolies. Who do we represent? Are we senators from Smithfield, ConAgra, or Cargill, which is a huge company in my state. Or, are we senators who represent family farmers in rural communities?"
~Senator Paul Wellstone, September 15, 1999

Living and working in rural Rice County, Senator Wellstone's early organizing activities related to farmers and their opposition to high-voltage powerlines running across their fields. The powerlines made it more difficult to work the land, and the health consequences of such powerlines was not known. In the 1980s, Wellstone organized family farmers who were losing their land to foreclosure. Wellstone led protests, orchestrated sit-ins at banks, and brought farmers to the state Capitol for rallies.

As stated in Bill Lofy's book, *Paul Wellstone: The Life of a Passionate Progressive,* "Wellstone had become fluent in the language of family farmers. He knew the prices of commodities, understood the causes of the farm crisis, and could communicate the concerns and demands of the farmers who were affected by the foreclosures." In fact his work with farmers led to his first and only arrest during a sit-in at a central Minnesota bank that was foreclosing on an area farm on August 6, 1984.

This knowledge of and passion for farming issues was evident throughout his years in the United States Senate, but was best demonstrated by a series of "mini-filibusters" that he made in 1999 to bring attention to the rise of large multinational agribusinesses and the loss of the family farm. Below is an excerpt of his floor speech on September 15, 1999, which was two hours and brought the Senate to a halt.

THE ECONOMIC CONVULSION IN AGRICULTURE
September 15, 1999

Mr. President, I was just at a gathering of family farmers from the state of Minnesota. I want to give a report on what many of these farmers from Minnesota had to say. I know the Chair has met with farmers from his state and is well aware of the economic pain.

This was a gathering of the Farmers Union farmers, although I think as they have traveled from Senate office to Senate office and House office to House office, they speak for many farmers in the country. Their focus is on what can only be described as an economic convulsion in agriculture.

I know this is not only a crisis in the Midwest but it is also a crisis in the South and throughout the entire nation. On present course, we are going to lose a generation of producers. Whether we are talking about farmers in Minnesota or farmers in Arkansas, many very hardworking people are asking nothing more than a decent price for the commodities they produce. These farmers, who want a decent price so they can have a decent standard of living and so they can support their children, are going to go under.

I will talk a little bit about policy, but, most importantly, I want to talk about families. I think it is important to bring this to the attention of the Senate. On the policy part, I would prefer, if at all possible, to avoid a confrontation about the Freedom to Farm bill. I thought it was "freedom to fail" when the bill passed in 1996. I thought it was a terrible piece of legislation; other senators at that time thought differently. Part of the legislation gave producers more flexibility, which was good. However, the problem we are facing now is the flexibility doesn't do any good because, across the board, prices are low and farmers can't cash-flow.

I don't know whether the Chair has had this experience in Arkansas. He probably has. Many farmers will come up to me, and often these farmers will be in their forties or fifties. They will say: Right now, I am just burning up my equity. I am digging into everything I have in order to keep going. I want to ask you a question: Should I continue to do that? Do I have a future, or should I just get out of farming?

People don't want to get out of farming. They don't want to leave. This is where they farm. This is where they live. This is where they work. The farm has been in their family for four generations.

We have to make a major modification in our farm policy. The modification has to deal with the problem of price. It is a price crisis in rural America. We have to get this emergency assistance package passed. Conferees must meet and report a bill to Congress so that we can get assistance out to farmers now. I think the emergency package must include a disaster relief piece. The Senate version includes no funding for weather-related disasters. Although I am supportive of an emergency relief package, I still don't think the Senate-passed version targeted the assistance towards those people who need the most help.

The point is, these producers want to know whether they have a future beyond one year. They can't cash-flow on these prices, whether it be for wheat, for corn, for cotton, for rice, for peanuts, or whether it be for livestock producers. They simply cannot cash-flow. They cannot make it. They can work twenty hours a day and be the best managers in the world, and they still won't make it.

I do think we have to raise the loan rate to get the price up. We have to do that. We have to have some kind of a way that our producers have some leverage in the marketplace to get a better price. I think we also need to have a farmer-owned reserve. A farmer-owned reserve would enable our producers to hold on to their grain until they can get a better price from the grain companies.

Whatever the proposal is, I say to all of my colleagues, for our producers—and I imagine it is the same in Arkansas—time is not neutral. It is not on their side. I don't think we can leave this fall without making a change. We have to pass the emergency assistance package, and we have to deal with the price crisis. I have heard discussion about how we are going to leave early. We cannot leave early.

I also want to talk about the whole problem of concentration of power. This is an unbelievable situation. What we have is a situation where our producers, such as our livestock producers, when negotiating to sell, only have three or four processors. They have the Smithfields, the ConAgras, the IPBs, the Hormels, and the Cargills. The point is, you have two, three or four firms that control over forty percent, over fifty percent, sometimes seventy to eighty percent of the market.

Pork producers are facing extinction, and the packers are in hog heaven. The mergers continue, and we have all of these acquisitions. We need to put free enterprise back into the food industry.

I have had a chance to review the Sherman Act and the Clayton Act and the work of Estes Kefauver and others. We have had two major public hearings, one in Minnesota and one in Iowa, with Joel Klein, who leads the Antitrust Division of the Justice Department, and Mike Dunn, head of the Packers and Stockyards Administration within the Department of Agriculture. Our producers are asking the question: Why, with these laws on the books, isn't there some protection for us? We have all sorts of examples of monopoly. We want to know, where is the protection for producers?

It is critical to pass some stronger antitrust legislation. I know Senator Leahy is doing a great job with his legislation. I am pleased to join with him. I know part of what the Leahy legislation is going to emphasize is that the U.S. Department of Agriculture can ask for a family farm rural community impact statement. It must address the impact these acquisitions and mergers will have on communities.

We want to see that USDA has the authority to review these mergers and acquisitions. We want to see that when people break the law and are practicing collusive activities, there are going to be very stiff penalties. We want to set up a separate division within the Justice Department that deals with agriculture and conducts an investigation and an impact study. Again, we need to have some strong antitrust legislation on the books.

This ought to be a bipartisan issue. I think this is one issue on which all the farm organizations agree. We must have some antitrust action. We must have some bargaining power for the

producers. We must put free enterprise back into the food industry.

Until we pass this legislation, I will have an amendment on the floor calling for a moratorium on any further acquisitions or mergers for agribusinesses with over fifty million dollars in revenue. We need to take a look at what is going on. We need to pass some legislation now or we need to have a moratorium for one year until we pass legislation. I think there is going to be a considerable amount of support for this. The reason I think there is going to be a lot of support is that I think many of my colleagues have been back in their states, and for those of us who come from rural states, from agricultural states, you can't meet with people and not know we have to take some kind of action.

I want to bring to the attention of my colleagues just what this crisis means in personal terms. I get nervous about the discussions we have about statistics. We talk about loan rates, we talk about target prices, deficiency payments and LPDs. I want to put this crisis in personal terms.

Let me talk, first of all, about the wonderful wisdom of a Kansas farmer.

I want to share a conversation I had with a Kansas farmer, who offered a great analogy that goes right to the heart of what is happening to our livestock producers, in particular, pork producers who are facing extinction while the packers are in hog heaven:

> Hogs can be mean, nasty and greedy animals. When a hog farmer raises hogs, he knows well enough to separate the big boars from the little hogs. No hog producer would put a boar in the same pen with small pigs. The boar would literally attack and kill the smaller pigs.

Yet while no producer would make such an illogical decision, we as a nation have shamelessly allowed the big boars within our own market pen. That is exactly what is happening. The large corporate "pigs" have been attacking and killing the smaller producers.

Now, let me just recite a little bit of historical context. These are words that were spoken on the floor. I read this piece and thought of the latest Smithfield effort to gobble up another company. These words were spoken on the floor of the Senate by Wyoming Senator John B. Kendrick in 1921, in support of the Packers and Stockyards Act:

> Nothing under the sun would do more to conduce to increase production in this country and ultimately to cheapen food products for the people of the Nation than a dependable market, one wherein the producer would understand beyond a shadow of doubt that he would not merely get what is called a fair market, but would get the market for his products based on the law of supply and demand. The average producer in this country is a pretty good sport. He is not afraid to take his chances, but he wants to know that he meets the other man on the dead level and does not have to go against stacked cards.

That is exactly what is at issue. Everywhere the family farmers look, whether it be on the input side, or to whom they sell, you have monopolies. We have to, as senators, be willing to be on the side of family farmers and take on these monopolies. Who do we represent? Are we senators from Smithfield, ConAgra, or Cargill, which is a huge company in my state. Or, are we senators who represent family farmers in rural communities?

I had a meeting with about thirty-five small bankers, independent bankers, community bankers, from rural Minnesota. It was unbelievable; all of them were saying they have not seen anything such as this crisis in their lifetimes. They said if we continue the way we are going right now, we are going to lose these farms. Our hospitals are going to shut down, our businesses are in trouble, our dealers and banks are in trouble. We are not going to be able to support our schools.

This is about the survival of many of our communities, and these bankers, they are right. I would, in 1999, like to associate myself with the remarks of Senator John B. Kendrick in 1921. He goes on to say:

> It has been brought to such a high degree of concentration that it is dominated by a few men. The big packers, so-called, stand between hundreds of thousands of producers on the one hand, and millions of consumers on the other. They have their fingers on the pulse of both the producing and consuming markets, and are in such a position of strategic advantage; they have unrestrained powers to manipulate both markets to their own advantage and to the disadvantage of over ninety-nine percent of the people of our country. Such power is too great, Mr. President, to repose it to the hands of any man.

I have been doing a lot of traveling during August meeting with farmers. I have been, certainly, to every single rural community in Minnesota and to gatherings in South Dakota, Iowa, North Dakota, Missouri, and Texas. Each and every time, I will tell you, it is incredible when you speak to farmers. You have 700 or 800 pork producers at a rally, for example, and they know from personal experience who the enemy is. They can't believe that IBP is making record profits while they are going under. How can it be these packers make all this money and the prices for our products don't go down in the grocery stores? Meanwhile, our family farmers, our producers, are facing extinction? What is going on?

When we passed the Sherman Act in late the 1800s, we did it to protect consumers; but, we also said we as a nation value competition. We thought the food industry was important. We thought we ought to have a lot of producers. We thought we ought to have a wide distribution of land ownership. We thought it was important to have rural communities. Somebody is going to farm land in America. When our family farmers in the Midwest or the South are driven off the land, the mentality seems to be not to worry about it.

The argument is made that somebody will farm the land. Somebody will own the animals. But the problem is that it will be these big conglomerates owning the land and the animals. The health and vitality of rural America is not based upon the number of acres of land somebody owns or the number of animals; it is based upon the number of family farmers who live in the community, buy in the community, care about the community.

As far as our national interest is concerned, this is a food scarcity issue. When these big conglomerates finish muscling their way to the dinner table and driving these family farmers out, what will be the price we pay for the food? Will it be safe? Will it be nutritious? Will there be land stewardship? Will you have producers that care about the environment? I think the answer is no.

This is a transition that America will deeply regret. We in the Senate must take action. We must take action to deal with this crisis, and it is a crisis. It is a price crisis. We have to get the loan rate up to get the price up. We have to have a moratorium on all of these acquisitions and mergers.

Eunice Biel from Harmony, Minnesota, a dairy farmer, said:

> We currently milk 100 cows and just built a new milking parlor. We will be milking 120 cows next year. Our twenty-two-year-old son would like to farm with us. But for us to do so he must buy out my husband's mother (his grandmother) because my husband and I who are forty-six-years-old, still are unable to take over the family farm. Our son must acquire a beginning farmer loan. But should he shoulder that debt if there is no stable milk price? We continuously are told by bankers, veterinarians and ag suppliers that we need to get bigger or we will not survive. At 120 cows, we can manage our herd and farm effective-

ly and efficiently. We should not be forced to expand in order to survive.

Lynn Jostock, a Waseca, Minnesota, dairy farmer, said:

> I have four children. My eleven-year-old son Al helps my husband and I by doing chores. But it often is too much to expect of someone so young. For instance, one day our son came home from school. His father asked Al for some help driving the tractor to another farm about miles miles away. Al was going to come home right afterward. But he wound up helping his father cut hay. Then he helped rake hay. Then he helped bale hay. My son did not return home until 9:30 p.m. He had not yet eaten supper. He had not yet done his schoolwork. We don't have other help. The price we get at the farm gate isn't enough to allow us to hire any farmhands or to help our community by providing more jobs. And it isn't fair to ask your eleven-year-old son to work so hard to keep the family going. When will he burn out? How will he ever want to farm?

Above and beyond that, I will just tell you that there is a lot of strain in the families. Families are under tremendous economic pressure, and they are under tremendous personal pressure.

As long as I am talking about families, I want to tell you that in my state of Minnesota there are farmers who talk about taking their lives. There are a number of people who are involved in the social services who are doing an awful lot of visits now to farms. And an awful lot of farmers are right on the edge. Do you want to know something? Their suffering is needless and unnecessary. This is not the result of Adam Smith's "invisible hand." This is not some inexorable economic law. It is not the law of physics. It is not gravity that dictates that family farmers must fall.

We have it within our power to change farm policy and to give these producers a chance. We should not leave. We should not go home until we write some new agricultural policy, a new farm policy that will really make a difference for people.

I am open to all suggestions. I am not arrogant about this. But I will tell you one thing I am insistent upon. I am going to be out on the floor talking about this issue. I am insistent that we take some action. We can't just turn our gaze away from this and act as if it is not happening.

Jan Lundebrek from Benson, a Minnesota bank loan officer:

> As a loan officer at a small town bank, I received a check for nineteen dollars for the sale of a 240-pound hog. I immediately went across the street to the grocery store and looked at the price of ham. The store was selling hams for forty-nine dollars. I wrote down that price and showed it to the producer. Then we decided to ask the grocer about the difference. Where does it go? Somebody is getting it, but it isn't the farmer.

We have policies to keep our country safe. We have a defense policy, we have an education policy, but we don't have a policy to protect our strength. We don't have a food policy that protects our farm communities and consumers who spend forty-nine dollars for a ten-pound ham that the farmer can't even buy through the sale of a 240-pound hog.

Now we have Smithfield that says it wants to buy Murphy. A merger of yet two more of these large packers is just outrageous. I want a moratorium on these mergers and acquisitions. I don't want these big livestock packers to be pushing around family farmers and driving them off the land.

* * *

Let me again point this out. You spend forty-nine dollars for a ten-pound ham, and this farmer is getting nineteen dollars for a 240-pound hog.

I mentioned the Sherman Act and the Clayton Act. I feel as if I am speaking on the floor of the Senate in the late 1800s. Where is the call

for antitrust action? Teddy Roosevelt, where are you when we need you? We have to get serious about this.

Richard Berg, [a] Clements farmer:

> My dad died when I was nine-years-old. Two years later, when I turned eleven, I began to farm full time with my older brother. He and I still farm together. This year I will bring in my forty-eighth crop. The farm we own has been in the Berg family for more than 112 years.
>
> When we began farming we would get up at 4:00 a.m. to do chores. Then we would go to school. During the evening, after we returned from school, we went back to work farming.
>
> My brother and I each own 360 acres. I never had a line of credit until the past five years. We always made enough to save some and buy machinery when we needed it. Now I have a line of credit against the land that I own that I am always using.
>
> I invested in a hog co-op a few years ago and a corn processing facility. I have a lot of equity tied up there. Neither venture is making money. They're losing money. There's no one after me who is going to farm .

Les Kyllo, Goodhue dairy farmer:

> My grandfather milked fifteen cows. My dad milked twenty-six. I have milked as many as 100 cows, and I'm going broke. They made a living out here, and I didn't. Since my son went away to college, my farmhands are my seventy-three-year-old father and my seventy-seven-year-old father-in-law who has an artificial hip.
>
> I have a barn that needs repairs and updates that I can't afford. I have two children that don't want to farm. At one point, in a thirty-mile radius, there were fifteen Kyllos farming. Now there are three. And now I'm selling my cows. My family has farmed since my ancestors emigrated to the United States.
>
> When I leave farming, my community will lose the $15,000 I spend locally each year for cattle feed; the $3,000 I spend at the veterinarian; the $3,600 I spend for electricity; or the

money I spend for fuel, cattle insemination and other farm needs.

By the way, I would like to thank these farmers. I don't know whether other senators realize this. I am sure they do. I am sure that people listening to our discussion on the floor realize this. But you know, when people tell you the story of their lives and allow you to talk about them and their strains, they do not do that except if they hope that if enough of us realize what is really going on, we will make the change. That is what they are hoping for. That is what they are hoping for, and that is what we should do.

Alphonse Mathiowetz, Comfrey farmer:

We were there forty-three years and it took forty-three seconds to take it all away." Alphonse and LaDonna, his spouse, farmed the same land in Comfrey for forty-three years. In the spring of 1998 a tornado tore through their community taking with it the work of their lifetime, their farm machinery, their buildings, their trees, their corn bins and their retirement. The Mathiowetz family lost more than $200,000 of equity to the tornado, none of which will be recovered.

Alphonse and LaDonna chose to rebuild their home on the farmstead. Not because they wanted to, but because if they did otherwise the reimbursement they received from their insurance company would have been highly taxed. It was the only financial decision available to the couple.

"I guess it's a blessing to retire, but not this way, watching the farm go away in bulk on an iron truck."

Steve Cattnach, Luverne small businessperson (insurance agent):

Two local farmers who raise hogs came in both in the same week to withdraw money from their Individual Retirement Accounts. During the course of ten days, the time it takes for the money to arrive, both were in twice asking about when their checks would arrive.

A local farmer who has 2 1,200-hog finishing facilities wanted to help his cash-flow by reducing the insurance coverage on his hog buildings from $180,000 each to $165,000 each. The terms of the policy allowed the coverage to be reduced, but the farmer's lender wouldn't allow the coverage to be reduced because the farmer, after three years of finishing hogs in those buildings, still owed $180,000 on each building. During those three years, he had only paid interest on the money he had borrowed.

Laura Resler, Owatonna farmer:

I have farmed with my husband for twenty years. When we started, we raised two breeds of purebred hogs and sold their offspring as breeding stock. Each animal sold for $300 to $500 per animal. But the increase in size of hog operations made our small breeding stock operation a money-losing venture. Also milked cows to produce manufacturing grade (Grade B) milk. But ten dollars per hundredweight is not enough to pay the bills, so we had to give up the cows. From the time my husband, Todd, was eighteen until now, when he's forty-one, he's worked for absolutely nothing. Now he works at a job in town so we have funds on which to retire. Our hope is to give our son the farm that's been in the family for generations and let our daughter have the house. But you can't cash-flow a 4-H livestock project. How can he cash-flow the farm?

Many of these youngsters growing up on these farms are not going to be able to farm because these farmers are going to be gone. I have heard people say: Senator Wellstone, you come out here and talk about this. What is to be done? Raise the loan rate; get the price up.

If Members don't want to do that, come out here and talk about other ways we can change policy in order to make it work.

Is there any senator who wants to come to the floor of the Senate, given the economic pain, the economic convulsion, the broken dreams, the broken lives and broken families in rural America, who wants to say stay the course? Is there any senator who wants to do that? I don't know of any senator who thinks we should stay the course.

If that is the case, let's have an opportunity for those who have some ideas about how to change this policy so people can get a decent price and there can be some real competition. We want an opportunity to be out here, to introduce those amendments, to introduce those bills, to have votes, and to try to change this. That is what I am talking about.

Darrel Mosel has been farming for eighteen years. When he started farming in Sibley County, which is one of Minnesota's largest agricultural counties, there were four implement dealers in Gaylord, the county seat. Today there is none. There is not even an implement dealer in Sibley County.

The same thing has happened to feedstores and grain elevators. Since the farm policies of the 1980s and the resulting reduction in prices, farmers don't buy any new equipment; they either use baling wire to hold things together or they quit. The farmhouses have people in them, but they don't farm. There is something wrong with that.

Again, when he started farming in Sibley County there were four implement dealers in Gaylord, the county seat. Today there is not one—not one. This isn't just the family farmers going under, it is the implement dealers, the businesses, our communities. This is all about whether or not rural America will survive.

Ernie Anderson, a Benson farmer:

Crop insurance has and is ruining the farmer. Because yields of disaster years are figured when calculating the premiums costs, a farmer's yield on which he can buy insurance decreases. As it decreases, it becomes apparent that paying a crop insurance premium doesn't make financial sense because when there is a loss, the claim

amount of damaged crops isn't enough to pay the price to put crops in the ground. Crop insurance is supposed to help me. It's not supposed to put me out of business.

Randy Olson, strong, articulate Randy Olson, a college student, beginning farmer, comes home from college each weekend to help on the farm. In March he came home from school and his parents looked like they aged five years. The price of milk had dropped from $16.10 in February to $12.10 in March. No business can afford a drop in price like that over a short period of time.

You love your parents, you see them hurt, and it makes you mad.

And prices are going up right now, but it is a heck of a dairy policy if, due to the drought in some areas of the country, Minnesota dairy farmers can do better. That is not a dairy policy.

Gary Wilson, an Odin farmer, received the church newsletter in the mail. What is normally addressed to the entire congregation had been addressed only to farmers. The newsletter said farmers should quit farming if it is not profitable. If larger, corporate-style farms were the way to turn a profit, the independent farmer should let go and find something else to do.

What he doesn't understand is that farmers are his congregation. If we go he won't have a church.

Not only that, Gary, but, again, I will just repeat it. The health and the vitality of our rural communities are not based upon how many acres of land someone owns or how many animals someone owns; it is how many family farmers live and buy in the community. The health and the vitality and the national interests of our nation are not having a few conglomerate exercising their power over producers, consumers and taxpayers.

✻ ✻ ✻

The reason I am on the floor today and I know this is inconvenient to other senators, is because it is my job to fight for people in my state. All of us do that. I am saying I want some assurance that we will have the opportunity to come out with amendments on legislation to change farm policy. All of us. That is point one.

The second point is, I certainly want to sound the alarm. I want to say to farmers and rural citizens in our states that are agriculture states: Put the pressure on. Don't let the Senate adjourn without taking action.

Don't let people say: We will do these appropriations bills, and we are out of here. That is not acceptable given what is happening to people. That would be the height of irresponsibility.

* * *

By way of apology to my colleagues for, in a way, bringing the Senate to a standstill for a little while, one of the reasons I do so, in addition to the reasons I have mentioned, is that when I was a college teacher in Northfield, Minnesota, I became involved with a lot of the farmers, I guess in the early 1970s, but in the mid-1980s, I did a lot of work with farmers, a lot of organizing with farmers.

There are several friends of mine who took their lives. There were a number of suicides. We had all of these foreclosures, and I used to sit in with farmers and block those foreclosures. It was always done with nonviolence and dignity.

I am emotional about what is now going on. I probably need to go back and forth between serious and not so serious, since I am taking some time to talk. I remember that in the mid-1980s, in the state of Minnesota, many people were losing their farms. This is where they not only lived but where they worked. These farmers didn't have much hope and didn't have any empowering explanation as to what was happening to them or how they could fight this. It became fertile ground for the politics of hatred.

The Chair and I don't agree on issues, but I respect the Chair. I don't think we engage in this type of politics. But that was really vicious politics of hatred, of scapegoating. When I say "scapegoating," it was anti-Semitic, and all the rest. I am Jewish. I am the son of a Jewish immigrant who fled persecution in Russia. My good friends told me one story about Minnesota and that I should stop organizing because these groups were kind of precursors to an armed militia.

When you are five-five-and-a-half, you don't listen to that. I went out and spoke at a gathering in a town we call Alexandria, Minnesota. The Chair knows our state. I finished speaking at this farm gathering, and this big guy came up to me and he said, "What nationality are you?"

I said, "American." I thought, what is going on here? I hadn't mentioned being Jewish in this talk.

He said, "Where are your parents from?" No, he said, "Where were you born?"

I said, "Washington, D.C."

He said, "Where are your parents from?"

I said, "My father was born in the Ukraine and fled persecution. My mother's family was from the Ukraine, but she was born and raised on the Lower East Side of New York City."

He said, "Then you are a Jew."

I tensed up. I mean, I was ready for whatever was going to come next. I said, "Yes, I am." He stuck out this big hand and he said, "Buddy, I am a Finn, and we minorities have to struggle together." That is one of the many reasons I have come to love Minnesota.

I think what is happening right now in our farm communities and in our rural communities is far more serious than in the mid-1980s. This is an economic convulsion. We are acting in the Senate and House as if it is business as usual.

* * *

I have some leverage as a senator that I can exert, I can focus on. I can call for a debate and insist on a debate. I have so many colleagues who care so much about this. I wish I knew agriculture as well as some of them. I know it pretty well. Some of the senators are immersed in it. Senator Daschle, our leader—I hear him speak all the time because he is a leader of the Democrats. When he talks about agriculture, it is completely different. We can see it is from the heart and soul. Senator Harkin, ranking minority member of the Senate Agriculture Committee—nobody cares more; no one is tougher; no one is more of a fighter. Both senators from North Dakota, Senator Dorgan and Senator Conrad—Senator Conrad always has graphs, charts, and figures; he is just great with numbers. He knows this quantitatively and knows it every other way. Senator Dorgan is on the floor all the time. Senator Johnson from South Dakota is unpretentious. He cares for people. It is great to have a member like that in the Senate.

I get sick of the bashing of public service. There are so many good people. Senator Grassley from Iowa—we don't agree on everything, but we had a hearing, that Senator Grassley and Senator Harkin were kind enough to invite me to in Iowa, dealing with the whole question of concentration of power. Senator Grassley asked a lot of tough questions about what is going on with all the mergers and acquisitions. There is Senator Blanche Lincoln. When she speaks about agriculture, it is unbelievable. It is her life, her farm, her family. There is nothing abstract about this to her. Or Senator Landrieu who was at our gathering today.

It is Midwest; it is South.

Senator Roberts from Kansas—I don't agree with him, but he cares. He is a capable senator. Senator Lugar, who I think is one of the senators who knows the most about foreign affairs, I do not agree with him on this policy question, but you can't find a better senator.

I am not here to bash senators; I am out here to say that I think this institution, the Senate, is on trial in rural America. This institution cannot afford to turn its gaze away from what is happening in rural America, to put family farmers and "rural people" and act as if that isn't happening. We can't afford to do this.

I come to the floor of the Senate today to make a plea for action. I come to the floor of the Senate today to say I am going to be coming to the floor of the Senate in these mini-filibusters. I call it a "mini" filibuster because I don't have that good of a back. If I had a good back, I could go for many more hours. I cannot stand for that long. As soon as I sit down, I lose the privilege to speak. However, I can come to the floor of the Senate several long hours at a time and keep insisting that, A, we have the opportunity to be out here with legislation to address this crisis in agriculture—that is not an unreasonable request, I say to the majority leader—and, B, to make it crystal clear that I will do everything I can to prevent the Senate from adjourning. I say this to my legislative director. We should not adjourn until we take this action.

* * *

Let me conclude.

I say to my colleagues, I have come to the floor of the Senate and have spoken for several hours to make a plea and to make a demand. I have tried to put this farm crisis in personal terms. I thank the farmers in Minnesota for letting me speak about their lives.

I have said that the status quo is unconscionable, it is unacceptable. I have said we have to change the policy. We have to give people a decent price. That we can do. I have said that the reason I have come to the floor of the Senate is to make the demand that: Yesterday, if not tomorrow, if not next week, we have the opportunity to bring legislation to the floor to deal with this crisis.

I have come to the floor of the Senate to say that we cannot adjourn—it would not be responsible, it would not be right—without taking action to help improve the situation for farmers. Why else are we here but to try to do better for people? What could be more important than for us, the Senate, as an institution—Democrats and Republicans—to pass legislation that would correct these problems and help alleviate this suffering and pain and make such a positive difference in the lives of so many people in Minnesota that I love—so many farmers in so many rural communities?

15

UNIONS, WORKERS, AND TRADE

> "Trade can lead to growth which benefits the majority of working people in all countries involved in that trade. Trade agreements can encourage the raising of labor and environmental standards to comparable levels. Trade agreements can make a positive link between respect for human rights and democracy and the granting of trade privileges. In my opinion, NAFTA should have these provisions and effects. I would be the first to embrace a NAFTA with such provisions and effects. . . . But this NAFTA does not."
>
> ~Senator Paul Wellstone, November 19, 1993

Paul Wellstone rose to prominence in the labor movement when he stood with seven hundred union meatpackers in Austin, Minnesota, in the fall of 1995 after a protracted dispute with Hormel Company. Meatpacker Local P-9 went on strike and were replaced. Tensions were high in the small southeastern Minnesota community, and violence broke out. The governor of Minnesota deployed the Minnesota National Guard to protect the replacement workers, and Wellstone found himself attempting to mediate a settlement. No settlement, however, was reached and the seven hundred union meatpackers lost their jobs.

Although the "fight" was arguably lost, Paul Wellstone's passion and pragmatism earned him respect. He got involved in a tense battle and picked a side, when other politicians stayed away. It was a pattern that repeated itself during the course of Senator Wellstone's tenure in the United States Senate.

THE CATERPILLAR STRIKE
April 8, 1992

Mr. President, I rise to address the Senate about a labor struggle. I think it is a historic labor struggle now taking place in our country between the United Auto Workers and Caterpillar, Inc. The work stoppage has lasted more than 150 days. I think that what we are witnessing in the country, Mr. President, really is not only historic but very serious in human terms.

I do not choose to speak on the floor of the Senate today about the specifics of the disagreement. But I do wish to express my concern on two fronts.

First of all, I am troubled by Caterpillar now calling in permanent replacements. Mr. President, I think that this just adds fuel to the fire. It concerns me that when workers are out on strike and there is some effort to try and get collective bargaining going, the company now hauls in other people, many of them desperate, to become workers and to become permanent replacements.

Mr. President, the problem is that ever since the Supreme Court's decision in Mackey versus Radio in the late thirties, we have had a situation in our country which simply does not work for working people, namely, that it is perfectly legal for a company to permanently replace someone who is out on strike. An employer cannot fire someone for going out on strike; that is illegal. But he can permanently replace his employees. That is a distinction without a difference.

Now for many, many years companies never did that, and we had a contract between labor and management, and it served our country well. But since the early eighties, what has happened in our country is that the right to strike has become the right to be fired, and working people have usually lost their collective bargaining rights. That is why this struggle is so significant.

So, Mr. President, what I want to suggest—and I believe it is constructive—is that there is an important role to play in this dispute for the Secretary of Labor.

I ask unanimous consent that a letter from Labor Subcommittee Chairman Metzenbaum, Labor and Human Resources Committee Chairman Kennedy, and many of us on the Labor Committee for Labor Department Secretary Martin urging her intervention in this strike be printed in the *Record*.

* * *

To summarize, I think that the import of this letter is that Secretary Martin really has a role to play; a positive, constructive role to bring in a neutral mediator to try and get the negotiations going again. Secretary of Labor Dole did that in the Pittston strike and it was very successful.

Mr. President, I believe that if this strike continues and, more importantly, if the company brings in permanent replacements, we are going to have a very volatile situation. It will be bad for our nation. It will be bad for the company, and it will be bad for the people that work in the plants. So I hope that Secretary Martin will take some real leadership here.

My second point, Mr. President, is that I think those of us in the Senate can also take some leadership. I have in mind support for S. 55. It is time for us to pass legislation which says to companies, "You can't hire permanent replacements. You can't haul in people during a strike and make those people permanent replacements and essentially wipe out jobs for people who have worked for your company, many for decades."

Mr. President, I believe that we must restore some kind of balance of power between management and labor. Of course, it will be good for unions. But far more importantly, it will be good for working people. It will encourage higher levels of productivity. It will prompt greater labor-management cooperation. That is what we have to do to get our economy going. Finally, and most important Mr. President, it will be the right thing to do.

I urge my colleagues to pay close attention to the situation in Illinois and elsewhere with the Caterpillar strike, and to support S. 55 when it comes before the Senate. We must take action now on this legislation so critical to the lives and livelihoods of American workers.

NORTH AMERICAN FREE-TRADE AGREEMENT ("NAFTA") IMPLEMENTATION ACT
November 19, 1993

Madam President. I regret that I cannot support President Clinton on a matter as important as this one. No vote that we have taken this year says more about our vision for the country's economic future. If this NAFTA is a precedent for other trade agreements to come, and is a model for the way we believe that business should be conducted in the world trading system, then few votes can as deeply affect the lives of our citizens and communities.

The debate here in Washington over NAFTA has been valuable. It has been passionate at times, usually reasoned, and it has generally focused on the proper questions. I believe it has focused on the proper questions in large part because the democratization of the NAFTA debate outside of Washington has transformed the way we now consider trade policy inside of Washington.

The dramatic increase in grassroots involvement around and study of NAFTA has surprised the experts, bureaucrats and business lawyers who previously had been accustomed to writing trade agreements by themselves, with little or no public input or accountability. This healthy development has forced attention to the questions that should matter most:

Will NAFTA improve the living standards of the majority of working people in the United States, Mexico, and Canada by encouraging a continental strategy of growth and global competition that is based on creating more, not fewer, high-wage/high-skill jobs?

Will NAFTA promote environmental and consumer protection?

Will it contribute to democracy and respect for human rights?

These interests have not in the past been the leading concerns in debate over trade agreements. The interests traditionally protected in trade agreements have been those of our financial and industrial sectors which seek safe investment opportunities and open markets for their products abroad.

Those traditional interests are assuredly addressed in this NAFTA. But in the NAFTA debate, citizens have brought additional concerns to the table. As a result, I believe that trade policy, thankfully, will never be the same.

The president has shown a lot of determination in the debate over NAFTA. And he showed considerable skill in using the power of his office to win passage of NAFTA in the House. I am sorry to say, however, that I believe that the president has missed a crucial opportunity to demonstrate the same kind of determination and to use the same kind of skills to pass a better agreement—an agreement which I believe it was possible to reach.

We are, as has been said many times in recent days, at an important historic moment for domestic and international leadership. In my opinion, this NAFTA does not promote the principles that America should stand for in the post-cold war world at this key moment. I believe that international agreements that we enter into in this period should demonstrate our leadership according to the best of American principles—the principles of raising living standards, of democracy and of human rights. This NAFTA does not do so.

I also believe that we are missing—by passing this NAFTA and not a better one which I think it was and is possible to reach—an important chance to address the legitimate concerns of the majority of working people in the United States, in Mexico, and in Canada.

By approving this NAFTA, we not only miss our chance to deliver a better agreement. We very likely also will preclude any chance of improving upon it when we consider additional agreements with other countries in Central and South America. NAFTA is a clear precedent for such further agreements.

Trade can lead to growth, which benefits the majority of working people in all countries involved in that trade. Trade agreements can encourage the raising of labor and environmental standards to comparable levels. Trade agreements can make a positive link between respect for human rights and democracy and the granting of trade privileges. In my opinion, NAFTA should have these provisions and effects. I would be the first to embrace a NAFTA with such provisions and effects.

A good agreement would have delivered on the president's promise to encourage the raising of labor and environmental standards. It would have included a principled link to human rights and democracy.

But this NAFTA does not. Unfortunately, this NAFTA is a backward-looking document. It seeks to revive at the continental level 1980s-style, trickle-down economics. It would place downward pressure on hard-won environmental and consumer standards. And it relaxes our principled linkage of trade privileges to human rights performance.

This NAFTA fails to tie trade to respect for labor and human rights—two elements which are directly related. That failure is NAFTA's most basic flaw. The poor record of respect for labor and human rights in Mexico is the basic reason why competition between United States and Mexican workers is not fair and why we should not institutionalize such a relationship through a trade agreement.

It is well known that the current Mexican government has held down wages and suppressed dissent in that country. This has been accomplished through the prevention of independent labor unions, through police and military repression, and through unfair elections. These combined policies have allowed Mexico to seek to attract investment on the basis of cheap labor.

Our workers can compete with workers anywhere in the world when that competition is fair. But competition is not fair when Mexican wages are held to one-seventh of United States levels through government policy, even when productivity and quality are comparable, as is more and more the case of Mexico's modern, high-productivity, export-oriented, new manufacturing sector. Holding down Mexican wages also, by the way, prevents Mexican workers from becoming a middle class which can purchase our consumer goods.

Unfortunately, the side agreements negotiated by this administration do little to improve on the original text. My consistent position on a trade agreement with Mexico and Canada has not been "No, never." It has been "Yes, if _____." I waited before taking a final position on NAFTA to examine the side agreements on labor and the environment that were announced in August. I wanted to give the president and Ambassador Kantor a chance to address the deep flaws in the text negotiated by the Bush administration. Ambassador Kantor assured me in March that he would deliver side agreements with real teeth.

But the side agreements contain no real effort to harmonize either labor or environmental standards upward. The enforcement mechanism in the side agreements is so weak that Mexican Secretary of Commerce Jaime Serra Puche reportedly assured the Mexican Congress that sanctions—the so-called teeth of the side agreements—would probably never be used.

When we compare the protections afforded to business in the text of the agreement itself—the investment protections, the intellectual property protections, both of which, by the way, strictly require upward harmonization on the part of Mexico—with the lack of real protection for workers and the environment in the side agreements, then the unbalanced character of this agreement becomes abundantly apparent. In fact, the enforceability of these side agreements has been even further challenged in recent days by the interesting analysis of Public Citizen and by the elements of the debate which has occurred here today over the issue raised by the senator from Alaska.

Madam President, I support more open global trade. I know that export industries provide jobs. I know that competitive imports benefit consumers and push our domestic industries to improve their quality and efficiency. I support the idea of a trade agreement with Mexico.

But this NAFTA will lead to a significant loss of U.S. jobs. By locking in incentives for United States firms to shift investment to Mexico to take advantage of lower wages and weaker regulation, NAFTA will depress wages in the country. It will place downward pressure on consumer and environmental standards.

Madam President, we could do much better.

AUTOWORKERS OF FLINT, MICHIGAN
July 16, 1998

Mr. President, for more than five weeks, the nation's largest industrial corporation has been locked in a labor dispute with workers in two of its Flint, Michigan, plants. I do not believe that we have had any discussion on the floor of the Senate about this. I want to speak about it.

The company and the workers are fighting over local issues—health and safety, speeding up the production lines, and sending work to outside suppliers—but these local disputes also highlight a broader national concern that affects millions of working Americans: how U.S. corporations invest, how they compete, and where they invest.

GM's hard-line stance and labor-war tactics endanger the livelihoods of tens of thousands of workers in the automotive industry and in the industries that rely on auto production for their business. Ironically, these hardball tactics also undermine the very competitiveness that GM says it wants.

Competitive firms need good labor relations; and good labor relations begin with a handshake, not a two by four.

Monday's *Washington Post* reported that high-level negotiations to end the strike broke down Sunday "amid signs the auto maker now may be willing to risk an all-out labor war." The company has asked an arbitrator to rule on the legality of the strike. The union has said fine. But GM's vice-president in charge of labor relations broke off negotiations, refusing to even participate further in talks to reach an overall solution to the strike. The *Post* further reported, a GM source said some top company officials are pushing for a form of drastic action to "send a clear message to the UAW. . . . Options reportedly under consideration, the source said, range from a legal action challenging the walkout . . . cutting off health-care benefits to all UAW members idled by the strike; or shutting down the two strike-bound parts plants in Flint, Michigan, and contracting out the work. Such a move," the *Post* explained, "would amount to an all-out war."

GM has taken the first step, filing a lawsuit against the union. GM would apparently rather sue than negotiate. They would rather fight than talk. The *Post* has reported that, "Company sources said the lawsuit is probably the first step in an escalating war between the company and the union."

This is no way for the nation's largest industrial organization to treat its workers and their representatives. The duly recognized representatives of GM workers, the United Auto Workers, had sought to negotiate a global settlement. GM senior representative should come back to the table.

Yes, GM has every right to seek to improve productivity and profits. But as yesterday's *New York Times* reported, "G.M.'s biggest productivity problem lies in its auto parts factories, which were . . . starved of investment during the 1980s . . . and have antiquated machinery as a result."

GM entered into agreements with the United Auto Workers to invest more in its American operations but has fallen short of making new demands on workers before it would comply with what it had already promised.

What is really at stake here are American jobs—good jobs, with good benefits. The workers at GM's Flint parts plants are fighting to preserve those American jobs. Over the next two years, in this act alone GM threatens to transfer about 11,000 of these jobs to subcontractors or out of the country altogether. GM's workers are justifiably concerned with what the *New York Times* calls "G.M.'s steady push to build factories overseas while slowing investment in its low-profit American operations."

GM should stop fighting its workers and get back to investing in the creation of those good jobs which bring good benefits right here in the United States. Strikes are hard on everyone—on the company, on the economy, and hardest of all on the men and women on the picket line. The best way for GM, or any corporation, to avoid picket lines is to address the underlying problems that lead to strikes, not to challenge the right of workers to strike.

The free world looked upon strikes in the 1930s with hope, because, as Franklin Roosevelt said in 1939, "Only in free lands have free labor unions survived." As long as there have been unions, we have known that the right to strike and liberty go hand in hand.

That is why, in 1860, Abraham Lincoln told striking New Haven shoe factory workers, "Thank God we have a system of labor where there can be a strike."

I have confidence in the auto workers of Flint, Michigan. Although I stand here today on the floor of the U.S. Senate, in my heart I stand with the auto workers of Flint, Michigan. They know the history of work, the auto workers of Flint, Michigan.

It was the auto workers of Flint, Michigan, who, on December 30, 1936, called another strike against the same company, General Motors. The goal of that strike was simple, too. All the strikers wanted was for GM to recognize the union. For over six weeks, the auto workers of Flint, Michigan, stopped production in the famous Sit-Down Strike of 1937. They slept on unfinished car seats and ate what food their families could slip through the factory windows.

The auto workers of Flint, Michigan, faced tear gas, heat shutoffs, and company security guards. Led by their new twenty-nine-year-old president of Local 174, a man named Walter Reuther, and the great union leader, John L. Lewis, the auto workers of Flint, Michigan, prevailed.

Because the auto workers of Flint, Michigan, were willing to strike, the auto industry was forever challenged. Because the auto workers of Flint, Michigan, were willing to strike, over the years the automotive industry became a source of good jobs with good benefits and the nation prospered. GM was the most successful auto maker in the world when it paid the highest wages, not the lowest. Americans want to be the beneficiaries of a more competitive firm, not their victims. And that is exactly why the auto workers of Flint, Michigan, walk the picket lines today.

JUSTICE FOR WORKERS AT AVONDALE SHIPYARD
June 16, 1999

Mr. President, I rise today in solidarity with the workers at Avondale Shipyard in Louisiana, who exactly six years ago exercised their democratic right to form a union and bargain collectively.

They voted for a union because that was the only way they knew to improve their working conditions, conditions that include more worker fatalities than any other shipyard in the country, massive safety and health violations, and the lowest pay in the shipbuilding industry.

Unfortunately, Avondale and its CEO, Albert Bossier, have refused to recognize the union

Avondale workers voted for back in 1993. For six years the shipyard and its CEO have refused to even enter into negotiations. According to a federal administrative law judge, Avondale management has orchestrated an "outrageous and pervasive" union-busting campaign in flagrant violation of this country's labor laws, illegally firing and harassing employees who support the union.

I met with some of the Avondale workers several weeks ago when they were here in Washington. What they told me was deeply disturbing. They told me about unsafe working conditions that make them fear for their lives every day they are on the job. They told me that job safety was the number one reason why they voted to join a union back in 1993. And they told me that Avondale continues to harass and intimidate workers suspected of supporting the union.

In fact, it appears that one of those workers, Tom Gainey, was harassed when he got back to Louisiana. Avondale gave him a three-day suspension for the high crime of improperly disposing of crawfish remains from his lunch.

The Avondale workers also told me that they are starting to lose all faith in our labor laws. For six years Avondale has gotten away with thumbing its nose at the National Labor Relations Board, the NLRB. The Avondale workers said they are starting to think there is no point in expecting justice from the board or the courts. And given what they have been through, I think it is hard to disagree.

In February 1998, a federal administrative law judge found Avondale guilty of "egregious misconduct," of illegally punishing dozens of employees simply because they supported the Avondale union. The judge, David Evans, found that Avondale CEO Albert Bossier had "orchestrated" an anti-union campaign that was notable for the "outrageous and pervasive number and nature of unfair labor practices."

In fact, Judge Evans found Avondale guilty of over 100 unfair labor practices. Specifically, Avondale had illegally fired twenty-eight pro-union workers, suspended five others, issued eighteen warning notices, denied benefits to eight employees, and assigned "onerous" work to eight others.

Judge Evans also found that, during public hearings in the Avondale case, Avondale's Electrical Department superintendent, a general foreman, and two foremen had all committed perjury. He further found that perjury by one of the foremen appears to have been suborned, and he implied that Avondale and its counsel were responsible.

Avondale's intimidation of its employees was so outrageous, so pervasive, and so systematic that Judge Evans came down with a highly unusual ruling. He ordered CEO Albert Bossier to call a meeting with Avondale workers and personally read a statement listing all of the company's violations of the law and pledging to stop such illegal practices. Judge Evans further ordered Mr. Bossier to mail a similar confession to workers at their homes.

Finally, Judge Evans fined Avondale three million dollars and ordered the shipyard to reinstate twenty-eight workers who had been illegally fired for union activities. Pretty remarkable.

What is even more remarkable is that Avondale still hasn't paid its fine, still hasn't rehired those twenty-eight workers, and still hasn't made any apology. Why not? Because instead of complying with Judge Evans' order, Avondale chose to challenge the NLRB in court.

Judge Evans' ruling concerned Avondale's unfair labor practices during and after the 1993 election campaign. A second trial was held this past winter on charges of unfair labor practices during the mid-1990s. Now the NLRB has filed charges against Avondale for unfair labor practices since 1998, and a third trial on those charges is scheduled to begin later this year.

This has been one of the longest and most heavily litigated unionization disputes in the history of the NLRB. After workers voted for the union in June 1993, Avondale immediately filed objections with the board. But in 1995 an NLRB hearing officer upheld the election, and in April 1997 the board certified the Metal Trades Council as the union for Avondale workers, once and for all rejecting Avondale's claims of ballot fraud.

At this point, you might think Avondale had no choice but to begin negotiations with the union. But they didn't. Avondale still refused to recognize the union or conduct any negotiations. So in October 1997 the NLRB ordered Avondale to begin bargaining immediately. Instead, Avondale decided to challenge the NLRB's decision in the Fifth Circuit Court of Appeals, and has succeeded in delaying the process for another two years, at least.

Safety problems at Avondale were the central issue in the 1993 election campaign. "We all know of people who have been hurt or killed at the yard," says Tom Gainey, the Avondale worker who was harassed after visiting Congressional offices several weeks ago. "That's one of the main reasons we came together in a union in the first place."

Avondale has the highest death rate of any major shipyard. According to federal records, twelve Avondale workers died in accidents from 1982 to 1994. Between 1974 and 1995, Avondale reported twenty-seven worker deaths. The New Orleans Metal Trades Council counts thirty-five work-related deaths during that period. One Avondale worker has died every year, on average, for the past thirty years.

It doesn't have to be that way. Avondale's fatality rate is twice as high as the next most dangerous shipyards. And it's more than twice as high as its larger competitors, Ingalls Shipyard and Newport News.

Avondale workers have died in various ways, many from falling or from being crushed by huge pieces of metal. Avondale workers have fallen from scaffolds, been struck by falling ship parts, been crushed by weights dropped by cranes, and have fallen through uncovered manholes.

Avondale's safety problems are so bad that it recently got slapped with the second largest OSHA fine ever issued against a U.S. shipbuilder. OSHA fined Avondale $537,000 for 473 unsafe hazards in the workplace. OSHA found that 266 of these violations—more than half—were "willful" violations. In other words, they were hazards Avondale knew about and had refused to fix.

Most of these violations were for precisely the kind of hazards that account for Avondale's unusually high fatality rate. These 266 "willful" violations involved hazards that can lead to fatal falls, and three of the seven workers who died at Avondale between 1990 and 1995 died from falls. Didn't Avondale learn anything from these tragedies?

OSHA found 107 "willful" violations for failure to provide adequate railings on scaffolding. Fifty-one willful violations for unsafe rope rails. Thirty willful violations for improperly anchored fall protection devices. Twenty-five willful violations for inadequate guard rails on high platforms. And twenty-seven willful violations for inadequate training in the use of fall protection.

OSHA also found 206 "serious" violations for many of the same kind of hazards. "Serious" violations are ones Avondale knew about—or should have known about—that pose a substantial danger of death or serious injury.

This is what Labor Secretary Alexis Herman had to say about Avondale's safety problems: "I am deeply concerned about the conditions OSHA found at Avondale. Falls are a leading cause of on-the-job fatalities, and Avondale has put its workers at risk of falls up to ninety feet.

The stiff penalties are warranted. Workers should not have to risk their lives for their livelihood."

OSHA Assistant Secretary Charles Jeffress said, "Three Avondale workers have fallen to their deaths, one each in 1984, 1993, and 1994. This inspection revealed that conditions related to these fatalities continued to exist at the shipyard. This continued disregard for their employees' safety is unacceptable."

And what was Avondale's response? True to form, Avondale appealed the OSHA fines. Avondale claimed that many of the violations were the result of employee sabotage. Avondale also tried to argue that the OSHA inspector was biased. In response, the head of OSHA observed that "it's very unusual for a company to accuse its own employees of sabotage, and it's very unusual for a company to attack the objectivity of OSHA inspectors."

OSHA had found many of the same problems back in 1994, the last time it conducted a comprehensive inspection of Avondale. In 1994 OSHA cited Avondale 61 times for 81 violations, with a fine of $80,000 that was later settled for $16,000.

There may be more fines to come. The OSHA inspection team will soon finish its review of Avondale's safety and medical records. This review was delayed last October when Avondale launched yet another legal battle to prevent OSHA from obtaining complete access to its records.

One of the Avondale workers who visited my office several weeks ago was there during the OSHA inspection, and told me how it happened. OSHA tried to inspect Avondale's Occupational Injuries and Illness logs. But Avondale refused complete access and, according to OSHA, "attempted to place unnecessary controls over the movements of the investigative team and their contact with employees."

When OSHA issued a subpoena for the logs, Avondale stopped all cooperation with OSHA and told the inspectors to leave the premises. OSHA had to go to New Orleans district court to get an order enforcing the subpoena.

The other main issue in the 1993 election campaign was pay and compensation.

Avondale workers have long been the worst paid in the shipbuilding industry. They have the lowest average wage of any of the five major private shipyards. According to a survey conducted by the AFL-CIO, Avondale workers make twenty-nine percent less than workers at other private contractors for the Navy, and forty-eight percent less than workers at the nation's federal shipyards. One Avondale mechanic, Mike Boudreaux, says, "It's a sweatshop with such low wages."

By way of comparison, look at Ingalls Shipyard, down the river in Pascagoula, Mississippi. The average pay at Ingalls is higher than the top pay at Avondale. Or look at wages in nearby New Orleans for plumbers, pipe fitters, and steamfitters. Their average wage is higher than the top pay at Avondale.

Avondale is also known for its inadequate pension plan. There are Avondale retirees with thirty years' experience who retire with $300 per month. And workers complain that they can't afford Avondale's family health insurance, which costs $2,000 per year. Avondale workers pay more for health care every week than Ingalls workers pay every month.

Unlike other shipyards, Avondale has had a hard time attracting workers, and inferior working conditions certainly have a lot to do with it. Avondale has responded to this labor shortage by using prison labor and importing workers from other countries. It imported a group of Scottish and English workers who were so appalled at the working conditions and low pay that they quit after three days. Nearby Ingalls shipyard, by contrast, has never had to import foreign workers on visas.

So why does Avondale pay so little? Because times are tough? Hardly. Avondale CEO Alfred Bossier has been doing quite well, thank you. In 1998, Mr. Bossier's base salary and bonuses totaled $1,012,410, up more than twenty percent from the previous year. His benefits increased to $17,884, up seventy-three percent from the previous year. And he got 45,000 shares of stock options, worth up to $1,927,791. The grand total comes to about three million dollars.

Meanwhile, the average hourly production worker at Avondale earns less than ten dollars an hour—or around $20,000 per year. So Al Bossier brings home about 150 times the salary of the average hourly worker.

The obvious question is how can Avondale get away with such appalling behavior? How can it be so brazen? The answer is depressing. Avondale gets away with it because our labor laws are filled with loopholes. Avondale gets away with it because the decks are stacked against workers who want to improve their working conditions by bargaining collectively.

Avondale gets away with it because they have enough money to tie up the courts, knowing full well that organizing drives can fizzle out in the five or six or seven years that highly-paid company lawyers can drag out the process. When asked how Avondale gets away with it, one worker laughed and said, "This is America. It's money that talks."

There's one other reason why Avondale gets away with it, and this is something I find especially troubling. They get away with it because American taxpayers are footing the bill. The Navy and the Coast Guard are effectively subsidizing Avondale's illegal union-busting campaign. Avondale gets about eighty percent of its contracts from the Navy for building and repairing ships. If it weren't for the United States Navy, Avondale probably wouldn't exist. This poster child for bad corporate citizenship is brought to you courtesy of the American taxpayer.

This is a classic case of the left hand not knowing what the right hand is doing. On the one hand, the NLRB and OSHA find Avondale in flagrant violation of the law. On the other hand, the Navy keeps rewarding Avondale with more contracts. Avondale has gotten 3.2 billion dollars in contracts from the Navy since 1993, when the shipyard first refused to bargain collectively with its workers.

To add insult to injury, Avondale is billing the Navy for its illegal union-busting. The Navy agreed to pick up the tab for anti-union meetings held on company time in 1993. Nearly every day for three months leading up to the union election, Avondale management called workers into anti-union meetings. Then they billed the Navy for at least 15,216 hours spent by workers at those meetings.

Some of these meetings were the same ones where Avondale illegally harassed and intimidated workers, according to Judge Evans. Yet the Defense Contractor Auditing Agency, DCAA, approved Avondale's billing as indirect spending for shipbuilding. And Avondale billed the Navy 5.4 million dollars between 1993 and 1998 for legal fees incurred in its NLRB litigation.

When the Navy looks the other way as one of its main contractors engages in flagrant lawbreaking, it sends a message. When the Navy keeps awarding contracts to Avondale, when it pays Avondale for time spent in anti-union meetings where workers are harassed and intimidated, when it pays for the legal costs of fighting Avondale's workers, it sends a message. It sends the message that this kind of behavior by Avondale is okay.

When Avondale continues to beat out other shipyards for huge defense contracts, that sends a message too. It sends a message that this is the way you compete in America today. You compete by violating your workers' rights to free speech and free assembly. You compete by illegally firing and harassing your workers. You compete by keeping your employees from bettering their working conditions through collective bargaining.

And that message is not lost on other companies. They see what Avondale is getting away with, and they draw the obvious conclusions. The AFL-CIO's state director pointed to another Louisiana company that initially refused to recognize the union its workers had elected. "Part of it is they're following Bossier's lead," she said. "After all, the guy's been at it for five years [now six] and he still gets all the contracts he wants."

Under federal regulations, the Navy is required to exercise oversight over the 3.2 billion dollars in contracts it has awarded to Avondale. And the Navy can only award contracts to "responsible contractors." The contracting officer has to make an affirmative finding that a contractor is responsible. Part of the definition of a "responsible contractor" is having a "satisfactory record of integrity and business ethics." So the Navy has to affirmatively determine that Avondale has a satisfactory record of integrity and business ethics.

Well, what exactly would qualify as an unsatisfactory record? Judge Evans ruled that Avondale management had orchestrated an "outrageous and pervasive" union-busting campaign consisting of over 100 violations of labor law and the illegal firing of twenty-eight employees. OSHA has found 473 safety violations—266 of them willful—and fined Avondale $537,000, the second largest fine in U.S. shipbuilding history.

The AFL-CIO has asked the Navy to investigate Avondale's business practices, as a first step to determining what steps should be taken. That doesn't sound so unreasonable to me. In fact, it seems to me that the Navy ought to be concerned when its contracts come in late, as they have at Avondale. It ought to be concerned when a contractor's working conditions are so bad that it suffers from labor shortages.

And it seems to me the Navy ought to investigate whether a company found to have orchestrated an "outrageous and pervasive" campaign to violate labor laws is a responsible contractor. Or whether a shipyard found to have willfully violated health and safety laws 266 times is a responsible contractor.

The Navy says it cannot take sides in a labor dispute. But nobody is asking them to do that. The problem is that they already appear to have taken sides. When the Navy finances Avondale's union-busting campaign, when it pays legal fees for Avondale's court challenges, when it certifies Avondale as a responsible contractor with a satisfactory record of integrity and business ethics, and when it rewards Avondale with Navy contracts, the Navy appears to be taking sides.

What has happened at Avondale should give us all pause. The NLRB's general counsel acknowledges that the Avondale case exposes the many problems with the system, caused in part by budget cuts and procedural delays. "It's hard to take issue with the notion that it's frustrating that an election that took place five years ago [now six] still hasn't come to a conclusion. It's something we're looking at as an example of the process not being what it should be."

Indeed, the Avondale case exposes glaring loopholes in our labor laws that make it next to impossible for workers to form a union and bargain collectively. In fact, this case provides us with a roadmap for putting a stop to rampant abuses of our labor laws.

First of all, we need to restore cuts in the NLRB's budget so that defendants with deep pockets can't delay the process for years and years. But beyond that, we need to improve our labor laws so we can put a stop to abuses of the kind we've seen in the Avondale case.

We need to install unions quickly after they win an election, the same way we allow elected officials to take office pending challenges to their election. Why should workers be treated any differently than politicians?

In addition, we need to strengthen penalties against unfair labor practices such as the illegal firing of union organizers and sympathizers. And we need to ensure that organizers have equal access to workers during election campaigns, so that companies like Avondale are not able to intimidate their employees and monopolize the election debate.

Senator Kennedy and I have introduced legislation that would do exactly that. Our bill—S. 654, the Right to Organize Act of 1999—would provide for mandatory mediation and binding arbitration, if necessary, after a union is certified. It would provide for treble damages and a private right of action when the NLRB finds that an employer has illegally fired its workers for union activity. And it would give organizers equal access to employees during a union election campaign.

The Avondale case sends a message to other companies and to workers everywhere, and it's the exact opposite of the message we should be sending. We should be sending a message that corporations are citizens of their community and need to obey the law and respect the rights of their fellow citizens. We should be sending a message that corporations who live off taxpayer money, especially, have an obligation to be good corporate citizens.

Avondale is making a mockery of U.S. labor laws and of the democratic right to organize. Instead of rewarding and financing the illegal labor practices of employers such as Avondale, I believe we should shine a light on these abuses and put a stop to them.

STEEL REVITALIZATION ACT
May 25, 2001

Mr. President, I rise to speak in support of the Steel Revitalization Act of 2001. This is the companion measure to H.R. 808 which, as of this moment, has 189 cosponsors in the House of Representatives. The measure represents a comprehensive approach to a serious crisis which is facing our domestic iron ore and steel industry.

Several of the provisions contained in this act are ones that my colleagues in the bipartisan Steel Caucus have introduced in the Senate. I particularly thank Senators Rockefeller and Specter for their work in co-chairing this caucus, and Senator Byrd for his unflinching support of the entire steel industry and his creative efforts on behalf of the industry's working families. A special thank you to Senator Rockefeller, who has been absolutely the leader on this issue.

The Steel Revitalization Act includes the following components:

First, there is import relief. We go back to a five-year period of quantitative restrictions on the import of iron ore. We go back prior to the import surge in 1997. We go to a three-year average. That is where we hold the line. Between February and March, 2001, there was a forty-percent surge in the import of steel or semifinished steel, way under the cost of production, constituting unfair trade and putting people out of work.

Second, there is creation of a steelworker retiree health care fund which is administered by the steelworker retiree health care board at the Department of Labor. This fund would be underwritten through a 1.5-percent surcharge on the sale of all steel products in the United States, both imported and domestic.

One of the awful things about what is going on is many of the retirees worked their whole life, thought they had health care coverage, and are terrified they will not have the health care coverage. A seventy-year-old struggling with cancer now is worried there will be no health care coverage.

Third, we have the enhancement of the current Steel Loan Guarantee Program which provides the steel companies greater access to funds needed to invest in capital improvements to take advantage of the latest technological advancements.

Finally, we have the creation of a 500-million-dollar grant program at the Department of Commerce to help defray the costs of environmental mitigation and the restructuring as a result of consolidation—again, assuming these companies make a commitment to invest in our country; again, assuming these companies make a commitment to the workers.

I think all senators can appreciate this legislation. The Iron Range of Minnesota, and if you think of our sister state of Michigan, this is a part of the United States of America with a proud history of providing key raw materials to the producers of steel for well over a century. In these taconite mines are some of the hardest working people you ever want to meet. LTV has closed down in Hoyt Lakes; 1,400 miners lost their work. They are steelworkers, but they work in the mines. These were good, middle-class jobs.

It is not just these workers who have lost their jobs; it has the ripple effect on all the small businesses, all the subcontractors, all the suppliers—all the families.

I am in schools all the time. There is such pain, such concern about the future of these families and concern for the future of their children. From my point of view, and I know I speak for Senator Dayton, there is probably not a more important piece of legislation to introduce.

The introduction of a piece of legislation is not symbolic politics. It does not mean it passes.

We have a lot of work cut out for us, but I will say to my colleague from Virginia, I thank publicly on the floor of the Senate—I certainly have called her—Secretary of Labor Chao. We are, again, in a situation right now where there is a lot of economic pain, a lot of economic desperation. The Secretary of Labor has provided the workers up there with at least some relief, which was extremely important. We were so hopeful we could get trade adjustment assistance benefits. The Secretary of Labor granted us an additional year, above and beyond unemployment benefits that workers receive through the state of Minnesota.

It is additional money for job relocation. For workers and their families to get that trade adjustment assistance is a lifeline. It gives them more time. It gives them an opportunity to think about what ladder there is for career development. It gives them some financial assistance for their families. I have told Secretary Chao—I don't know if I will get her in trouble with the administration by being so glowing about what I have to say about her—I so appreciate it and so do the people in the State of Minnesota. I want to publicly thank her.

I also want to say we are now waiting, of course, for the administration on a decision—Secretary Evans will make a decision soon—as to whether or not we will be taking some trade action to really make sure we have a future for this industry. The next big decision is going to be in mid-June about whether or not the taconite workers on the Iron Range in Minnesota are going to have a future. This industry will not survive if it is continually faced with unfair trade practices, if it continues to face this import surge of slab or finished steel. Our taconite workers on the Iron Range of Minnesota ask nothing more than to have a level playing field. We wait for a decision mid-June.

I think steelworkers and industrial workers all across the country—and I think they will have a lot of allies—will in a strong voice say you have to take some action. For the Iron Range in Minnesota, northeast Minnesota, time is not neutral. Time moves on. It is extremely important, above and beyond this lifeline assistance, that we get serious about a fair trade policy so these workers and their families have a future.

There is companion legislation in the House. Very important work has been done by Senator Rockefeller and Senator Specter. I think we can get some strong bipartisan support, but it is not going to be enough to just introduce a bill. We will need action from the administration and we will need legislative action if there is to be a future for this extremely important industry—which, by the way, I think is essential to our national security.

This legislation is legislation near and dear to my heart because it is so connected to the lives and people I truly love, that is to say the steelworkers and their families on the Iron Range of the state of Minnesota.

16

CAMPAIGN FINANCE REFORM

> "Mr. President, in the cafes in Minnesota, quite often people would say to us: When it comes to our concerns, Paul and Sheila, about affordable child care, jobs and decent wages, and affordable health care, about the power of insurance companies, the way in which we are denied coverage, about the concentration of power in banking, about the concentration of power in agriculture, about affordable education, when it comes to our concerns, we don't think our concerns are of much concern in the Halls of the Congress. I think the main reason that people have reached this conclusion is that they are so disillusioned about all the ways in which they see big money dominating politics. Indeed, I think that is the ethical issue of our time."   ~Senator Paul Wellstone, October 7, 1997

In Paul Wellstone's first campaign for the United States Senate, he was outspent by incumbent Senator Rudy Boschwitz seven to one. Millions of dollars were spent on television advertisements attacking and distorting Wellstone's opinions on Social Security and Medicare. As stated by former Vice-President Walter Mondale, Boschwitz engaged in a "relentless, brutal, heavily financed, and, in my judgment, untruthful television assault." Boschwitz's money came largely from corporate Political Action Committees, which opposed the ideas that Paul Wellstone felt the most strongly about.

It was no surprise, then, that after Paul Wellstone was sworn in as a United States senator, he was an early and outspoken advocate for campaign finance reform. For over a decade, Senator Wellstone pushed for campaign finance reform. It was not until March 27, 2002, that the Bipartisan Campaign Reform Act, otherwise known as the McCain-Feingold Act, passed and was signed into law.

HEALTH CARE AND CAMPAIGN FINANCE REFORM
August 8, 1994

Mr. President, I want to speak today on health care, but I want to focus on health care within the framework of campaign finance reform because I think if there ever was an issue that really should focus attention on the mix of money and politics, and why it is just imperative that we pass a strong campaign finance reform bill this session, it is health care.

Mr. President, a couple of months ago I was invited to speak to a gathering, a group of doctors. It was their annual association meeting. It was an 8:30 engagement, and I got there at 8:25. I was having a cup of coffee in the back of the room, at which point the director of this organization was talking to his members. There were about 350 doctors who came from around the country. He said: When you go to see your representative or your senator, you cannot give them a PAC check in their office. That is not legal. So they might want to just tell you where to send it instead.

And then he hesitated and he said in kind of an awkward way, "But they will take it," at which point there was this uneasy laughter in the room. But it was not just cynical laughter; actually, it was awkward laughter because, after all, as much as the doctors and the people in this organization did not like the taking of the money, they were doing the giving. I mean, if they thought something should not feel right about this, they were a part of it.

So, Mr. President, it was now my turn to speak, and I was trying to figure out how to make this transition. First, I thanked them for their work as surgeons, having been involved in athletics for a long time, and I said to them: I was listening to your conversation, and I have to tell you in all honesty that I really believe that throughout this whole debate on this health care bill, I have said that I do not think representatives or senators should take any health care PAC money. I wish there would be a moratorium on it. Nor do I think we should take any large, individual contributions from the health industry, broadly defined, over $100.

Mr. President, at that point, I was certain that I would be met with a kind of wall of hostility, and I was really surprised because people literally came to their feet, and there was this tremendous applause. And then I looked at these doctors, who were not particularly political. They all came to Washington because they had been told this is where you come at this moment in this debate.

And I said to them: Having been a teacher for twenty years, I am pretty good at reading faces, and I now know what is going on here. We are all trapped in this same awful system, those of us in the Senate, whether we are Democrats or Republicans, who are told that the benchmark figure we are supposed to raise is $13,000 a week to be viable for reelection, or thereabouts. This is an obscene money chase, in which people are too often told that you actually have to come to Washington, checkbook in hand, to have influence. No wonder people feel so ripped off; no wonder people feel so angry.

Mr. President, as we start this health care debate, I just want to say to my colleagues that there is nothing more important that we can do to improve our policy process than to enact tough, far-reaching campaign finance reform. The focus of the congressional debate during the next few weeks, on health care reform, really brings this to the forefront.

Mr. President, I say to my colleague from Illinois, if we were talking about a soccer game, as my good friend and long-time campaign reform advocate Phil Stern used to say:

If you were talking about a soccer game or football game, and you saw the opposing teams pouring in money to the referees or the officials before the game took place, there is not a person in this country who would believe that those officials or those referees were going to be able to make an objective, fair decision. They would feel like something was wrong with that whole process.

That is what is going on right now, Mr. President. In the 1992 presidential and congressional elections, political contributions from the medical industry stood at a record high of forty-one million dollars. This was in the 1990-1992 cycle, 26.4 million dollars from doctors; 7.3 million dollars from the insurance industry; four million dollars from drug manufacturers; and almost three million dollars from other providers. The rest came from HMOs, lobbyists, mental health professionals, medical suppliers, and others.

Mr. President, according to an FEC analysis by Citizen Action, in the last eighteen months, 26.4 million dollars has poured into the U.S. Congress from political action committees and individual special interests:

Twenty-six point four million dollars over the last eighteen months, Mr. President. That is over one million dollars a month.

In March, these organizations contributed a staggering four million dollars. Let me repeat that one more time—four million dollars, in March alone, pouring into the U.S. Congress from the health industry.

Mr. President, on the one hand, we are supposed to have this debate, we are supposed to make objective decisions, we are supposed to make the kinds of decisions that will enable us to do well for the people we represent; and, on the other hand, you have all of this money pouring into the Congress at an unprecedented rate.

Mr. President, I just think it looks awful. It just looks awful.

Mr. President, I am not talking about the wrongdoing of individual officeholders. I am not arguing that any of us is personally corrupt.

What I am saying, Mr. President, is that this system does not work. We must put a stop to all this money pouring in here. We must clean up our act. We must have real, tough campaign finance reform now.

When four million dollars is contributed from the health care industry in March alone and over the last eighteen months over one million dollars a month has poured in, how can we hope that people we represent will believe that the final reform bill we pass will not, in one way or another, have been affected by these huge special interest contributions?

Mr. President, all too often, senators and representatives, rather than being the bold agents of health care change, have become timid agents of interests. And what is interesting to me is that when we look at the analysis or hear about what is wrong, we have the doctors who want to blame the lawyers; we have the employers who say that the problem with the health insurance industry is they do not want to insure anybody unless they are wealthy or healthy. And then we have the insurance companies who blame the doctors. And then, of course, we have this analysis that blames the consumer.

The one kind of issue that has not been focused on—and I really wish it would be, because I think it is so important that we have campaign finance reform this session—is the way in which money and politics have intersected on this issue with such force, with people attempting to buy access to influence and power.

I wish it was not happening because I think it has a corrosive effect on the political process in our country. And I think it is one of the reasons, by the way, Mr. President, that people feel so out of the loop.

I see the senator from Illinois has a question; if I could just add one statistic, then I will yield to the senator from Illinois.

Common Cause recently issued some telling data on this question. They concluded that from January 1987 through December 1993, business PACs contributed slightly more than seventy-two million dollars to U.S. Senators. Labor PACs over the same six years contributed sixteen million dollars. That is a four-to-one business-over-labor margin.

And we wonder why there is opposition in the Senate to employers paying their fair share for universal health care coverage?

Let me repeat that. A Common Cause study found that between 1987 and 1993, seventy-two million dollars was contributed from business PACs, and sixteen million dollars from labor PACs: a four-to-one margin. And people wonder why it is so difficult to push a health care reform bill through that calls upon employers to pay their fair share.

By the way, these business PACs out-gave, if that is the right way of putting it, to Democratic senators by a two-to-one margin over labor. Very interesting. Business PACs in this six-year period gave thirty-two million dollars to Democrats; labor PACs, fifteen million dollars. And people wonder why we are having such a time having employers pay their fair share.

I yield to the senator from Illinois.

CAMPAIGN FINANCE REFORM, McCAIN-FEINGOLD
October 7, 1997

I thank my colleague for his strong words. He has been a very strong reformer in the Senate.

Mr. President, let me try to not repeat the arguments that have already been made on the floor and instead draw from conversation that my wife, Sheila, and I have had with people in cafés in Minnesota. We had the opportunity, in August, to spend about a week just dropping in cafés in the morning around breakfast time and lunch time and just talking with people and listening to what people had to say.

I say to my colleagues that one disturbing conclusion from these discussions with people is that I think many people in our country, certainly many Minnesotans, are now pretty well convinced that way too much of politics, way too much of government is dominated by wealthy people and special interests, that too few people have way too much wealth, power, and say and that too many people—that is to say the majority of people—are locked out.

Mr. President, in the cafés in Minnesota, quite often people would say to us: When it comes to our concerns, Paul and Sheila, about affordable child care, jobs and decent wages, and affordable health care, about the power of insurance compa-

nies, the way in which we are denied coverage, about the concentration of power in banking, about the concentration of power in agriculture, about affordable education, when it comes to our concerns, we don't think our concerns are of much concern in the Halls of the Congress.

I think the main reason that people have reached this conclusion is that they are so disillusioned about all the ways in which they see big money dominating politics. Indeed, I think that is the ethical issue of our time.

Mr. President, so that nobody has any illusions here, I don't think that people view this as corruption as in the wrongdoing of individual officeholders, but they view it as systemic. They really believe that there is an imbalance of power where the wealthy few and powerful interests pretty much dominate the political process. Mr. President, you know what? I think they are right. I don't think it is just a perception. I think they are absolutely right.

If you believe in representative democracy, then you believe in the idea that each person counts as one and no more than one. We don't have that any longer. We have auction block democracy, government going to the highest bidder. People are disillusioned. That is the meaning of the last election, where over fifty percent of the people in the country didn't even vote. The party of the disaffected is the largest party in our country. Therefore, I don't understand, for the life of me, why my colleagues on the majority side introduced an amendment—the majority leader introduces an amendment which basically destroys this campaign reform effort.

Now, Mr. President, I want to thank senators McCain and Feingold for their very strong leadership. I think this is the most important issue before us. I think it is the core question; it is the core issue. Every year since I have been here in the Senate, I fought it out on these reform issues because I really think this goes to the very heart of whether or not we really have a democracy or whether we just have a pseudo-democracy. What we have before us really is not the McCain-Feingold original formula, but the extra-mild version, which I don't think has enough zing in it, but at least it represents a step forward.

With the McCain-Feingold effort here, we have a ban on soft money contributions to the parties. This is the sort of unaccountable money, if you will. We have in addition, some real standards on this issue advocacy—and this has been gone over, which is a terribly important part of this legislation—and by the way, if you ban soft money to the parties and don't do anything about the issue ads, really pseudo-fake ads, the money will just shift there, and in addition, you have some standards dealing with tighter standards dealing with independent expenditures. So it is a step forward. That is why we should pass it.

My hope is that it will whet the appetite of people in the country for more because the truth of the matter is, in the spirit of compromise, the one provision that was actually dropped—that is why we have McCain-Feingold extra-mild now, it had [to] do with us, with reducing the amount of money spent in campaigns in Senate races. I mean, I thought that was the most important part that we would somehow reduce the amount of money spent in exchange for discounts when it comes to access to TV time or direct mailing, you name it.

Now, Mr. President, I mean, I think the criteria ought to be, let's stop this obscene money chase, let's stop the obscene amount of money all of us have to spend and the time we have to spend raising money. Let's lessen the special interest access and influence. There is way too much of that. The vast majority of people really are locked out of this process, and let's try and have a level playing field, where challengers have a shot at winning. By that criteria, the McCain-Feingold bill doesn't go far enough. But if this piece of legislation is passed—and that is why it is such an important bill, even this stripped-down version is so important—people in the country, I think, will say, look, the Congress has finally taken some action. This is a step forward.

People aren't fools. People aren't going to see this legislation as the be all and end all. They are not going to see it as Heaven on Earth, as ending all special interest access; they are not going to see it as ending the huge amounts of money spent in politics. But people will see it as a step forward. I say to my colleagues that what we have here when it comes to the majority leader's amendment—quite frankly, I am surprised that some of my colleagues in the majority party have essentially followed the lead of this amendment. I hope they won't. If we have a vote that is going to be very revealing.

If in fact people vote for this Lott amendment and continue to insist that it became part of a reform bill knowing that it is, as everyone has said, the "poison pill" amendment, then we may very well have no reform bill passed at all.

So this becomes a vote which tells people in the country where all of us stand and on what side each party stands on when it comes to this fundamental question of reform.

If we come here this afternoon and what we have happen is that we have the Lott amendment out there—I don't know why we can't have a separate vote on the Lott amendment. I thought we would. I think we can vote it down. If that doesn't happen, then there is no cloture, and then we go to the McCain-Feingold bill and we can't get cloture, that is blocked by senators in the majority party, then what happens is we again reach an impasse, and people in the country become disillusioned.

As a Democrat, I will just say to the members of the majority party that, frankly, I think people will be very angry. I think they will not appreciate this amendment. I think they will not appreciate the effort on the part of the majority leader to kill campaign finance reform. But I would say, not as a Democrat but as a Minnesotan, as an American citizen, ultimately we all lose. If we do not take advantage of this moment in time where we can pass a reform bill, albeit it still doesn't do enough, then we will be making a huge mistake, and this will just add to the disillusion of the people in the country.

The good news is that we can pass a reform bill. I hope we do. I hope we do not squander this opportunity. The good news is that all around the country there is a lot of energy for reform.

I introduced a bill with Senator Kerry which is a clean-election, clean-money option which essentially gets all of the private money out of politics. It is really strong. People in Maine have supported it. People in Vermont have now supported it. There are going to be initiatives around the country on this. There is a lot of energy in states all across the country. So I think people in the country are going to continue to put the pressure on.

But we ought not to miss this opportunity to do something good. We ought not to miss this opportunity to at least begin to make some changes in the way in which all of this money is spent on politics. We ought not to miss this opportunity to pass the McCain-Feingold bill and give people in the country a clear message that we hear them. We ought not to miss this opportunity for reform. We ought not to miss this opportunity to reassure people in the country that we are committed to a political process that is more open, with more integrity—and not just the heavy hitters, the big givers, the invested and the well-connected running the show. We better not miss this opportunity.

I say to my colleagues in the majority party that I hope some of you will have the courage to vote against this Lott amendment, if we have that chance, or have the courage to join us and pass the McCain-Feingold bill, which would be a historically significant step in the right direction in leading our country toward more democracy, toward more participation and more involvement as opposed to this awful system we have right now which absolutely needs to be changed.

17

IMPEACHMENT

> "It is a supreme irony that the most conservative forces in our politics today have for months wielded the most radical option made available in the Constitution against this president: impeachment and removal."
> ~ Senator Paul Wellstone, February 12, 1999

In 1998, President William Jefferson Clinton became only the second United States president to be impeached by the House of Representatives. The impeachment was based upon allegations that President Clinton lied under oath in a civil sexual harassment case brought by Paula Jones. Once a president is impeached by the House of Representatives, the matter is referred to the United States Senate for trial. The "jury" is comprised of the sitting United States senators, and, in this case, Chief Justice William H. Rehnquist presided over the "trial." The Constitution required two-thirds of the United States Senate to vote in favor of the removal of President Clinton from office. The final vote, largely along party lines after a twenty-one-day trial, fell well short of a two-thirds majority. Senator Paul Wellstone voted not guilty on both the charges of perjury and obstruction of justice.

THE IMPEACHMENT OF PRESIDENT WILLIAM JEFFERSON CLINTON
February 12, 1999

Mr. Chief Justice, I want to explain my views publicly on the impeachment articles sent to us by a partisan vote of the House of Representatives, and on the removal of the president from office which they would prompt.

First, I am shocked and saddened that our Republican colleagues persistently have blocked our efforts to have open and public debates and discussion in our deliberations in this matter, and most especially in our deliberations on the final votes on whether to remove the president. Whatever their motives, this is not what a free, representative, accountable democracy is all about. Simply publishing partial transcripts of our proceedings, which include only some formal statements made by senators and not the deliberations themselves—and doing so only at the end of the trial—is, in my view, a great leap sideways.

I also want to describe what I think—and frankly have thought for months—is a more appropriate mechanism to express our disapproval of the president's behavior: a tough, bipartisan censure resolution which makes clear our contempt for what he's done in lying to his family, his friends, his staff, and the American people about his relationship with Monica Lewinsky; and the disgrace which those lies have placed upon his presidency for all time.

In recent months, hundreds of Constitutional scholars—including many respected conservatives—have argued that, in their view, the Constitution does allow this censure vote; the Senate's precedents allow it; we have done it before. It's true that the Constitution is silent on the question of what else we can do in addition to removal; it is also true that the Constitution in no way prevents us from moving forward on censure. The argument that we are somehow blocked Constitutionally from censuring the president is contrived, and fraught with partisan pleading.

Even so, if we are ultimately blocked by a filibuster from a vote on censure, the president will not have escaped the judgment of Congress or the American people. Any senator, in any venue they choose, can offer their own forceful, public censure of the president, repeatedly if they like. I certainly have. A corporate expression of the Senate's condemnation of the president's actions, while of course preferable, is not essential, for all of us already have made known our views.

We all condemn the president's behavior. It has been said so many times, it hardly bears repeating, were it not for the wilful, partisan attempts to mischaracterize a vote against removal as a vote to condone what the president has done. That is, of course, preposterous; the president has been impeached by the House. That has only happened once before in our history. The trial has gone forward, and every member of this body has condemned the president's behavior as unacceptable, meriting only scorn and rebuke.

It is clear that the president already has paid a terrible price in the eyes of history, not least in the shame and humiliation that this permanent mark on his presidency has caused him, his family, his friends and supporters, and his Administration. The message is clear, including to our

young people: When one fails to tell the truth, there are real, sometimes even awful consequences and costs. The president's behavior was shameful, despicable, unworthy, a disgrace to his office. And in this long, sordid, painful process, I believe he has been held accountable for what he has done.

Pursued overzealously by Kenneth Starr and by House Judiciary Committee Republicans, the articles were then approved by the full House in a grossly unfair and partisan proceeding that was destructive both of our polity and our politics. All of us should be deeply troubled by it, and all should work together to put it behind us. In my view, these allegations should never have reached the Senate. But they have, and the trial has now been held. It has changed few, if any, minds on the basic facts, on how the law should be applied to those facts, or on the high bar for removal set by the Constitution.

Finally we bring to a close this long, sad year of investigations, hearings, and speeches. It has been a painful year. In many ways, it has been a lost year. Think of what we might have done this past year, had we not done this. Think of the news we could have made, had not all seen this. Think of the good laws that we could have written, had not this stood in the way. Think of the opportunities lost, the hopes staved off. We must ask with Langston Hughes, "What happens to a dream deferred?"

Sadly, so many opportunities for better, more prudent and proportionate judgment fell by the wayside. First, and most important, the president should have avoided this sorry relationship. Then, a little over a year ago, the president could have been more forthcoming and told the whole truth, instead of misleading us all. The American people could have handled it. Then, the Independent Counsel could have shown greater discretion in judging whether to bring this case forward. The leadership of the House of Representatives could have allowed a vote on censuring the president, instead of pushing the case forward to impeachment. They were wrong to thwart the will of what I expect would have been a House majority in so doing. And the Senate could have voted to dismiss the case and promptly and resolutely censured the president.

Instead, against better judgment, against all indications of the people's will, and against any shred of charity, an ardent and zealous minority pressed on. They had the right. They had the power. But they were wrong, and I believe history will so judge them. It is a supreme irony that the most conservative forces in our politics today have for months wielded the most radical option made available in the Constitution against this president: impeachment and removal. Aware of its dangers, our founders designed Constitutional protections against its abuse. This process has shown that those protections are not perfect; they require reasoned judgment in their application; judgment that has been missing in this process from day one.

Let us resolve to learn the lessons of this long, sad year. Let us learn now, having come this far, the wisdom of the founders that impeachment is and must be a high barricade, not to be mounted lightly. Let us learn that because it requires the overwhelming support of the Senate to succeed, it cannot and should not proceed on a merely partisan basis. Let us learn that the desire to impeach and remove must be shared broadly, or it is illegitimate.

Let us learn that the subject matter of impeachment must be a matter of great gravity, calling into question the president's very ability to lead, and endangering the nation's liberty, freedom, security. Let us learn that the case against the president must be a strong and unambiguous one in fact and in law, for even a president deserves the benefit of our reasonable doubts.

The charges brought against President Clinton do not rise to those levels. And even if

they did, the case against him is neither strong nor unambiguous. As the White House defense team has made clear, there are ample grounds for doubt about both the facts and law surrounding each of the two articles before us.

It is true that the impeachment process has further alienated millions of Americans from their government, and that is a tragic harm for which the president bears considerable responsibility. It is also true, as we were told by Chairman Hyde yesterday, that the nobility and fragility of a self-governing people requires hard work, every day, to get it right, to fight the good fight, to discern the common good. But I believe, unlike him, that it is the impeachment process itself, both here and in the other body—its partisanship, its meanness and unfairness, its leadership by those who want to win too badly—which has increased people's cynicism; not the prospect of the president's "getting away" with something.

Our nation was founded on the Jeffersonian principle, "that government is the strongest of which every man feels himself a part." What Jefferson and the other founders feared was the warning of their counterpart Rousseau: "As soon as any man says of the affairs of State 'What does it matter to me?' the state may be given up as lost." But while the many signs of disaffection among our people are growing, I do not think we have reached the point of no return; there is time in this Congress to recover from this episode, and to move on.

Despite the claims of pundits that Americans have simply tuned out, I think a deeper reality is present in their reactions, and in the polls. In fact, most Americans, in their wisdom, have reached a subtle, sophisticated judgment in this case, and have already moved beyond it. As is so often the case, they're way ahead of Washington. It is true that they abhor the president's behavior, but don't believe it merits his removal. In addition, they believe that there are larger issues facing the nation than the misdeeds that nearly all now concede the president committed: peace in the Middle East; the hunger of children; the health of Americans; saving our social security safety net; debating whether hundreds of billions of dollars of surplus should go to bolster Medicare, or to some combination of universal savings accounts or tax cuts. These are the things that the people sent us here to work on. These are the things that I hear about when I return to my state.

So let us now bring to a close, with our votes, this long, sad year of investigation and impeachment. And let us resolve that there shall be many a year before we have another one like it. It is time for our country to pull together to seek an end to the fractious partisanship that has defined this period, and to re-engage a full-throated, genuine debate about our nation's future that can help us find again that common ground that unites us as Americans, and that can serve as a firm foundation for resolving the many serious problems that still face our country—impeachment or not—today and tomorrow.

We should, as White House attorney Charles Ruff said, listen to the voices not merely of the advocates who have been before us, but of Madison, Hamilton, and the others who met in Philadelphia 212 years ago; of the generations of Americans since then; of the American people now, and of future generations of Americans. And if we do, we will do the right thing.

Congressman John Lewis observed in his final impeachment speech, in the end, we are "one house, one family, one people; the American house, the American family, the American people." We are called together to come to judgment on this president, and then to return promptly to the pressing issues that lay before us, and that require our urgent attention. That judgment is by now clear: Bill Clinton should remain president;

the censure of this body, and the historic impeachment that will ever attach to his name, will leave a permanent mark on his presidency.

I thank you, Mr. Chief Justice, for the fine work that you have done, and I thank both the majority leader and the minority leader for their leadership. I said to Senator Lott, I think yesterday, I am still furious that we are in closed session and will say that, but I appreciate the way in which you have kept us together. I thank the two of you.

I was thinking I might do something a little different, because even if I were to give a great speech to the best of my ability, I don't know that there are any more arguments that can be made. I was thinking like, I might agree—actually I have a printed statement—I might agree to just have my statement included in the record and not speak any further, if I can get some support for some legislation. (Laughter.)

Just on some children's legislation. Does it look like we are at that point? It does? Well, I like that show of support, and I think, Mr. Chief Justice, what I will do is give to you in a moment a full statement and just simply say to everybody here about three things in two minutes.

One, I wish we had done this in open session, and I cover that more in my full statement.

Second of all, I think that a decision to acquit is certainly not a decision to condone the president's behavior which I think merits scorn and rebuke.

Third of all, I think that the standard, and I want to say this to Senator Domenici, talking about children, to me the standard is guilty beyond a reasonable doubt. I think the evidence has to be unambiguous and strong. I don't think it was. Senator Levin said that very well, so I don't need to repeat any of those arguments.

Fourth of all, Tim Hutchinson, Senator Hutchinson, I like what you said about the polls. I actually make a different argument. I raised the question earlier when we were raising questions about popular will and does it matter. I actually meant about the last election, it seems to me if it ever does, it is on such a decision. I think before you overturn an election, you really have to meet a very high threshold. I don't think the House managers have done so.

Finally, I think a lesson that I have learned as a political scientist, when I teach class again, is I do not think the articles work and this process works when it is clearly not bipartisan. I think it becomes illegitimate. It just doesn't work.

You did not have broad support coming from the House, and you do not have it here. That is why I think it was doomed from the start.

Finally, it has been a long, sad year, and I wish—I just wish—that those who could have really rendered decisions with judgment had done so, starting with the president and his sorry affair. He could have told the truth to the people in the country. The people would have appreciated that. I could also talk about Starr, and I could also talk about the House, and I could also talk about us. But I do not think I need to do so.

Let's get on with the work of democracy. We have had some strong views here, but I am looking forward to working with you.

18

THE ECONOMY, TAX CUTS, AND THE PROTECTION OF WORKING FAMILIES

> "What I am worried about is deficit reduction based on the path of least political resistance, because I think that is exactly what we did in the last Congress. That is to say, we are afraid to take on powerful interests, so, instead, what we do is we go after the people who are not the heavy hitters, who are not the big givers, who are not well connected, and those people, all too often, in the Senate are voiceless and they are faceless and they are powerless and they are disproportionately poor children in America." ~Senator Paul Wellstone, February 10, 1997

The theory of "economic justice" is at the root of many of Senator Wellstone's opinions, but it is most evident in his speeches related to "investments" in low-income communities, raising the minimum wage, bankruptcy, and taxes. Senator Wellstone often spoke for working people that did not have the benefit of lobbyists and Political Action Committees. Economic justice was really a matter of fairness: What do we need to have a society that values every person? And then, who is in the best position to pay for that society?

AN ECONOMIC GROWTH STRATEGY FOR THE NINETIES
January 23, 1992

Mr. President, I think that politics in our country has become very concrete. What we call the bread-and-butter issues have kind of walked into people's living rooms now and are staring them in face, and the economic pain in our country cuts across a very broad section of the population.

What we have in the United States today is a submerged middle class. I look up and see some younger people in the gallery today. We also have on our present course, maybe, as we look at our younger people, a downwardly mobile generation. That would be a historic trauma for the United States, because all of us believe that our children will do better than we have done economically, that they will have more opportunity.

Therefore, Mr. President, I think that anyone—Republican, Democrat, it makes no difference—who engages in any kind of symbolic politics about these issues which are so important to people and their loved ones is making a huge mistake.

People in our country really are expecting us in the U.S. Senate to come through for them in a very concrete and very real way. And I would like to add my voice to those in the U.S. Senate who have emphasized the importance of an investment-led recovery. I think that is so important.

I do not oppose tax cuts for middle-income or working people from the point of view of equity, from the point of view of people who feel the squeeze and deserve some relief. But I do not think it is a very rigorous analysis to suggest that these tax cuts as a matter of fact will be enough, or are the answer, in order to give a short-run stimulus to our economy—much less lead us down the path of long-term productivity.

So I emphasize the importance of an investment-led recovery with investment in two decisive areas—really, in no particular order of importance. They are both equally important.

Investment in physical infrastructure. Let me emphasize today on the floor of the Senate that when we are talking about roads or bridges or repairing water systems or repairing sewer systems or cleaning up the environment, we are not only talking about investment for the sake of "jump-starting the economy." I do not much like that metaphor. We are talking about investment that is important for our country at all times, and clearly has an economic multiplier effect, and absolutely is crucial if we are going to see the economy move forward with some decent jobs for people.

What do I mean by decent jobs? I mean jobs that people can rely on; namely, jobs that pay a decent wage with some decent fringe benefits.

The second kind of investment I want to talk about today is human capital investment. That is kind of a high-faluting way of saying that we will not be strong as a nation until we invest in the people who live in our nation. Let us get that down to the level of individual men and women and, oh, what a price we have paid for well over a decade of neglect. We have not invested in our young people, and I want to argue that if we are going to have citizens in the United States of America who can compete in an international economy, then we have to talk about women and men who have the skills.

We have to talk about a literate, skillful, productive work force. And I think that the vast majority of people in our country know—sometimes I think better than we know—that the new definition of "national security" is going to be whether or not the United States of America can compete economically in the 1990s and in the next century.

So I want to put a lot of emphasis on investment in education and job training and all of the rest as being so terribly important.

Mr. President, I joined with Senator Kennedy in introducing a piece of legislation that talked about a forty-billion-dollar short-term stimulus in the remaining months of fiscal year 1992 divided equally between physical infrastructure and human capital investment. I think it is a must.

We can talk about 170 billion dollars over the next seven years and that altogether would come from 210 billion dollars transferred from the military budget.

Let me be clear. Where the money comes from is a question we have to answer. People do not want to see us try and dance at two weddings at the same time and call for investments in physical infrastructure and investment in our people and then when asked, where does the revenue come from, silence. That really is the voodoo economics practiced both by presidents Reagan and Bush.

We can get the money from one of two ways: Either we can go into more debt—and we should not—or we can raise taxes. If there are going to be taxes for middle and working people, we have to add them to those with high income. The main place we can do it is through a transfer and that is why it is so compelling that an important item of business for all of us is to essentially eliminate that budget agreement, not spend more, but bring down that firewall and transfer some money from the military budget to these domestic needs in a new world.

By the way, 210 billion dollars over seven years is really a rather modest cut in the military budget, certainly less than fifteen percent.

Mr. President, let me conclude my remarks this way this morning. I want to give a perfect example of why I feel so strongly that we take this action and back our rhetoric with action.

We have an education bill that we have been dealing with, and I think the work of Senator Kennedy has been very important. But all of us know that it is really barely adequate. We are still not funding nutrition programs for women expecting children. That is what we call human capital investment. We are still not fully funding Head Start. We are not bringing the class sizes down in elementary school, and our younger people still cannot afford higher education.

So later on today I am going to introduce a sense-of-the-Congress resolution to that education bill which says this is fine. But we know that if we are going to back our rhetoric, we are going to have to transfer resources, and the first item of business is going to begin to get at that budget agreement and bring down that firewall.

Mr. President, I thank you for this opportunity to speak. I thank the senator from South Dakota.

I feel so strongly about these issues. I believe in public service, and I think people in the country are waiting for us to do something good for them. I believe we can do that if we focus on these economic issues.

Balanced Budget Amendment to the Constitution
February 10, 1997

Mr. President, let me read this amendment slowly and carefully because I am hoping to get a very strong vote in favor of this amendment, and I hope it will be an up-or-down vote. This is a pretty important matter amending the Constitution, and if this is going to be done—it may or may not be done—we better do it well, we better do it carefully.

This amendment says:

It is the policy of the United States that, in achieving a balanced budget, federal outlays must not be reduced in a manner that disproportionately affects outlays for education, nutrition, and health programs for poor children.

What this amendment is saying, and I will give plenty of historical and economic context for it, is that we should go on record and make it very clear that if, in fact, this constitutional amendment to balance the budget is passed, which then locks us into this goal, will make the commitment that we are not going to, as we did in the last Congress, disproportionately cut programs that affect, quite often dramatically, the nutritional or health or educational status of poor children in America.

The reason that I offer this amendment is that I think we need to have some focus on this question. There can be arguments made, and there have been, on whether or not we ought to amend the Constitution. There can be arguments made about whether or not this is a mistake vis-a-vis our fiscal and monetary policy to make sure recessions don't become depressions. There are arguments both ways.

Senator Durbin has an amendment on the floor that says, look, if we need to move forward with an economic plan that puts the budget out of balance during a downturn in the economy, it should just be a requirement of a majority vote. I think that amendment is on the mark.

I see the budgets over the years. There could be an argument of whom to blame. I wasn't here during the decade of the eighties or prior to that time. We can argue it both ways. I think historians are going to write about a piece of legislation which was euphemistically called the Economic Recovery Act which dramatically cut tax rates. I think it became rather regressive, because most benefits went to higher income citizens, at the same time of dramatically increased expenditures in the Pentagon. I think President Bush once called it voodoo economics. All of it was to lead to economic growth. People would have more money with a tax cut, productivity, jobs. It would lead to eliminating the debt. Actually, quite the opposite happened.

That was actually borrowed money and borrowed time. It was politics of illusion. I really appreciate the focus of Senator Hatch on no longer having that illusion and the message from the people in the country that we should get our economic house in order and our political house in order. But what I am asking senators to do, because I think we really owe it to the people we represent, is to make a commitment that one more time, as we go about achieving a balanced budget, federal outlays must not be reduced in a manner which disproportionately affects outlays for education, nutrition and health care programs for poor children.

I hope this amendment will not be tabled. I offer this amendment with passion and with commitment to a matter that I think is very important. I think there should be an up-or-down vote, and I hope it will be adopted.

Mr. President, why the amendment? Well, because of recent history. The Center on Budget and Policy Priorities issued a report entitled "Bearing Most of the Burden: How Deficit Reduction During the 104th Congress Concentrated on Programs for the Poor."

I will just read a few of their conclusions: More than ninety-three percent of the budget reductions in entitlements have come from programs for low-income people. The Congressional Budget Office estimates that legislation enacted during the 104th Congress reduced entitlement programs by 65.6 billion dollars from 1996 to 2002. Of that, almost sixty-one billion dollars

out of the 65.6 billion dollars comes out of low-income entitlement programs, the largest reductions in the supplemental security income program and programs for the elderly and the poor.

Please remember, I say to my colleagues, that one out of every five children in America today is poor. Mr. President, I read an article the other day with great interest of how you, as the senator from Missouri, have teamed up with other senators, like Senator Coats, and you have your own commitments to really not turning our gaze away from the concerns and circumstances of one out of every seven Americans, many of them children, but you are committed to doing something.

We might have different ideas of what to do. I think that is commendable, and I know you well enough to know that you have that commitment. What I am worried about is deficit reduction based on the path of least political resistance because I think that is exactly what we did in the last Congress. That is to say, we are afraid to take on powerful interests, so, instead, what we do is we go after the people who are not the heavy hitters, who are not the big givers, who are not well connected, and those people, all too often, in the Senate are voiceless and they are faceless and they are powerless and they are disproportionately poor children in America.

I hope my colleagues will at least support this amendment. If this passes, it happens one time. Let's get it right. If we are going to lock ourselves into balancing the budget and deficit reduction, let's lock ourselves into humane and fair priorities that we are not going to disproportionately cut programs that affect the educational and nutritional and health care status of children.

Mr. President, other than entitlements, thirty-four percent of the reduction in nondefense programs that are not entitlements came from nonentitlement programs for people with low incomes.

Those low-income people programs accounted for only twenty-one percent of overall funding, but they were disproportionately cut as well.

Just looking at the 104th Congress, I offer this amendment to make sure that we make a commitment that we are not going to cut such vital programs. Sometimes we are just too generous with the suffering of others. Let's not be too generous with the suffering of poor children in America.

The Concord Coalition had this to say. Martha Phillips the executive director, on November 26, 1996: Balancing the federal budget— And this has been a goal of the Concord Coalition— and keeping it in balance is critically important, but balance ought not to be achieved principally on the backs of the poor. Every program should be on the budget cutting table. No programs, groups or special interests should be exempt or get a free ride when the budget is being balanced. But neither should the needy be singled out to bear a disproportionate share of the load.

They go on to say—this is the Concord Coalition, I say to my colleagues, committed to deficit reduction. The Concord Coalition goes on to say, under the able leadership of Senator Rudman and Senator Tsongas, who passed away—a real loss for our country—the Concord Coalition goes on to say: Even though the 104th Congress, which passed the laws, and the president, who signed them, did not plan to target deficit reduction efforts on programs affecting low income people, that was nevertheless the result of both actions that were taken and those that were not.

Mr. President, there is another interesting statement from the Committee on Economic Development. By the way, I would like to congratulate the business community in our country. The Committee on Economic Development over and over and over again, over the last several years, have said, from the point of view of economic performance for our nation, we must invest in the health, skills and intellectual character of our children. We must do that.

I quote, as a part of a letter that was written November 26, 1996, by the senior vice president and director of research of the Committee on Economic Development:

Second, in an unfortunate surrender to misplaced ideology and political opportunism, our leaders in both political parties have increased the magnitude of the financing problem by insisting that tax reductions be included in their balanced budget plans.

That was their view. By the way, I think we are going to have to look very closely at some of those budget proposals. My understanding is the Joint Tax Committee, in projecting the majority party's tax cuts over the next ten years, has identified close to 500 billion dollars in the first five years more targeted toward middle-income people and the second five years more targeted toward wealthy, high-income people.

What is going to be the offset? Cuts in the nutritional and educational and health care programs for poor children in America? If that was the case, that would be unconscionable. If there was some sort of budget deal that leaves these children out in the cold, that would be unconscionable.

The senior vice president of the Committee on Economic Development goes on to say:

Third, as a result of the fiscal pressures created by these two factors, the burden of budget austerity has fallen disproportionately on those parts of the budget, and those parts of society, that offer the least political resistance.

Actually, I have been saying that over and over again. I guess we are in agreement. I am pleased to hear them actually state it that way.

For the budget that means that the discretionary annually appropriated programs, including those public investment activities for a society—it quite simply means the poor.

Now the quote: As David Stockman observed a decade ago, politics triumphs over policy in seeking out weak clients rather than weak claims.

This amendment asks us not to let politics triumph over policy. This amendment asks us to seek out the weak claims, not the weak clients.

This amendment says we go on record that when we balance the budget, we will not cut disproportionately those programs that affect the health care, nutritional and educational status of poor children. We ought to have 100 senators voting for that. We can go forward to balance the budget. We can go forward with deficit reduction. But given the way we did it in the last Congress, and the evidence, I must say to my colleagues, it is irreducible and irrefutable that we ought to at least make this commitment.

* * *

Can't we make a commitment as a Senate knowing full well the importance of family and community? But can't we at least get some resources for the communities and neighborhoods and families so that we can support our children?

I will tell you something. I am absolutely convinced that when historians write about this time period of the decade of the 1980s moving into the decade of the 1990s, the ultimate indictment of our country will be the way in which we have abandoned our children and devalued the work of adults who work with those children. Think about it for a moment.

I am not off the topic. I love to take my grandchildren to the zoo. But if you work at the zoo, you get paid twice the salary, twice the wage, that a woman or a man makes working in a child care center. We pay people who work for the zoo twice as much money as we pay men and women who work with children. What in the world does that say?

When I was a teacher at Carleton College in Northfield, Minnesota, I would meet students, and they would say, "In all due respect, we do not want to be college teachers. We want to work with these children when they are young, one, two, three, or four years of age, because we know that is such a critical time." But many of them would then go on and say, "But we can't. We can't support the family. We would make six dollars an hour with no health care benefits."

What are we saying? Let us dig into our pockets. Let us not spend money on wasteful programs. Let us cut. Let us balance the budget. Let us be fiscally responsible. But, please, let us make a commitment with this amendment that we are not going to balance the budget on the backs of poor children. Please let us invest in certain areas of life in America, starting with our children.

Marcus's teacher said:

> I just don't know what could be done for him. I know that he needs a lot of one-on-one attention and love, but I just do not have the time or the resources. Every day I feel him slipping, and, frankly, it breaks my heart. He is a good boy and a smart boy. I feel as if he is being punished for what we did not do for him. I am worried that he will always hate school and suffer until he can leave. He tries so hard. Sometimes I want to cry.

That is what this debate is all about. It is about people. It is about children.

I say to my colleague from Utah that I really believe there can be 100 senators voting for this. I am not bringing this amendment to the floor because I want to point the finger at other colleagues. I am not bringing this amendment to the floor to force an embarrassing vote. I am bringing this amendment to the floor in good faith and in good conscience really hoping that my colleagues will support it because, otherwise, I will just tell you, given our track record of deficit reduction based on the path of least political resistance, we are, with this constitutional amendment to balance the budget, going to lock ourselves into very stoic priorities, and we will make these cuts, and I believe in the absence of some commitment, we will make cuts in these very programs that affect these very children.

By August of 1996, in West Monroe, Louisiana, there was already a waiting list for Head Start for August 1997. Zora Cheney has been a Head Start teacher there since 1965. She was there at the very beginning. Not only does she see the need for it, but she lives the success. According to Zora, without Head Start the lives of many children would be in words "a disaster."

I visit Head Start programs all across Minnesota. Another outstanding feature is parental participation—high-participation parents—in meeting with the teachers and in talking about the children. This program is a really important investment in poor children.

We get kids here, so many kids here, that need us and would not endure later school years without it. I have seen some kids who come in, and it is obvious they are not cared for enough and that the home family needs help. While Zora's program emphasizes the traditional things that we discuss with Head Start, like building on language, learning shapes and colors and developing social skills, it does so much more. Says Zora, "We are concerned with everything about that child. We want the parents to learn how to feed them, how to dress them, how to parent them."

She continued, "I have had children come to school, and I know they have been sleeping on the floor. I know they need so much at home. We work with other groups. We refer the families to get things like furniture and doctor appointments." When asked the most significant contri-

bution that Head Start in West Monroe, Louisiana, has made to the community Zora replies, "For many its the first place that they feel safe."

I have other examples that I will go through tomorrow, but I just wanted to give some examples of some children, and I am going to be doing this over and over and over again, actually thanks to the people in Minnesota—I am just going to bring to the floor of the Senate the lives of children so that we can get some votes on their behalf because I will tell you something. For example, the Senator from Utah—and this is not meant to challenge him—on these children's issues he is effective, and he is a powerful senator for children. I know that. So I do not feel like I am spitting in the wind when I come out here to speak or I do not think I make a mistake with this amendment. I am just trying to get my colleagues to make this commitment because I know so many of them care so deeply about children.

The amendment says we make a commitment that we will not put into effect disproportionate cuts in programs that affect education—I talked about that—nutritional and health care programs for children.

IN SUPPORT OF AN INCREASE TO THE MINIMUM WAGE
September 22, 1998

Mr. President, I am pleased to be on the floor with my colleague, Senator Kennedy, in support of this amendment.

Let me say to my colleagues on the other side—perhaps we can have some discussion and debate about this—that I find it very interesting what is going on here. If I am wrong, I am sure my colleagues will try to prove me wrong. I don't actually think they can prove me wrong. Here is what is going on.

The reason that the vast majority of the people in our country have made it crystal clear that they are for an increase in the minimum wage, that they think to go from $5.15 an hour to $6.15 over a two-year period is imminently reasonable is because they think this is a family-value issue. This occurred the last time we went through this debate and this time as well. Most people in Minnesota and most people in the United States of America believe that it is our responsibility as senators and as Democrats and Republicans to create a climate whereby they can do their best by their kids because when they do their best by their kids, they do their best by our country. One of the ways they can do best by their kids is to have a decent job and a decent wage so they can support their families. That is what this debate is all about.

Mr. President, we have these arguments trotted out here. I do not like where they come from. We have the same old song. I understand that for a variety of different reasons some of my colleagues are opposed to raising the minimum wage . I understand this may be a difficult vote. So we have to figure out other arguments to make. I don't think it looks good.

I am going to sort of break from the traditional boundaries of debate and say this: I don't think it looks good.

In this past year we gave ourselves a cost of living raise of $1.50 an hour on top of giving ourselves, several years ago, a $30,000 increase. We in the Senate went from $100,000 to $130,000-plus.

At the time, I had colleagues come up to me and say, "We need to do it. We have two places. We have children. They are in college. It is tough. It is very difficult to make ends meet." So we voted ourselves a $30,000 increase, and then, on top of that, we vote ourselves a $1.50-an-hour cost of living increase. Yet, we say it is just outrageous to increase the minimum wage for people who are working full-

time, playing by the rules of the game, fifty-two weeks a year, forty hours a week, and are making poverty wages. People who work full time ought not to be poor in America. They ought to be able to make a decent wage and support their children. $100,000 to $130,000 for us is fine, but to raise the minimum wage one dollar over two years is not fine.

That is a tough argument to make for people in the country, because most people in the country believe that it is our job to make sure that when people play by the rules of the game and work hard that they earn a decent living. Most people in this country believe that those people ought to have that chance. Thus, the arguments come out.

And so we heard that we are going to lose all these jobs, but that didn't happen. Here are the figures from the Bureau of Labor Statistics. I am not bringing out any particular conservative group or liberal group. I am just going by BLS data. When we went from $4.25 to $4.75 over this first year, 394,000 new jobs were added to the economy. Then when we went from $4.75 to $5.15, 517,000 new jobs were added to the economy.

When I am finished I look forward to my colleagues refuting this; to just explain away the data. Sometimes we don't know what we don't want to know. But these are the facts from the Bureau of Labor Statistics. Where is the evidence that this increase in the minimum wage that helped so many people in our country—ten million-plus people, 140,000 people in Minnesota, helped people do better by themselves and better by their kids— where is the evidence that it led to a decrease in jobs?

In the state of Wyoming, since the federal minimum wage was increased, unemployment in Wyoming dropped by eight percent. Where is the evidence that the increases in the minimum wage lead to a sharp drop in the number of jobs in the state of Wyoming? It is just the opposite. According to BLS, fifteen percent of the workforce in

Wyoming will benefit from our increase—30,000 workers.

So I don't understand this whole argument about how it will lead to a decrease in jobs. For reasons I can't understand, I think it is just sort of "blind ideology" that my colleagues don't want to support this. We are glad to have a big increase for ourselves. Then I say, "Okay. What could be the reasons?"

Here are the arguments that are brought out to the floor. One is we will see all of these jobs disappear. But precisely the opposite is happening.

Until I hear to the contrary, I don't quite understand that argument.

My colleague from Wyoming, who I enjoyed hearing, said we didn't have any hearings. The chairman of the Committee on Labor and Human Resources, my good friend, said we would be pleased to have hearings.

So we don't have hearings. Hearings are denied and then that is used as an argument why we shouldn't take action.

Then I hear my good friend from Utah make the argument that these jobs are not just about earnings. They are about learning, and that we should recognize the dignity of work. I agree. But do you want to know something? The best way that we can recognize the dignity of the work is to make sure there is some value to the work and make sure that these men and women who are taking care of our children, taking care of our parents, providing us with food, cleaning buildings, and you name it, are provided with a decent wage.

A lot of people, no matter how hard they work, are poor because wages are too low. To talk to them about the dignity of their work and how this is great for learning just misses the point, if we won't talk about earnings.

I don't know what reality we are dealing with here. We are dealing with the phenomenon of many working poor families in our country with the head of household working full-time, and those families are still poor.

I am hearing colleagues talk about how we are opposed to raising the minimum wage because somehow we think it will undercut the dignity people have. Or we are opposed to raising the minimum wage because we really think this is as much about learning as it is earning. I just do not understand these arguments.

Mr. President, we know that this especially helps women because they are disproportionately among the low-wage workers. We know that this disproportionately helps adults. We dealt with the mythology that this is all about teenagers. Then we get into the argument: But there are a percentage of these workers who are younger people, high school age, college age.

Again, I don't know what reality my colleagues are focused on here. But do you know, they work for compelling reasons as well. In case anybody hasn't noticed, higher education is an expensive proposition.

Many high school students and college students are working—I meet many college students who are working two and three minimum-wage jobs. That is why it takes them six or seven years to graduate. They are not doing it just on some lark. They are doing it because this is key to their being able to finance their education or help their parents finance their education. Or, if they are older—since many of the students are older and going back to school—it is even more critical.

I heard my colleague from Utah refer to a study that showed when you have a higher minimum wage, welfare mothers stay on welfare a longer period of time. That does not make any sense to me. I would love to know what there is to that story. Because, frankly, if you are going to talk about the importance of going from welfare to workfare, presumably one of the key things you want to make sure of is that the jobs are there that pay a decent wage so those mothers and children will be better off.

For some reason, states with higher minimum wage—or I guess the argument is supposed to be that by raising the minimum wage we have discouraged these parents from moving from welfare to work? It just makes no sense. I would love to know a little bit more about that finding.

So, my conclusion—and I say this with some indignation—we just have all the sympathy in the world when we have oil companies coming out here asking for special breaks, but we have very little sympathy when it comes to these working poor families.

I yield the floor.

TAX CUTS

February 6, 2001

Mr. President, I will say to the majority leader that I think his last set of remarks may be the basis of bipartisanship between the two of us. We will keep this civil.

I will also say to the majority leader and others that I can't wait for the debate because he focuses on the $30,000-a-year family. But anybody who looks at the distribution of benefits of President Bush's tax cut plan will see—I don't know—forty percent of the benefit going to the top one percent of the top five percent, which is ridiculous. It is like Robin Hood in reverse. Yes, we will make sure there is a set of tax credits to go to middle-income and working-income families. Absolutely.

I will point out one more time—and I didn't hear the majority leader respond to this at all—I want to hold President Bush accountable for these numbers—a 3.1-trillion-dollar non-Social Security surplus becomes 2.6 when you put

Medicare trust money aside, which we will do. It becomes two trillion dollars when extending tax credits, and we also provide payments to farmers and other people, which we will do without doubt. The tax cuts go from 1.6 trillion to two trillion dollars, when you now have to pay the interest on the debt, when you are not paying the debt down, in which case I want to know where are the resources to leave no child behind.

I say to the majority leader that I am more than willing to debate after we provide tax cuts for middle-income working families, whether or not we, in fact, provide some benefits so elderly people can afford prescription drugs versus tax cuts for the wealthy, whether we can expand health care coverage versus tax cuts, or whether or not we will live up to the words of leaving no child behind and make investment in child care and in Head Start and in our schools and fund the IDEA program versus tax cuts for the wealthy.

I think the message President Bush is trying to convey and the majority leader echoes to the people in the country—I all of a sudden find myself being a fiscal conservative—is that we can do it all. There is no free lunch. We can't do it all. We can't have tax cuts disproportionately to the wealthy, erode the revenue base, and at the same time say we are going to leave no child behind; we are going to make an investment in education; we are going to make an investment in covering prescription drugs for the elderly. We can't do both. The people in the country are smart enough to figure that out, and I hope Democrats will engage this administration. The sooner the better. I don't think we need to wait one more day to have this debate.

Senators and President Bush: You cannot proclaim the vision and the value of leaving no child behind and keep this on a tin cup budget. If we are real about this, we will make the investment in the intellect, the skills, and the character of our children.

This budget is not real. It does not make that commitment to leaving no child behind.

In Opposition to the Bankruptcy Abuse Prevention and Consumer Protection Act of 2001

July 12, 2001

Mr. President, normally I do not do it this way. I try not to rely too much on notes. But I want to try to be as detailed and as thorough as I can because what I am asking the Senate to do today is to step back from the brink and decline to go to conference with the House on the so-called bankruptcy reform.

I am going to be in this chamber a number of times over the next week, maybe over the next several weeks. There is a lot that I want to say. There is a lot I think I should say as a senator from Minnesota because I think Congress is about to make—or is headed toward—a very grave mistake.

So I will not attempt to say it all today. What I will do, however, is to speak, at least in a broad way, about why I feel so strongly in the negative about this bill.

I ask unanimous consent that several pages I have of titles of editorials about the bankruptcy bill be printed in the *Record*.

＊　＊　＊

"Bad Timing on the Bankruptcy Bill," Robert Samuelson, *The Washington Post*, March 14, 2001; "A Bad Bankruptcy Bill," *San Francisco Chronicle*, March 15; "A Debt Bill Bankruptcy of Decency," *The Chicago Sun Times*; "Deeper Hole for Debtors," *Los Angeles Times*; "Business Dictated Bankruptcy Law," *New York Times*; "Congress, President Side with Banks, Not Consumers," *The Atlanta Journal Constitution*; "Compounding Debt," *The Boston Globe*; "A Bankrupt Law?" *Businessweek*; "Bankruptcy Overall Hits Needy as Well as Greedy," *The Miami Herald*; "Congress Pushing Usury," *Bismarck Tribune*; "Hammering Bankrupt Consumers," *Chattanooga Times Free Press*; "Down on Your Luck? Tough," *The Chicago Sun Times*.

These are just kind of random samples:

"Bankruptcy Bill is Anti-Family Measure," *Intelligencer Journal*; "A Flawed Bankruptcy Bill," *The Milwaukee Journal*; "Banking on Politics," the *News Observer*; "In Bankruptcy Bill, Money Talks," the *Oregonian*; "Why Campaign Finance Reform? Look at Bankruptcy Bill," the *Palm Beach Post*; "Bankrupt Bill; This Reform Will Hurt Americans Who Are Struggling," *Pittsburgh Post-Gazette*; "Bankruptcy Bill, So-Called Reforms Make Reckless Lending More Profitable," *Sacramento Bee*; "Bankruptcy Bill Helps Guess Who?" *San Jose Mercury News*; "Bad Piece of Legislation," *Buffalo News*; "Taking Care of Business," Bob Reich in the *American Prospect*. The list goes on and on.

I have for over two years been fighting this bill, with some of my colleagues: senators Kennedy, Boxer, Durbin, Schumer, Leahy, and Feingold. I will give myself a little bit of credit as to why we are still debating this bill and it has not passed. In truth, a great deal of the credit goes to the proponents of the bill because it has been their consistent refusal to compromise on the legislation that has made the job easier. I will go into some of the greedier aspects of this legislation in a moment.

Some have argued that the tactics have been extreme, that I have been at this over and over and over again in trying to block it. I would rather be spending my time not stopping the worst but doing the better. I much prefer to do that. But this is a disastrous piece of legislation. What has been done with this very harsh legislation is basically shredding one of the important safety nets, not just for low-income people but for middle-income people as well. Shredding that safety net so that people can no longer rebuild their financial lives is truly egregious.

To argue that the reason we need to do this is because a lot of people have been filing Chapter 7 in order to get out of repaying their debt and that they are untrustworthy, they don't feel any stigma, et cetera, simply doesn't hold up under any kind of scrutiny.

We know in the vast majority of cases, fifty percent of the people who file bankruptcy in this country file bankruptcy because of medical bills. Is somebody going to say they are lazy or they are slackers or cheats? We know beyond that one of the major causes of bankruptcy is loss of a job. More and more people are losing their jobs now; 1,300 taconite workers at LTV Company on the Iron Range of Minnesota just lost their jobs.

Is it divorce? Not surprisingly, many of our citizens who find themselves in the most difficulty are women after a divorce. They are the ones who are taking care of the children in most cases.

It hardly holds up that these are a bunch of slackers and a bunch of cheats we are going after. As a matter of fact, the evidence is clear—I will refer to studies later on—that at best there is maybe three percent abuse. What about the other ninety-seven percent of the people?

Major medical illness is a double whammy because not only do you have to pay the doctor and the hospital charges, but in addition quite often you can't work. If it is your child, even if it is not you, it is the same issue: it is the medical bills. But then you are home taking care of the child. Now you have no other choice. You are trying to rebuild your life and file for Chapter 7, and you can't do it any longer.

As I said, you can't argue that people overwhelmed with medical debt or sidelined because of an illness are deadbeats. This legislation assumes they are. It would force them into credit counseling

before they could file, as if a serious illness or disability is something that could be counseled away. I had an amendment to this bill that would have created an exclusion for people who were filing for bankruptcy because of medical bills. It did not pass.

Women single filers are now the largest group in bankruptcy. They are one-third of all the filers. They are the fastest growing. Since 1981, the number of women filing increased by 700 percent. A woman single parent has a 500 percent greater likelihood of filing for bankruptcy than the population generally.

Divorce is a major factor in causing bankruptcy in America. Are single women with children deadbeats? This bill assumes they are.

The new nondischargeability of credit card debt will hit hard those women who use the cards to tide them over after a divorce until their income stabilizes. The "safe harbor" in the House bill, which proponents argue will shield low- and moderate-income debtors from the means test, will not benefit many single mothers who most need the help because it is based upon the combined income of the debtor and the debtor's spouse, even if they are separated, the spouse is not filing for bankruptcy, and the spouse is providing no support for her, for the debtor and her children.

In other words, a single mother who is being deprived of needed support from a well-off spouse is further harmed by this piece of legislation which will deem the full income of that spouse available to pay debts for determination of whether the safe harbor and means test applies. It makes no sense whatsoever, and it is incredibly harsh.

Over the past two years, any pretense that this piece of legislation is urgently needed has evaporated. Now proponents and opponents agree that nearly all the debtors resort to bankruptcy not to game the system but, rather, as a desperate measure of economic survival and that only a tiny minority of Chapter 7 filers, as few as three percent, can afford any debt repayment, according to the American Bankruptcy Institute.

Yet low- and moderate-income families, especially single-parent families, are those who need most the fresh start provided by bankruptcy protection. The bill will make it harder for them to get out from under the burden of crushing debt, and that is why I oppose it.

The second reason why I oppose this legislation is that the timing of this bill could not be worse. Basically people are not going to be able to file for Chapter 7. Chapter 13 is going to be made more unworkable for many debtors. We had a situation where four years ago, when we first started this debate, the big banks and credit card companies were pushing so-called bankruptcy reform in good economic times. The stock market was soaring. The unemployment rate was coming down. But given the economy we find ourselves with right now, given the fact that we no longer have the same boom economy, that people are now out of work or underemployed, that these are harder times, rushing this bill through seems completely divorced from reality.

What is the most cited reason for filing for bankruptcy? Job loss, and the unemployment rate is rising. What is the second most cited reason? Excessive medical bills, and the cost of health care is rising, as are the number of uninsured. At the same time, we are going to make it impossible for people to file for Chapter 7 and rebuild their lives.

While the bill will be terrible for consumers and for regular working families even in the best of times, its effects will be all the more devastating now because we have a weakening economy. It boggles the mind that at a time when Americans are most economically vulnerable, when they are most in need of protection from financial disaster, we would eviscerate the major safety net in our society for the middle class, and that is precisely what this legislation does. It is the height of insanity that we would be contemplating doing what we are doing given this economy.

It may be the case that the Congress and the president will ignore the plight of these families. Each one of them by themselves is not that powerful. Most folks assume this is never going to happen to us. Most people and most families never expect they are going to have to file for bankruptcy, but at least my colleagues should care about the effect on the economy.

This bill could be a disaster, but I do not want you to take my word for it. I want to quote some excerpts from a column by Robert Samuelson in the March 14 *Washington Post*. To put it delicately, Mr. Samuelson and I rarely agree on anything. In fact, he likes—I want to be intellectually honest about it— he likes the substance of the bankruptcy bill. All the more reason, I say to my colleagues, to pay attention to him. The title of the editorial is "Bad Timing on the Bankruptcy Bill." He writes:

> The bankruptcy bill about to pass Congress arrives at an awkward moment: the tail end of a prolonged boom in consumer borrowing. From 1995 to 2000, Americans increased their personal debts by about fifty percent to roughly 7.5 trillion dollars—a figure including everything from home mortgages to student loans.

Now comes the bankruptcy bill, which would make it slightly harder for consumers to erase debts through bankruptcy. Although the bill is not especially harsh, it could perversely worsen the economic downturn.

I do not agree with part of his characterization. I am now focusing on his argument about the effect of the economy.

He concludes:

> The real pressures of high debt are now being compounded by scare psychology. "Drowning in

Debt," says the cover story of the latest *U.S. News & World Report.* "Why you're in so deep—and how to get out before it's too late." The bankruptcy bill sends a similar message: Be prudent, don't overborrow. The message is now about four years too late. Now it may simply amplify the growing gloom. This is not a bad bill, but it certainly is badly timed.

There you have it, I say to my colleagues. Not an opponent but a supporter suggesting that now is not the time, that we could end up prolonging or actually worsening the downturn in the economy.

He is not the only one. A May 21 issue of *Business Week* had an article titled "Reform that Could Backfire." The article begins:

> Just as bankruptcy reform seemed headed for certain passage, the economic omens point to a sharp rise in personal bankruptcies over the next few years. The likely results, says economist Mark Zandi of Economy.com, Inc., will be "much pain for hard pressed households, little if any gain for lenders, and, in the event of even a mild recession, major problems for the overall economy."

Again, this is not some leftwing rag; this is the magazine of note for corporate America—*Business Week.* If *Business Week* and Paul Wellstone are in agreement on an issue, then I ask you: How can we be wrong?

The article concludes:

> The drop in bankruptcies in recent years partly reflected the booming economy. Now, with sharply rising unemployment and slowing income gains, Zandi expects high household debt to take its toll. Especially at risk, he believes, are lower income families, for whom debt repayment dictated by the pending bankruptcy reform would entail tremendous hardship. "If the economy becomes mired in recession or sluggish growth," he warns, "the loss of the spending power could significantly retard the recovery."

I ask my colleagues, I ask the majority leader—I am not in agreement with him—what is the rush? Why do you want to do this to the economy? Why do you want to do this to families? Why are you prepared to go to such ridiculous lengths to move this legislation?

Mr. President, I do not really get this. One of the arguments being made is that, what we are going to see is an increase in bankruptcies because of a slowing economy and high consumer debts that are overwhelming families and, therefore, we need to pass legislation to curb access to bankruptcy relief. Try that on for size.

For two years, while the good times were rolling, the proponents of this bill were citing the number of bankruptcy filings as a reason to pass the bill, although there actually was a dramatic drop in filings taking place. I never understood that argument.

Now they are turning around and saying we need to rush to do this because the economy is slowing down and many hard-working people, through no fault of their own, are going to find themselves in dire circumstances; therefore, we had better pass legislation that will curb their access to bankruptcy relief.

It is amazing: Increasing hard times, a lot of people finding themselves in these impossible financial circumstances, and now they want to make it harder for them to get a fresh start. The logic of this argument completely escapes me.

The point Mark Zandi makes in the *Business Week* article, as other economists have done, is that restricting access to bankruptcy protection will actually increase the number of filings and defaults because banks will be more willing to lend to marginal candidates. Indeed, it is no coincidence that the single largest surge in bankruptcy filings began immediately after the last major pro-creditor reforms were passed by Congress in 1984.

This is not a debate about winners and losers because we all lose if we erode the middle class in this country. We lose if we take away one of the critical underpinnings for middle-class people. Sure, in the short run big banks and credit card companies may pad their profits, but in the long run our families will be less secure and our entrepreneurs will become more risk adverse and less entrepreneurial.

The whole point of bankruptcy is to allow people to get a fresh start. Bankruptcy disproportionately affects the financially vulnerable, but it also disproportionately affects the risk takers, small businesspeople or entrepreneurs. Our bankruptcy system ensures that utter insolvency does not need to be a life sentence, but it can be an opportunity to start over, and that is what this bill erodes.

This is not a debate about reducing the high number of bankruptcies.

No one can will a piece of legislation that can do that. Indeed, by rewarding—I make this argument—the reckless lending that got us here in the first place, we are going to see more consumers burdened with that.

It is amazing; there is hardly a word in this whole piece of legislation that calls for these credit card companies or lenders to be accountable as they continue to pump this stuff out to our children and grandchildren every day of every week. But this is perfect for them because they don't have to worry any longer. They get a blank check from the government. No, this is a debate about punishing failure—whether self-inflicted—and sometimes it is—or uncontrolled or unexpected. This is a debate about punishing failure.

If there is one thing this country has learned, it is that punishing failure doesn't work. You need to correct mistakes. You need to prevent abuse. But you also need to lift people up when they have stumbled, not beat them down. This piece of legislation beats them down.

Both the House and Senate bills basically give a free ride to the banks and credit card companies, that deserve much of the credit—you would not know it from this legislation—for the high number of bankruptcy filings because of their loose credit standards. Even the Senate bill does very little to address this issue.

There are some minor disclosure provisions in the Senate bill. But even these don't go nearly as far as they should. Lenders should not be rewarded for reckless lending. Where is the balance in this legislation? If we are holding debtors accountable, why don't we hold lenders accountable as well? I know the answer. These financial interests have hijacked this legislative process. As high-cost debt and credit cards and retail charge cards and financing plans for consumer goods have skyrocketed in recent years, so have the bankruptcies. As the credit card industry has begun to aggressively court the poor and vulnerable, is anybody surprised that bankruptcies have risen?

Credit card companies brazenly dangle literally billions of dollars of credit card offers to high-debt families every year, and they are not asked to be accountable. They encourage credit card holders to make low payments toward their card balances, guaranteeing that a few hundred dollars in clothing or food will take years to pay off. The length to which the companies go to keep customers in debt is absolutely ridiculous, and they get away with murder in this legislation. After all, debt involves a borrower and a lender. Poor choices or irresponsible behavior by either party can make the transition go sour.

So how responsible has the industry been? It depends on how you look at it. On the one hand, consumer lending is unbelievably profitable, with high-cost credit card lending the most profitable of all, except for perhaps the even higher costs on payday loans. We don't go after any of these unsavory characters. So I guess by the standard of the bottom line, they are doing a great job. This industry is thriving. These credit card companies are making huge profits.

On the other hand, if your definition of responsibility is promoting fiscal health among families, educating them on the judicious use of credit, ensuring that borrowers do not go beyond their means, then it is hard to imagine how the financial services industry could not be a bigger deadbeat. The financial services industry is the big deadbeat. The problem is that it is the heavy hitter, the big giver, and it has so much money that it dominates the politics in the House of Representatives and the Senate. That is part of what this is about.

Theresa Sullivan, Elizabeth Warren, and Jay Westerbrook wrote a book called *Fragile Middle Class*. I recommend it to everybody. They write:

> Many attribute the sharp rise in consumer debt—and the corresponding rise in consumer bankruptcy—to lowered credit standards, with credit cards issuers aggressively pursuing families already carrying extraordinary debt burdens on incomes too low to make more than minimum repayments. The extraordinary profitability of consumer debt repaid over time has attracted lenders to the increasingly high risk-high profit business of consumer lending in a saturated market, making the link between the rise in credit card debt and the rise in consumer bankruptcy unmistakable.

Credit card companies perpetuate high interest indebtedness by requiring—and there is not a senator who can argue against this practice—low minimum payments and, in some cases, canceling the cards of customers who pay off their balance every month. Using a typical monthly payment rate on a credit card, it would take thirty-four years to pay off a $2,500 loan. Total payments would exceed 300 percent of their original principal. That is really what this is all about. A recent move by the credit card industry to make the minimum monthly payment only two percent of the balance rather than four percent further exacerbates the problem of some uneducated debtors.

These lenders routinely offer "teaser" interest rates which expire in as little as two months, and they engage in "risk-based" pricing which allows them to raise credit card interest rates based on credit changes unrelated to the borrower's account. It is just unbelievable what they get away with.

Even more ironic, at the same time that the consumer credit industry is pushing a bankruptcy bill that requires credit counseling for debtors, the Consumer Federation of America found that many prominent creditors have slashed the portion of debt repayments they shared with credit counseling agencies—in some cases by more than half. This may force some of these agencies to cut programs and serve even fewer debtors.

Well, Mr. President, I am sorry. I am glad there aren't a lot of senators on the floor because it is hard to say this because you feel as if you are engaging in personal attacking. I don't mean it to be that way. I can't say enough about the hypocrisy of this legislation—not of individual senators but the content of this legislation. It is incredible to me the way in which these banks and credit card companies have rigged this system, and we have this harsh piece of legislation in increasingly difficult economic times that is going to make it impossible for many families to rebuild their lives. The vast majority find themselves in these horrible circumstances because of medical bills, having lost their jobs, or divorce.

Do you know what. This legislation doesn't do anything about the egregious greed, the exploitive practice of this industry. All of us who have children know what they send out in the mail every day.

So the question is: Paul, if the bill is as bad as you say, how come it has so much support?

This is a lonely fight. Just a few senators are in strong opposition. I don't mean it in a self-righteous way, and it doesn't make us closer to God or the angels. I don't understand why the bill is going through. The bill has a lot of support in the Congress, and some of those who are supporting it, such as Senator Sessions and others, are worthy senators. We have an honest disagreement. The president says he supports it. But the fact of the matter is—and I am not talking about a specific senator; I don't do that because that is not what it is really about. At the institutional level, I believe the reason this legislation has so much support—I will repeat that—at the institutional level, I believe the reason this legislation has so much support is that it is a tribute to the power and the clout of the financial services industry in Washington.

Let's call it what it is. Might makes right. It is the financial might of the credit card companies and the big banks that are big spenders, heavy hitters, and investors in both political parties. It doesn't mean individual senators support this legislation for that reason. I can't make that argument. People can have different viewpoints. But if I look at it institutionally, I can look at the amount of money those folks deliver, their lobbying coalition, and the ways in which they march on Washington every day, and I can't help but say that is part of what this is about.

Why has the Congress chosen to come down so hard on ordinary working people down on their luck? How is it that this bill is so skewed against their interests and in favor of big banks and credit card companies? These editorials in a lot of newspapers that say the Congress—the House and Senate—comes down on the side of binge banks, not consumers, are right. Well, maybe it is because these families don't have million-dollar lobbyists

representing them before the Congress. They don't give hundreds of thousands of dollars in soft money to the Democratic and Republican parties. They don't spend their days hanging outside the chamber to bend a member's ear.

Unfortunately, it looks as if the industry got to us first. The truth is that, outside of this building, the support for this bill is a pittance. I mean the truth of the matter is that if you go outside this building, support for this bill is very narrow.

The support has deep pockets. Apparently the Congress responds to deep pockets—not apparently; it does. Everybody knows that. People know it in Nebraska; they know it in Alabama; they know it in Minnesota.

We can agree or disagree about this legislation, but that is the view people have. They say when it comes to our concerns about ourselves and our families, our concerns are of little concern in Washington. Part of that is the mix of money in politics. That is why the vote in the House is important and why everybody should know that McCain-Feingold and Meehan-Shays is just a step. Lord, we will have to do much more.

I am trying to win on a cloture vote on which I will get beat badly. Outside of this building, and I will stake my reputation on this—I hope I have a reputation—outside this building there is no support for this, or very little. People are not running up to us in coffee shops in Nebraska and saying, please pass that bankruptcy bill because, by God, that is the most important thing you can do that will help us.

People are talking about health care costs, childcare costs, good education for their children, a fair price for family farmers, how we can keep our small businesses going, the cost of higher education, the cost of prescription drugs, concern people will not have a pension, what happens when you are seventy-five or eighty, in poor health, and you have to go to the poorhouse before you get help in a nursing home or home-based care and receive medical assistance. That is what people talk about. They don't say, please pass a bankruptcy bill so when we get into trouble, no fault of our own, because of medical bills or we lost our jobs, we will not be able to rebuild our lives. There isn't any support for this legislation outside this building. The deep-pocket folks got to the Congress first, as they usually do.

There is opposition. You can know something about a bill by who the enemies are. Labor unions oppose the bill. Consumer groups oppose the bill. Women and children's groups all oppose the bill. Civil rights organizations all oppose the bill. Many members of the religious community oppose the bill. Indeed, it is a fairly broad coalition that opposes this. Behind them are millions of working families who have nothing to gain and everything to lose from this legislation. That is why I have been blocking this bill for over two years.

I come from the state of Minnesota. We had a great senator and vice-president, Hubert Humphrey. He once said that the test of a society or the test of a government is how we treat people in the dawn of life, the children, in the twi-light of their lives, the elderly, in the shadow of their lives, people who are poor, people who are struggling with an illness, people struggling with a disability.

By this standard, this bill is a miserable failure. There is no doubt in my mind this is a bad bill. It punishes the vulnerable and rewards the big banks and credit card companies for their own poor practices. For all I know, this legislation will only get worse in conference. I hope that is not the case but it is my fear.

Earlier I used the word "injustice" to describe this bill. That is exactly right. It would be a bitter irony if creditors used a crisis, largely of their own making, to talk Congress into this legislation.

Colleagues, it is not too late to reverse the course of the bill. It is never too late to pull back from the brink until we have leaped. We have not leaped yet. Let's step back. Let's do reform the right way. Let's wait until we are not adding to the economic pain that too many American families are already feeling. Let's not prolong the pain.

I urge the Senate to change the course. If I lose on this vote, then we will have to have another cloture vote, which will be next week, and there will be more discussion. From there, we will see.

19

IN MEMORY OF . . .

"I close very simply in honor of the memory of this very great politician. We all are better off because of his life."
~Senator Paul Wellstone
January 19, 1999

Senator Wellstone gave hundreds of speeches recognizing individual constituents, volunteers, and world leaders. The most poignant, however, were Senator Wellstone's remembrances of people who had passed away. Sometimes they were political and other times they were personal, but each time they were heartfelt. The speeches also provided insight into Senator Wellstone himself, such as his memorial to Mike Epstein, a close aide and advisor who died of cancer.

RONALD SKAU
November 13, 1991

Mr. President, I rise today to honor a man who a short time ago came to Washington to fulfill his dream of many years. His name is Ronald Skau and he is a Vietnam veteran. Ron was diagnosed with lung cancer in June of this year. The cancer spread rapidly to his liver, brain, bones, and lymph system. Later in June, Ron was given three months to live. He came to Washington to see the Vietnam Veterans Memorial while still alive.

Ron started his career in the Army on January 31, 1962. On July 14, 1966, he left for Vietnam as part of the Seventy-fifth Ranger Battalion. He served for 366 days in the Tay Nin Province in the Iron Triangle with the Seventy-fifth as well as with the 196th Light Infantry Brigade. During this time, Ron was injured twice in the line of duty. He has received a Purple Heart, the Vietnam Service and Campaign Medals, an Occupation Medal, and two Good Conduct Medals.

Ron returned from Vietnam on July 15, 1967. Upon his return, Ron went through the problems of readjusting that so many veterans faced then and still face today. After fourteen years of drifting from city to city and job to job, Ron was diagnosed as having posttraumatic stress disorder (PTSD) and was hospitalized for three months to deal with his severe emotional and psychological problems.

It is an accomplishment for anyone to face and overcome PTSD. Many people who become plagued with PTSD retreat into themselves. The severe emotional and psychological problems associated with PTSD can ruin a life as easily as the worst of physical diseases. What has attracted me most to Ron is the way he has dealt with having PTSD.

While he was still in the hospital in 1981, Ron turned his energies toward helping other veterans who suffer from PTSD. Along with his friend George Buck, Ron founded the Vietnam Veterans Awareness Council to help other veterans suffering from PTSD. The council was based in Minneapolis and offered a wide range of services including counseling, information and referral, crisis intervention and emergency food and shelter for up to six months.

The Awareness Council was the first in a series of examples of Ron's devotion to helping others. The most recent was his willingness to allow a photo-journalist to accompany him and his wife on their trip to Washington. The journalist is working on a project that will be a study of the dying process. She will be a constant companion of the Skau's until Ron's death and will continue to meet with Ron's wife, Roseanne, after Ron dies to study the grief process.

When Ron came to my office with his wife, Roseanne, and son, Nathan, he did not come to complain about his life and he did not use his health as a crutch. Instead, he came to my office to tell his story and ask me to help him revive the Vietnam Veterans Awareness Council and specifically to help him start a shelter for homeless veterans. Even in a wheelchair and on oxygen, Ron wants to continue helping other veterans experiencing hardship. I told him it was the absolute least I could do for him.

I asked Ron if I could use his story and our conversation in my speeches and actions on behalf of veterans. His story should be held up as an example to us all. The desire to give of himself to help others has spanned his entire life and will effect others even after he is gone.

I would like to take this opportunity to thank Ron on behalf of myself and my family and on behalf of the state of Minnesota and the U.S.

Senate for this service to his country and to his fellow veterans.

As Ron and his family were leaving my office, he gave me a copy of a poem he wrote in a hospital bed in Yang Tau, Vietnam, about the pain of being injured, then helplessly watching his best friend die. I would like to read this poem now:

I remember walking down that blood strewn trail,
In a jungle far from home,
Thinking of my Minnesota white,
And thanking God I'm not alone.
Minnesota snow so cool and white,
Where a body can forget his fright,
A good warm land to live and love,
God please help this warrior dove, with Minnesota white.
A flash of red screams from the dark,
An angry bee strikes my best friend's heart,
I slam some rounds into the night and make my mind think of
Minnesota white, Oh Lord, Minnesota White!
I scream and cry, get mad as hell,
For there is no one I can tell,
Of how I felt from where I lie,
And watched as my best friend died!
Minnesota white, God please give me Minnesota white.
The night explodes into fire and hate,
I take my gun, don't hesitate,
Sweat streaming into my eyes, Lord I know quite well,
Tonight I die in this burning hell,
Minnesota white, Oh please, Minnesota white.
I force myself to stand and fight,
My body shaking from it's fright,
I look around, I've got four men down,
Come on mind with Minnesota white,
Beautiful Minnesota white.
The warriors dove counts his kill,
He feels his body growing cold and still,
He fights as a tuned machine throughout the night,
He's psyched his mind with Minnesota white,
Thank God and Minnesota white.
The new dawn breaks calm and bright,
The warrior dove seems all right,
He checks his gun and cleans his wounds as he sits,
All alone, with a soul that's dead and a mind of
Minnesota white and back home.

MAYA KOPSTEIN
January 24, 1995

I thank the Chair. Mr. President, sometimes we speak on the floor of the Senate—Democrats and Republicans—not because we have an amendment to offer, not because it is our legislative agenda, but because we just cannot be silent and we feel that it is important as senators, given the honor of being senators, to speak about those issues and those peoples that we feel very strongly about.

In today's *New York Times*, there is a picture that tells more than a thousand words: A friend of Sergeant Maya Kopstein, a nineteen-year-old victim of a suicide bombing, mourned at her grave yesterday and held the flag from her coffin.

Mr. President, nineteen Israelis were murdered in a Palestinian suicide bombing. All but one of these soldiers were barely old enough to vote.

This one young woman over here in this picture, as I talked with a very close friend of mine—we become close with the staff we work with—my legislative director, Mike Epstein, said: "Just look at her face, this young woman, young girl. It looks as if she's saying, 'What kind of a world do I live in?'"

Israelis murdered, ". . . all but one of them soldiers barely old enough to vote."

I have three children, and my youngest is now twenty-two. These were children who were murdered. I do not know when all this violence will stop, but I want to speak on the floor of the Senate today—and I did have a chance to also talk to the Israeli Ambassador—to convey not only my sadness and sympathy but also my outrage. I believe that this is a sentiment that I express for all senators, and I send this to the people of Israel. I want them to know that all of us care fiercely about what has happened, that all of us, on both sides of the aisle, condemn murder.

And, Mr. President, I today hope and pray—I use those words carefully but I think those words apply—I hope and pray that the Israelis, Palestinians, all of the peoples in the Middle East, find a way, first of all for security and protection, to stop this, and, second of all, a way to move forward—to move forward—with the peace process. There has to come a day when children are not murdering children. There has to come a day when this violence ends. There has to come a day of reconciliation.

The sad thing is that the extremists have figured out the most effective way of trying to destroy this process. The extremists have figured out perhaps the most effective way of trying to make sure that there never will be peace. But my hope and my prayer today is for all of the families of all of these young people that have been murdered. My hope and prayer today is for the Israelis and the Palestinians, and for all the people in the Middle East—that there will be reconciliation. And as an American senator and as an American Jewish senator, I want to speak on the floor to express these sentiments. I want my country to be as helpful as possible, our government to be as helpful as possible at this time. I want us to extend our friendship and our support to Israel. I never want any of us to turn our gaze away from this kind of outrageous slaughter of young people, of children.

Murder, Mr. President, is never legitimate. Murder by anyone is never legitimate.

ANNIVERSARY OF THE DEATH OF ROBERT F. KENNEDY
June 5, 1998

Mr. President, on June 6, 1968, at 1:44 a.m., Bobby Kennedy passed away. I would like to speak about Senator Kennedy. First of all, I just recommend for people in Minnesota and our country a wonderful documentary that will be shown this week on TV on the Discovery Channel, "Robert F. Kennedy, A Memoir." This was done by Jack Newfield and Charlie Stewart. My wife, Sheila, and I had a chance to see two hours of this, a preview. It is very powerful.

I thought what I would do is read from a book which just came out, written by one of Bobby Kennedy's children, Maxwell Taylor Kennedy. The title of it is *Make Gentle the Life of the World.* This is an excerpt from one of Bobby Kennedy's speeches: Let us dedicate ourselves to what the Greeks wrote so many years ago, "to tame the savageness of man and make gentle the life of the world."

Thus the title, *Make Gentle the Life of the World.*

Let me just say at the beginning, before quoting from some of Bobby Kennedy's speeches, that I believe—this is just my opinion—that the senator who really most lives this tradition, of course in a very personal way, but in terms of his just unbelievable advocacy for people and the kind of courage and power, the effectiveness of his advocacy for people, of course, is Senator Ted Kennedy.

Behind me is the desk of President John Kennedy, which is Senator Edward Kennedy's desk. I can't think of any senator who better represents the words I am now about to quote.

Bobby Kennedy gave a speech. I believe it was at the University of Kansas. He wanted to talk to students and young people. He wanted to talk about the way in which we measure ourselves as a people. It is one of my favorite speeches, and I quote a part of it: Yet, the gross national product does not allow for the health of our children—

In other words, do we measure how we are doing as a country just by the economic indicators.

Yet, the gross national product does not allow for the health of our children, the quality of their education or the joy of their play. It does not include the beauty of our poetry or the strength of our marriages, the intelligence of our public debate or the integrity of our public officials. It measures neither our wit nor our courage, neither our wisdom nor our learning, neither our compassion nor our devotion to our country. It measures everything, in short, except that which makes life worthwhile. And it can tell us everything about America, except why we are proud that we are Americans.

Mr. President, another speech that Senator Kennedy gave is relevant to our times:

There are millions of Americans living in hidden places whose faces and names we never know, but I've seen children starving in Mississippi, idling their lives away in the ghetto, living without hope or future amid the despair on Indian reservations with no jobs and little help. I've seen proud men in the hills of Appalachia who wish only to work in dignity, but the mines are closed and the jobs are gone and no one, neither industry nor labor nor Government, has cared enough to help. Those conditions will change, those children will live only if we dissent. So I dissent, and I know you do, too.

Interesting words about crime:

Thus, the fight against crime is, in the last analysis, the same as the fight for equal opportunity, or the battle against hunger and deprivation, or the struggle to prevent the pollution of our air and water. It is the fight to preserve the quality of community which is at the root of our greatness, a fight to preserve confidence in ourselves and our fellow citizens, a battle for the quality of our lives.

About the importance of work: We need jobs, dignified employment at decent pay. What many today call living-wage jobs.

The kind of employment that lets a man—And I add, and I am sure Senator Kennedy would add, a woman—say to his community, to his family, to his country and, most important, to himself [or herself], "I helped to build this country; I'm a participant in this great public venture; I am a man"—And, I add, "I am a woman." The importance of work—

Community:

Today, we can make this a nation where young people do not see the false peace of drugs. Together, we can make this a nation where old people are not shunted off, where regardless of the color of his skin or the place of birth of his father, every citizen will have an equal chance at dignity and decency. Together, Americans are the most decent, generous and compassionate people in the world. Divided, they are collections of islands—islands of blacks afraid of islands of whites; islands of northerners bitterly opposed to islands of southerners, islands of workers warring with islands of businessmen.

Government:

Governments can err, Presidents do make mistakes, but the immortal Dante tells us that divine justice weighs the sins of the cold-blooded and the sins of the warm-hearted in a different scale. Better the occasional faults of a government living in the spirit of charity than the consistent emissions of a government frozen in the ice of its own indifference.

Courage—I think the pages will especially like this:

It is from numberless, diverse acts of courage and belief that human history is shaped. Each time a man stands up—Or a woman stands up—for an ideal or acts to improve the lot of others or strikes out against injustice, he sends forth a tiny ripple of hope and crossing each other from a million different centers of energy and daring those ripples build a current which can sweep down the mightiest walls of oppression and resistance.

These are really beautiful words.

Mr. President, I had an opportunity about a year ago to travel just to a few communities Senator Kennedy visited. I started out in the delta, Mississippi, and actually just this past Friday, a week ago, I went back to Tunica in the delta, just by myself, mainly to teach classes. I went back because there was a marvelous teacher, Mr. Robert Hall, who said a year ago at a community meeting, "I wish you could come back around graduation time, because only about fifty percent or just a little bit more of our students graduate, and our students need to have more hope."

In Tunica, the public high school is all African-American, and the private schools are all white. So I came back. I landed, and a man named Mr. Young picked me up at the airport. He said, "Before you go to the high school, you will be addressing the third and fourth graders." I say to the chair, I thought to myself, addressing the third and fourth graders the last day of school, like a policy address? It didn't sound like this was going to work very well.

I went to the elementary school, and the third and fourth graders were all sitting in the auditorium. A principal, a young man, introduced me, and we were high on the stage. I told the principal, "I think I will not stay on the stage." I went out to where the students were.

This one young girl helped me out so much because we were talking about education and school and why you like school. She said, "I like it because a good education will help me be all I want to be in my life." Then forty hands went up at one time. That is a teacher's dream, and these children had all sorts of dreams—doctors, lawyers, psychiatrists, professional wrestlers, boxers, football players—you name it—teachers, on and on and on. I thought to myself, this is what it is about. The only problem is that for too many children, that is the way they start out, and then this just gets taken away from them. The same spark isn't there later on by the time they get to high school.

I then went to East L.A. and to Watts and went to public housing projects in Chicago and inner-city Baltimore and Letcher County, Kentucky, and inner-city Minneapolis, Phillips neighborhood, rural Minnesota. The point is there are heroines, and heroines are doing great work. That is my point.

The other point is, everywhere I went, I really believe—and these are my words, I summarize it—what part of the people were saying with a lot of dignity was, "What happened to our national vow of equal opportunity for every child? We don't have it in our communities."

And the jobs—where are the jobs with decent wages? That is what we want to be able to do. Just think about Robert Kennedy's words, about the importance of work. That is what people are saying today. "We want to have jobs at decent wages so that we can earn a decent living and we can give our children the care we know they need and deserve."

Really, Mr. President, as I think about that travel—and travel in any community—this is the focus: On jobs and education, health care, earning a decent living, being able to do well for your children. That is the focus.

Different people think about Senator Kennedy's career, Bobby Kennedy, and what he stood for, and different people in different ways, to try to use that inspiring example to do good work. I want to just raise one question before the Senate today, as I feel that this is very connected to Senator Kennedy's life and what he tried to do for our country. And this is the question. I pose this question for my colleagues and the people in the country: How can it be that in the United States of America today—not June of 1968—June of 1998, how can it be the richest, most affluent country in the world, at the peak of our economic performance—we are all writing

about how well the economy is doing—how can it be that we are still being told that we cannot provide a good education for every child, that we cannot provide good health care for all of our citizens, that people still cannot find jobs at decent wages that they can support their families on, that we cannot at least reach the goal of making sure that every child who comes to kindergarten is ready to learn? She knows how to spell her name; she knows colors and shapes and sizes; she knows the alphabet; she has been read to widely; and she or he is ready to learn. And we are still being told we can't reach those goals as a nation?

And how can it be that in our peak economic performance today, one out of four children under the age of three are growing up poor in America—under the age of three; and one out of every two children of color under the age of three are growing up poor in our country? How can this be?

How can it be that we have a set of social arrangements that allow children to be the most poverty-stricken group in America? That is a betrayal of our heritage. The impoverishment of so many children is our national disgrace.

I just feel—and I am just speaking for myself—as I think back about Robert Kennedy's life, he would surely say today that this is not acceptable and that we can do better. He would probably say, "We can do betta." And I think those words are very important.

One final point, if my colleague would indulge me.

I had a chance to speak at a baccalaureate at Swarthmore College this last weekend. And I was saying to the students—a lot of people have given up on politics. A lot of people, it is not that they don't care about the issues, they care deeply, they care desperately, but they don't think there is much of a connection between their concerns and our concerns. They read all about money in politics, and they just do not think it is that important.

A friend of mine was telling me he was teaching a seminar class on electoral politics, and he was talking about presidential races and some of his involvement in the past, and students said, "Well, that's when elections mattered." Elections do matter. All of us in public service, I think, believe that, even if we have different viewpoints.

I said to the students—and I want to conclude this way, in just talking with young people, not at young people—that I read—and certainly this was the case in Swarthmore College—an incredibly high percentage of students in our colleges and universities are involved in community service, and also high school students. It is not true that young people do not care about community, do not want to serve our country. There is a tremendous amount of good work being done. The problem is that I think many young people say community service is good and politics is unsavory.

I just say today, on the floor of the Senate, to the young people: We need you to be mentors and tutors. We need your community service. We need you to volunteer at battered women's shelters. If my wife, Sheila, was here, she would say, "Mention that, Paul." We need you to be advocates for children. We need you to help other children. We need you to do community work. When you go on to college and universities and get degrees, and you are lawyers and businesspeople, we need you to take some of your skills and give it to the community. We need you to do that. But we also need you to care about public policy. We need you to care about good public policy, and we need you to make sure that our nation does better.

Mr. President, I want to say today—since I wanted to take a few minutes to speak about Robert Kennedy and his life, the meaning of that life, to me and I think to many Americans—I think that the final point that I would want to make—feels right to me, at least—is to say, especially to younger people, the future is not going to belong to those who are content with the present. The future is not going to belong to cynics; it is not going to belong to people who stand on the sidelines; it is not going to belong to people who view politics as a spectator sport.

The future is going to belong to people who have passion and people who are willing to make a personal commitment to making our country better. And the future is going to belong—these are not Bobby Kennedy's words; these are Eleanor Roosevelt's words—"The future is going to belong to people who believe in the beauty of their dreams."

Bobby Kennedy had many beautiful dreams. His life was cut short, and he was not able to realize all those dreams. But his dreams and his hope and his work for our country is as important to our nation today as it ever was while he was alive.

I yield the floor.

ANNIVERSARY OF THE DEATH OF HUBERT H. HUMPHREY
January 19, 1999

Mr. President, I rise to speak today to honor a great Minnesota senator and a great American.

U.S. Senator Hubert H. Humphrey died on January 13, 1978. On that day, a piece of Minnesota died—a piece of the nation died.

In many ways, Senator Humphrey embodied the best of our state and our nation. He was a visionary who never lost sight of people in the here and now; he was a prophet who spoke with authority and compassion; he was a leader who never lost sight of the ". . . extraordinary possibilities in ordinary people." Whether as the mayor of Minneapolis or the vice-president of the United States, Senator Humphrey was a person of dignity, integrity and honesty.

Even during our darkest days of segregation and war, he never lost his humor or his commitment to improve the lives of people. And this Happy Warrior did improve the lives of countless people throughout my state and our country. Indeed, he fulfilled his own pledge that "we must dedicate ourselves to making each man, each woman, each child in America a full participant in American life."

My state and our nation owe a debt to Senator Humphrey that can never be paid.

I owe a debt to Senator Humphrey: In the back of my mind, I continually aspire to the standard he set for Minnesota senators. I attempt to fulfill his goal that our "public and private endeavor ought to be concentrated upon those who are in the dawn of life, our children; those who are in the twilight of life, our elderly; and those who are in the shadows of life, our handicapped."

My thoughts on Senator Humphrey's passing are even more poignant this year because his wife—Senator Muriel Humphrey—died this past fall. As friends and family gathered at her funeral, I was struck by how blessed we were to have these two incredible people pass through our lives.

I close very simply in honor of the memory of this very great public man: We all are better off because of his life.

MIKE EPSTEIN
May 3, 2000

Mr. President, let me thank the leadership of both parties for allowing the Senate to talk to a very dear friend, Mike Epstein. I want you to know, Mike, and your family, that a lot of our staff are back here as well with me. I think this is a little unusual, that the Senate stops its business and focuses on an individual in this way. But I think there are some things that many of us want to say to Mike.

I want to start out this way. When I mentioned in the past couple of days to senators, but also support staff everywhere here, that my friend Mike was struggling with cancer, I just could never have anticipated the reaction. Mike, I want you to know I can think of at least four or five times where someone said to me: Mike? He's an institution.

I know Mike's priorities, so let me be clear about the people who talk about Mike as an institution. And, Mike, I know you; this was real. This was real.

Some of the people who said Mike is an institution were support staff. People said to me: Mike just treats everybody so well. He is such a nice, good person. He is great, just because of the way he treats people.

Mike, that is the best compliment of all.

Then senators said to me: Paul, Mike Epstein is an institution in the Senate. Some may have been thinking about history. Some in the Senate—I do not think that many because we have had a lot of new senators—know of Mike's role with the Church committee and the important investigative research he has done.

There are others who are familiar, Mike, with the kind of work you have done with Senator Kennedy. Mike did some of the most important investigative research on HIV infection and AIDS early on when other people in the country did not even want to focus on this.

Then other senators said to me: Paul, we are going to come to the floor and talk to Mike today because we have worked with him on the Senate Foreign Relations Committee when he was chief counsel to the committee.

Then way down on the list of priorities—because I am talking to you, Mike, about great work that you do—has been the work that Mike and I have done together. Mike, I know you will not like me saying this, but I am going to say it anyway because it is true. I believe from the bottom of my heart that everything I have been able to do as a senator that has been good for Minnesota and the country is because, Mike, you have been there right by my side, 1 inch away from me.

A lot of the people in the Senate know that. As a matter of fact, I say to my colleagues on the floor, I will never forget one time when I finally learned at least a little bit of the rules and I was able to come to the floor and fight very hard a number of years ago for some assistance for victims of a tornado that hit Chandler, Minnesota, and other small communities. Mike was there as my tutor, as my teacher, teaching me, as you do, Mike.

It worked out well, but afterwards, Alan Simpson, a former senator from Wyoming, came up to me and said: Paul?

I said: Yes?

He said: You see those fellows on the other side of the aisle?—pointing to the Republicans, and I think Nancy Kassebaum was there as well.

I said: Yes.

He said: They have been looking at you.

I said: Yes. Mike was a ways behind me about where Tinker is sitting right now.

He said: He has been right next to you the whole time. It doesn't look good. It looks like you can't do it yourself. It looks like he is doing it for you. Paul, the trick is this: You want to have Mike far enough away from you so that it looks like you are doing it yourself but close enough to you in case they throw a whizzer on you, he can be one inch away from your side.

That has basically been my methodology as a senator. I had Mike far enough away so it looked like I was doing it on my own, but Mike was close enough so that always when I needed the advice, I got it.

Mike Epstein, I speak on the floor today in the Senate, and others are coming out to speak, because you are an institution and I want to make sure you and your family hear these words loudly and clearly.

* * *

I thank all of the senators who spoke for Mike and his family. There are other senators who will be speaking who could not work into this timeframe. It is quite amazing to have so many people come down.

Mike, I want you to know that the Parliamentarian, staff, Republican, Democrat, everybody here has a look on their face, an expression of love and support for you and your family.

I finish this way, Mike. It has not been our friendship—the relationship is not like I hired somebody to be my assistant; it is more like I hired somebody who has been my teacher. Maybe that is why we are joined at the hip.

Sometimes when I come to the floor, probably I make mistakes, maybe get too intense, feel too strongly. I will ask Mike, how have I done? He will be willing to give me quite a bit of constructive criticism. But sometimes I will be down on the floor with other senators and I will go back to the office and I will go to Mike and look for approval. I will say: Mike, how did I do? And he will say: That was just right.

Mike, I hope you think this was just right.

20

Veterans

> "Sick Persian Gulf veterans shouldn't be kept in limbo, waiting years for the completion of research that should have been done years ago on the long-term health effects of low-level exposures to chemical and other agents."
> ~Senator Paul Wellstone, January 28, 1997

The connection between Senator Paul Wellstone and veterans is not immediately apparent. It is assumed that a senator with an outspoken record of opposing military action and large expenditures for defense programs would not devote a significant amount of time to veterans' issues. This, however, was not true.

After initially alienating veterans' groups with his press conference in front of the Vietnam Memorial opposing the Gulf War in January 1991, Senator Wellstone apologized and then became their champion. Wellstone met with both national and local veterans' groups and listened to their concerns. He learned that their need, related to health care, mental health and chemical dependency treatment, and education upon leaving military service, aligned closely with the issues that he felt passionately about.

Over the course of twelve years, Senator Wellstone fought for increased benefits for veterans, recognition for the sacrifice of "atomic veterans," and successfully led efforts for Congress to pass legislation that mandated resources to "reach the national goal of ending veterans' homelessness within the decade."

Senator Jay Rockefeller (D-WV), chair of the senate committee on Veterans' Affairs, described Senator Wellstone as one of his strongest allies on the committee. "With the passing of my dear friend Paul Wellstone, the nation's veterans have lost one of their strongest allies in the Senate and in the country," Rockefeller said in a statement after his death. "When Senator Wellstone was committed to a particular cause, he wouldn't rest until he achieved victory. But, the victories were never for himself, they were for the millions of veterans across the country who desperately needed a voice in Washington. Whether they were veterans who suffered from radiation exposure, or veterans who were homeless, Paul didn't rest until they received the assistance they needed and had earned."

Jesse Brown Will Not Be Silenced
November 18, 1995

Mr. President, yesterday morning there was an article in the *Washington Post*. It dealt with some of the debate that is now taking place about the budget and veterans. We can agree to disagree, but there was one piece in this article that really captured my attention, as a senator from Minnesota. This was:

> The conferees sent what they called a "strong message" of displeasure to Veterans Affairs Secretary Jesse Brown, in the form of sharp cuts in his office's staff and travel budget.

Mr. President, I would like to talk a little bit about Jesse Brown, Secretary of Veterans Affairs. Jesse Brown is one of our nation's most able and outspoken veterans advocates. He is a man who is a Marine combat veteran, a Marine combat hero who served our country with honor and distinction. Mr. President, he is a disabled veteran who, long before he became secretary of what he calls "For Veterans Affairs," was one of the most important voices and strongest voices for veterans, especially disabled veterans in the United States of America.

I would like to make it very clear, as a senator from Minnesota, that I do not believe these kinds of attacks, petty attacks on his personal office travel budget, will silence Jesse Brown. My colleagues are sadly mistaken, they are profoundly mistaken, if they believe any form of retaliation will silence this secretary, who is such a powerful advocate for veterans, based upon his own personal life, based upon his service for this country, and based upon his position.

Since taking office in 1993, let me just list a few of the impressive accomplishments of Secretary Jesse Brown, "Secretary for Veterans."

Agent Orange—in 1993, a VA-sponsored review conducted by the National Academy of Sciences found that certain cancers and illnesses could be caused by agent orange exposure. The VA promptly responded by presuming service-connection for these diseases—long overdue.

Mr. President, homeless veterans convened the first National Summit on Homelessness among Veterans. It is a scandal that such a large percentage of our street people and homeless people are veterans.

This Secretary, Jesse Brown, will not be silenced.

Persian Gulf veterans fought hard to make sure Persian Gulf veterans were not forgotten, to compensate certain Persian Gulf veterans with undiagnosed illnesses.

Mr. President, Secretary Jesse Brown will not be silenced.

Streamline and make the VA more responsive, a plan to decentralize the VA national health care system, which is now being implemented.

Mr. President, Secretary Jesse Brown will not be silenced.

Women veterans: He implemented a series of health care initiatives for women, established eight women veterans Comprehensive Health Care Centers.

Mr. President, Secretary Jesse Brown will not be silenced.

There are many more accomplishments that I could list, but I want to just end with one personal story, which I think tells a very large story about Secretary Jesse Brown.

Tim Gilmore fought for our country in the Vietnam war. He suffered from agent orange exposure, and he died of cancer. Toward the end of his life, Tim Gilmore was tormented by one fact. He knew he would not have long to live, but he had not received any compensation. By the rules that we operate under, if he did not receive any compensation before he passed away, there was a very real question whether his family would ever receive any compensation. He was tormented by this.

When Secretary Jesse Brown came to my state, this family made a personal appeal to him, the veterans community made a personal appeal to him to somehow, please, cut through the bureaucracy and please have some compassion and please be an advocate for Tim Gilmore and his family.

Mr. President, I made the same appeal. Time went by, Tim Gilmore became weaker, and it was very clear he was going to pass away soon. A very short period of time before Tim Gilmore passed away, Secretary Jesse Brown made sure that he received compensation, made sure that his family would receive that compensation.

That family has never forgotten that. To Tim Gilmore, a Vietnam vet who died from agent orange exposure, that was one of the most important things before he passed away. I will be indebted, as a senator from Minnesota, to Secretary Jesse Brown forever, for his compassion and his strength and commitment to people.

I will say to my colleagues, you can do whatever you want to his travel budget or personal budget, but you are not going to silence him. He is going to continue to talk about this budget and how it affects veterans.

I will mention one point I have been focused on, as a U.S. senator, and I will be pleased to debate this with anyone. I think what we are doing here in the health care field puts way too many veterans in very serious jeopardy for the following reason: Our veteran population is also becoming an aging population. We all know that.

If you have reductions in Medicare—and we continue to go through this debate about whether it is lessening the rate of increase or a cut. I do not even want to get into the semantics. I want to tell you, there is only one way you look at it. Look at the year 2002; ask how many people are going to be sixty-five years of age or over, how many of them are going to be eighty-five years of age or over; you ask what kind of services they are going to require, and you ask whether or not you are investing the resources to make sure they get them. We are not.

If you have those reductions in Medicare and reductions in medical assistance, you are going to have more of the elderly people coming to the veterans health care system for health care. Then, if you have the reduction in the VA health care system as well, it becomes a triple whammy.

Secretary Jesse Brown is going to continue to be a strong advocate for veterans. I will say to my colleagues, he is going to continue to challenge your budget and he is going to continue to say, "Why don't you ask the oil companies to sacrifice a little bit, or the coal companies, or the tobacco companies, or the pharmaceutical companies? And how come you give all this money to military contractors, above and beyond what the Pentagon asked for? And how come you have all these rapid depreciation allowances and cuts in capital gains?"

I listened to my colleague from Mississippi speak with considerable intelligence the other day about this. He is a very able senator. But this secretary of Veterans Affairs is going to continue to challenge these priorities. He should.

We do not need any hate, I think all of us agree. But we will have the debate. It will be an important debate for this country. I believe Secretary Jesse Brown will be a very powerful voice in that debate. I come to the floor of the Senate to speak in his behalf today.

Atomic Veterans
October 1, 1996

Mr. President, I rise to announce my intention to introduce in the 105th Congress a companion bill to the provisions of H.R. 4173 which was introduced last week by Congressman Lane Evans, who is an exceptionally dedicated and effective advocate for all veterans, including atomic veterans.

This important legislation would grant atomic veterans the presumption of service-connection for eight additional illnesses: Bone cancer; colon cancer; nonmalignant thyroid nodular disease; parathyroid cancer; ovarian cancer; brain and central nervous system tumors; unexplained bone marrow failure; and meningioma. Were this bill to be enacted, it would ensure that atomic veterans receive compensation for six diseases for which Marshall Islanders now automatically receive compensation under the Marshall Islands Nuclear Claims Tribunal Act and two diseases the VA accepts as radiogenic but does deem to be presumptively service-connected.

I am convinced that enactment of the provisions of H.R. 4173 would help to rectify an injustice or, to put it more accurately, a series of injustices inflicted by our government over the past fifty years on atomic veterans who served our country bravely, unquestioningly, and with great dedication.

If there's any doubt about the need to expand the list of presumptive diseases, it should have been dispelled by the final report of the President's Advisory Committee on Human Radiation Experiments, which was issued almost a year ago. The report's recommendations echoed many of the complaints that atomic veterans have had for years about the almost insuperable obstacles they face when seeking approval of their claims for VA compensation. The report urged an interagency working group to work "in conjunction with Congress"—I repeat in conjunction with Congress—to promptly address the concerns expressed by atomic veterans. Among these concerns cited by the committee are several that I've long believed need to be urgently addressed, including:

- The list of presumptive diseases for which atomic veterans automatically receive VA compensation is incomplete and inadequate.
- The standard of proof for atomic veterans without a presumptive disease can't be met and are

inappropriate given the incompleteness of exposure records retained by the government.
- Time and money spent on contractors and consultants in administering the claims program, particularly the dose reconstructions required for most atomic vets filing claims with the VA, would be better spent on directly aiding veterans.

With regard to the last two concerns, it is important to note that the Advisory Committee found that the government didn't create or maintain adequate records regarding the exposure, identity, and test locale of all participants. This finding casts serious doubt on the ability of the government to come up with accurate dose reconstructions on which the approval of claims for VA compensation of many atomic veterans depend.

In sum, there's no doubt that the report of the President's Advisory Committee strongly buttresses the case for expanding the list of radiogenic diseases for which atomic veterans must receive the presumption of service-connection and, therefore, for enacting the provision of H.R. 4173 in the next Congress.

Mr. President, for almost three years I've been deeply moved by the plight of our atomic veterans and their families, and frankly dismayed and angered when I have learned of the many injustices they've experienced over the past fifty years. My mentors on this issue have been Minnesota atomic veterans, particularly veterans of the U.S. Army's 216th Chemical Service Company who participated in "Operation Tumbler Snapper," a series of eight atmospheric nuclear tests in Nevada in 1952. They are an extraordinary group of Americans who despite their many trials and tribulations have not lost faith in this country and believe and hope they will one day receive the recognition and compensation that is due them.

Mr. President, since January 1994, I have had numerous meetings and contacts with the men of the "Forgotten 216th" and their families. Since their problems typify those of other atomic veterans nationwide, permit me to tell you about veterans of the U.S. Army's 216th Chemical Service Company and about why they now term themselves the "Forgotten 216th."

When the men of "The Forgotten 216th," about fifty percent of whom were Minnesotans, participated in "Operation Tumbler Snapper," they believed their government's assurances that it would protect them against any harm, but now are convinced they were used as guinea pigs with no concern shown for their safety.

Many were sent to measure fallout at or near ground zero immediately after a nuclear bomb blast, encountering radiation so high that their geiger counters literally went off the scale while they inhaled and ingested radioactive particles. They were given little or no protection, sometimes even lacking film badges to measure their exposure to radiation and were not informed of the dangers they faced. Moreover, they were sworn to secrecy about their participation in nuclear tests, sometimes denied access to their own service health records, and provided with no medical follow-up to ensure that they had not suffered adverse health effects as a consequence of their exposure to radiation. Many members of the 216th have already died, often of cancer, some as long as twenty years ago. It should be obvious to all why these men now refer to themselves as "the Forgotten 216th."

For fifty years, atomic veterans have been one of America's most neglected groups of veterans. For almost forty years there were no provisions in federal law specifically providing veterans compensation or health care for service-connected radiogenic diseases. Even now, with laws on the books covering radiogenic diseases on both a presumptive and non-presumptive basis, the rate of VA approval of atomic veterans' claims is abysmally low.

Mr. President, in this connection, permit me to quote from the testimony of Mr. Joseph Violante of the Disabled American Veterans before a House subcommittee on April 30, 1996:

The DAV believes that a great injustice has been done to America's Atomic veterans and their survivors. . . . Only ten percent of those atomic veterans who seek compensation for . . . disabilities are granted service connected benefits, although the VA cautions that "it cannot be inferred from this number that service-connection was necessarily granted on the basis of radiation exposure." . . . As of April 1, 1996, VA statistics show that there have been a total of 18,515 radiation [claim] cases. Service connection has been granted, as of April 1, in 1,886 cases. . . . Statistics current as of December 1, 1995, demonstrate that of the total number of cases in which atomic veterans have been granted service-connection, 463 involve the granting of presumptive service connection . . .

To sum up, if we were to exclude the 463 veterans who were granted presumptive service connection, atomic veterans had an incredibly low claims approval rate of less than eight percent. And of this low percentage, an indeterminate percentage may have had their claims granted for diseases unrelated to radiation exposure. Moreover, in the roughly seven-year period following the 1988 enactment of a law granting atomic veterans service connection on a presumptive basis for certain radiogenic disease to a degree of ten percent disability or more, only 463 claims of presumptive diseases have been improved. By any standard, the VA's record of approving veterans' claims based on disabilities linked to radiogenic diseases is a sorry one.

Mr. President, permit me to quote further from the eloquent and persuasive testimony of Mr. Violante:

It cannot be overemphasized that radiation claims are wrongfully denied because of inaccurate reconstructed dose estimates used as the basis for the determination that the estimated minimal level of exposure experienced by the atomic veteran was insufficient to cause the cancer or other disease ravishing the atomic veteran's body. The reality is that atomic veterans are fighting a losing battle, not only with the disease or diseases that have taken away their good health, but with the very government that put them in harm's way. . . . . Why are only fifteen diseases given a rebuttable presumption of service connection for atomic veterans while Marshall Islanders receive an irrebuttable presumption for twenty-five medical conditions [now twenty-seven conditions]? Why does our government continue to put the needs of its veterans behind those of other groups, such as the Marshall Islanders? . . . Congress should consider making all the recognized "radiogenic diseases" and any other disease, illness or disability that others, such as the Marshall Islanders are being compensated for, diseases for which presumptive service connection is granted.

I couldn't agree more with the DAV's cogent analysis and this is one of the reasons I'm determined to ensure that atomic veterans are granted service-connected compensation for all radiogenic diseases.

The cover of every copy of the *Atomic Veteran's Newsletter*, the publication of the National Association of Atomic Veterans, contains the simple but eloquent statement: "the atomic veteran seeks no special favor . . . simply justice."

Mr. President, I urge my colleagues from both sides of the aisle to join me in supporting the valiant and long struggle of atomic veterans for justice by strongly backing the bill that I plan to introduce next year and in fighting for its enactment.

I dedicate this statement to the members and families of "The Forgotten 216th" who have educated me about the plight of atomic veterans and whose courage and perseverance I shall always admire.

I ask that excerpts of the statement of Mr. Joseph Violante of the Disabled American Veterans before the Subcommittee on Compensation, Insurance and Memorial Affairs, House Committee on Veterans' Affairs, April 30, 1996, be printed in the *Record.*

BENEFITS FOR GULF WAR SYNDROME
January 28, 1997

Mr. President, I am pleased and proud to introduce a bill today that will address a serious problem faced by many Persian Gulf veterans—the denial of their claims for VA compensation based solely on the fact that their symptoms arose more than two years after they last served in the gulf. This bill is a companion to H.R. 466 introduced recently by Congressman Lane Evans, ranking minority member of the House Veterans' Affairs Committee and an outstanding, energetic, and dedicated veterans' advocate.

This bill would extend from two to ten years the time by which a veteran must develop symptoms after departing the gulf to be eligible to file for VA disability compensation.

While this legislation is simple and straight forward, there are a number of reasons that I am introducing it that require some elaboration.

Over a month ago Congressman Evans and I sent a joint letter to VA Secretary Jesse Brown asking him to administratively extend the presumptive period from two to ten years. We pointed out that the VA had denied about ninety-five percent of Persian Gulf veterans' claims for undiagnosed illnesses and noted that in House testimony last March Secretary Brown himself said that "most of the people we are denying, a large percentage of the people that we are denying, do not have a disease within the two-year period." The secretary added that there was a need to examine health problems emerging after that time period.

Mr. President, our letter also noted that continuing disclosures about possible exposures of our troops in the gulf to chemical weapons make it clear that it may take many years before we have a full understanding of what occurred during the Persian Gulf war and how these events affected our veterans. In closing, we stressed that Gulf War veterans must be given the benefit of the doubt.

Although Secretary Brown has not yet replied to our letter, I know that he is a fearless and deeply committed advocate of our nation's veterans and fully shares my view that America's veterans must always be given the benefit of the doubt. Under his leadership, the VA is now reviewing 11,000 cases to ensure that Persian Gulf veterans are indeed given the benefit of the doubt in the development and adjudication of their compensation claims.

Secretary Brown, at the request of President Clinton, is formulating a plan to expand the deadline for compensation which is to be submitted to the president in March. I anticipate that the administration will extend the deadline and believe that when this occurs they'll want congressional authorization. This bill is intended to grant them that authority.

Mr. President, so that my colleagues on both sides of the aisle will better understand my reasons for introducing this bill and why I believe the administration must and will extend the deadline for filing Gulf War claims, permit me to list some of the key factors involved:

Sick Persian Gulf veterans shouldn't be kept in limbo, waiting years for the completion of research that should have been done years ago on the long-term health effects of low-level exposures to chemical and other agents.

In this connection, the experience of atomic veterans for over fifty years is hardly encouraging, with disputes among scientists persisting about the long-term effects of exposure to low-level radiation and about the validity of U.S. government-funded radiation dose reconstructions—dose reconstructions which continue to be a major factor in denial of the vast majority of atomic veterans' claims for VA compensation.

While I'm pleased that research is finally taking place after a delay of over five years stemming from DOD's contention that there were no chemical exposures and that low-level exposures had no health effects, I fear there is a possibility that the etiology of Persian Gulf illnesses may never be known because needed scientific data was not collected immediately after the war and because of the complexity of figuring out the synergistic effects of various combinations of harmful agents present during the Gulf War.

DOD and CIA are developing new information about possible chemical and other exposures during the Gulf War that could further complicate the search for the causes of illnesses, while the media sometimes carry contradictory reports on such exposures that add to the uncertainties and anxieties of veterans and their families.

There are a number of serious diseases that are not manifested until ten years or more after initial exposure to harmful agents.

In closing, Mr. President, I would like to pay tribute to the brave Minnesota veterans of Operation Desert Shield/Desert Storm whom I met with over a month ago. These Minnesota veterans who are my mentors told me about the illnesses and symptoms they developed after the war, including skin rashes, hair loss, reproductive problems, memory loss, headaches, aching joints, and internal bleeding. They said that they are scared to death about their health problems. I was deeply moved by their accounts and pledged to do all I could to help them. Moreover, I was distressed to learn that as of last month, out of 171 Minnesota gulf veterans who had filed disability claims, only eighteen were receiving full or partial disability benefits.

As part of an action plan to help Minnesota gulf veterans, I told them that Congressman Evans and I were writing to Secretary Brown to extend the two-year period to ten years. This initiative was supported both by Minnesota Persian Gulf veterans and state veterans' leaders and the bill I'm now introducing is a logical followup to the letter sent to Secretary Brown.

I am very pleased to note that this legislation is supported by the American Legion and the Vietnam Veterans of America, and I urge my colleagues to join these organizations in strongly supporting this bill.

I dedicate this bill to the patriotic and courageous Minnesota veterans who served in the Persian Gulf war.

21

TERRORISM

> "I believe people in our country will come together and that one message for these terrorists who have committed this murder on a mass scale is that they will not change our values. They will not change our way of life. They will not change who we are as Americans. We will never give way to the politics of hatred. We are a diverse people of many different colors and religions and backgrounds. We will continue to respect and support one another."
> ~Senator Paul Wellstone, September 12, 2001

On Tuesday morning, September 11, 2001, four passenger airplanes were hijacked by nineteen men. The hijackers did not fit the stereotype of Middle Eastern extremists. Most suicide bombers are young, poor, uneducated, and carefully supervised. The nineteen hijackers were older and well-educated.

At 8:46 a.m., the first plane, American Airlines Flight 11 struck the North Tower of the World Trade Center. Flight 11 departed from Logan International Airport in Boston, Massachusetts, and was originally scheduled to go to Los Angeles, California. Sixteen minutes later, United Airlines Flight 175 struck the South Tower. It had also departed from Boston and was scheduled to fly to Los Angeles, and also carried a two year-old child who was the youngest victim of the September 11th terrorist attacks.

Thirty-five minutes later, American Airlines Flight 77 crashed into the Pentagon. Flight 77 had left Washington Dulles Airport in Washington, D.C., and it was also bound for Los Angeles, California. Then, United Airlines Flight 93 crashed into a field in rural Pennsylvania at 10:03 a.m. Flight 93 had left from Newark Liberty

International Airport in Newark, New Jersey, and it was scheduled to fly to San Francisco, California. The 9/11 Commission determined, after reviewing tapes of passenger phone calls and other information, that the hijackers crashed the plane into the field in order to keep the crew and passengers from gaining control.

Not including the nineteen hijackers, approximately 3,000 people were killed as a result of the September 11th terrorist attacks.

TERRORIST ATTACKS AGAINST THE UNITED STATES
September 12, 2001

Madam President, as a senator from Minnesota, I rise to thank the religious community, the faith community in my state—Christians, Jews, and Muslims—for coming together and for their prayers for all of the men, women, and children who were murdered in our country. That is the very best of Minnesota. That is the very best of our country.

Let me also thank and pray for all of the loved ones of our firefighters and law enforcement community who have lost their lives in trying to protect people and save people's lives.

I believe people in our country will come together and that one message for these terrorists who have committed this murder on a mass scale is that they will not change our values. They will not change our way of life. They will not change who we are as Americans. We will never give way to the politics of hatred. We are a diverse people of many different colors and religions and backgrounds. We will continue to respect and support one another.

President Bush is certainly right when he says we will leave no stone unturned in getting to the bottom of who committed this act of murder. As a senator, I certainly believe we must hold them accountable.

Most importantly, we have to do everything within our power, regardless of political party, to take the steps and to do what is necessary to make sure people in our country are safe and secure.

Madam President, one more time, I want to finish up in the few minutes I have by saying that murder is never legitimate, and this was a mass murder of men, women, and children. I think the thing that I will never be able to get out of my mind is that so many innocent people, so many innocent Americans could be murdered in a single day in our country. To me, in my adult life, yesterday was the worst day for our country, and there are going to be many more difficult days because we don't even have a sense of the loss of life.

I am absolutely convinced this will bring out the best in us. I am absolutely convinced that Americans will be their own best selves. I am absolutely convinced that these terrorists will see Americans coming together and I hope the whole international community that represents civilization will come together so these kinds of acts of murder can never be committed again.

MINNESOTANS MOBILIZE
September 14, 2001

Mr. President, there are many times to speak in this chamber. Today I speak from the Senate floor to make the remarks of one senator from Minnesota part of our historical record. The senator from South Dakota is right, it is a very somber time. The unthinkable happened.

We have witnessed the slaughter of parents and their kids. I want to talk about this in the following way: First of all, it sounds so political to do this, but I want to thank the people of Minnesota for mobilizing the way they have mobilized: the blood banks, the offers of assistance, the prayers. Nothing could be more important.

As a senator from New Jersey, as someone who worked in the World Trade Center, the chair has probably a more direct understanding of the agony and the hell of so many families, but I am very proud that the people of Minnesota, in every way possible, are there for support.

This represents the best in our country. I say this because I want to say, drawing on the Minnesota example, that I do not want to let these terrorists ever take away from us as Americans the greatness of our country, including the values by which we live. I am talking about the civil liberties of Americans, and I am talking about the freedom that is so important to each and every one of us.

I say this as well because unlike these terrorists who slaughtered parents and kids, let us be clear, as we pass a resolution and move forward, that when we respond, our intention is to target the people that are responsible for this. Unlike these terrorists and what they did to Americans, we care about innocent civilians. We care about parents and kids.

Our effort must be focused on the people who are responsible, their network, their organizations. Our greatness, even in carrying out military action, is always to do everything we can to make sure innocent people do not lose their lives.

These are our values. This is what we are about. Whether it be how we now conduct ourselves as a nation, or the kind of military action that we are going to be taking, we will never let these terrorists take away from us what has made our country great.

As the son of a Jewish immigrant who fled persecution from Russia, I have always cherished our freedoms, and I always will. I hold that dear, and I believe that Americans hold it dear. As the son of a Jewish immigrant who fled persecution from Russia, I have always believed the greatness of our country is the value we place on human life. I am not responding to anybody's particular comments. But of course we will always care and make sure that to the maximum extent possible there will not be loss of lives of innocent people, wherever they live. That is what we are about.

Our effort is going to be targeted to these terrorists, targeted to their organization, targeted to their infrastructure. As many people have written in the papers, as Tom Friedman said today in the *New York Times*, which was right on the mark, and as I think Secretary Powell has been trying to say, our efforts will not be a single action, and may not be done right away. It is going to be a long, difficult struggle. I believe people in our country and in Minnesota are united in this, but we need to do this the smart way. We need to do this the right way.

THE RESPONSE TO TERRORISM
September 25, 2001

Madam President, I would like to, in ten minutes, cover three topics. First, I want to talk a little bit about September 11 and now. And I want to just say, in an ironic way—not bitterly ironic—the days I have had in Minnesota have maybe been some of the better days I have had because—and I am not putting words in anybody's mouth; and I do not do damage to the truth; I have too much respect for people, even when we disagree—most of the people with whom I have spoken back in Minnesota have said a couple things.

First of all, they have said we need to do a better job of defending ourselves. Who can disagree with that? Second of all, they have said— they have not been jingoistic; and they have not said we need to bomb now—we need to do this the right away. Many of them have expressed concern that we not let terrorists define our morality and that we should take every step possible to minimize the loss of life of innocent civilians in Afghanistan, or any other country, starting with innocent children. I am proud of people in Minnesota for saying that.

People in Minnesota have also said they understand this is not going to be one military action. They know this is going to be a long struggle. They know we are going to need a lot of cooperation from a lot of other countries. They think it should be international.

Above and beyond the way people come together to support each other, I am so impressed with the way I think people are really thinking deeply about this and want us to stay consistent with our own values as a nation. I just want to say that. That is my view.

I find myself kind of on two ends of the continuum. I had a discussion with some friends who were telling me that I should speak out more about the underlying conditions and causes of this violence, this hatred and violence. I told them there is a divide between us because I cannot do that because there are no conditions or explanations or justification for the mass murder of innocent people. I do not even like to talk about war because I do not think warriors murder people. Warriors are not involved in the slaughter of innocent people; criminals are.

A second point, which now gets closer to the defense authorization bill: On economic recovery, we have to really focus on economic security. I believe, and will always believe, we should have included assistance for employees in the package we passed last Friday.

I say to the senator from Massachusetts, when I went home to Minnesota, I heard about that. People were not bitterly angry, but they said: How could that happen to us and our families who are out of work? That has to be a priority, along with safety, to get help to employees.

I would argue, maybe it is a sequence; you can't do everything at one time. It is easier to give a speech than to actually do it. But above and beyond help for employees and employment benefits and making sure people can afford health care needs and making sure there is job training and dislocated worker funding and, I would argue, having to deal with some child care expenses, I want to say one other thing.

The truth is, I think we have to also think about an economic recovery package. And that should include, I say to my colleague from New Jersey, a workforce recovery package because not only are we going to need to extend the lifeline to people by way of helping them—when people are flat on their back, government helps them; that is what government is for—it is also true that that is part of an economic stimulus because you do not want to have a lot of people—people who work in hotels and restaurants and small businesspeople, all of whom now are really hurting—you do not want to have a whole lot of people shut down and not able to consume at all.

So we need to think about this package in broader terms as well.

Finally, on the defense authorization bill, if I had my own way, there are at least a couple of provisions I wish were in it. One of them Senator Levin worked so hard on, and other colleagues support it. It made it clear that if President Bush requested funding for missile defense tests that violated the ABM Treaty, he would need congressional approval to spend those funds. I wanted that language in this bill in the worst way. If I had time, I would argue over and over again, but I don't want to impose my own agenda on what our country is facing right now. But we need to reorder some of our priorities, and clearly more of the money—some of the money in this bill that I don't think we need for certain items I would put into homeland defense and helping families with economic security.

I think there are a lot of threats our country is faced with that come way before a rogue nation sending missiles our way by suitcase, by boat, by plane, chemical, biological—there are lots of other threats with a much higher priority. I wish we hadn't dropped that language. I understand that the majority leader and Senator Levin and others made a commitment that we will come back to that language and that provision.

I believe missile defense doesn't make the world more secure; it makes it less secure for our children, grandchildren, and for all God's children. I could argue that for the next five hours. I don't have five hours.

I congratulate senators on both sides of the aisle for the way in which we have worked together. We probably need each other as never before. There will be some sharp disagreement on policy issues—some of the issues that deal with education and health care, prescription drugs, you name it. Frankly, I am sure there will be questions many of us have as we go forward. But for right now, I want to just dissent on missile defense and say to my colleagues we need to get back to that debate. I think we are going to have to see more of an emphasis on priorities, including some of the money from some weapons systems that are not necessary to what we are talking about now by way of our own national security and homeland defense.

I say to Senator Levin and others, I appreciate the additional support for the armed services, especially when they are about to go into harm's way. I want to say to every senator that we did not do well for too many people in this package for the industry, which was necessary. I don't think the companies and CEOs were crying wolf, but we didn't help the employees, and the economic security of these working families has to be the next step, along with safety. That has to happen soon.

Finally, I believe we are going to have to have a broader workforce recovery bill as part of economic recovery legislation, as a part of how we deal with this recession in hard economic times, because there are a lot of other people who are really hurting right now. The government should be there to help people when they are flat on their backs through no fault of their own. That is going to be a big part of our work as well.

REFUGEE CRISIS IN AFGHANISTAN
October 1, 2001

Mr. President, I want to talk about an amendment that I hope will be part of the Defense authorization bill. But as long as we are talking about the resolution for a moment, I want to borrow from a piece I just finished writing. I will not go through the whole piece, but that which deals with the humanitarian catastrophe that is now taking place in Afghanistan. I think it is relevant to talk about this.

You have a situation on the ground that is unimaginable: four years of relentless drought, the worst in three decades, and the total failure of the

Taliban government to administer to the country. Four million people have abandoned their homes in search of food in Pakistan, Iran, and elsewhere. Those left behind now eat meals of locust and animal fodder. This is in Afghanistan.

Five million people inside this country are threatened by famine, according to the United Nations. As President Bush made clear, we are waging a campaign against terrorists, not ordinary Afghans—I think that is an important distinction to make—who are some of the poorest and most beleaguered people on the planet and who were actually our allies during the Cold War.

Any military action by our country must be targeted against those responsible for the terror acts and those harboring them. And we must plan such action to minimize the danger to innocent civilians who are on the edge of starvation.

Let me repeat that one more time. Any military action must be targeted against those who are responsible for the terror acts and those who have harbored them. And we must plan such action to minimize the danger to innocent civilians who are on the edge of starvation. And we must be prepared to address any humanitarian consequences of whatever action we take as soon as possible.

Mr. President, I ask unanimous consent that a piece that I just finished writing be printed in the *Record*.

There being no objection, the material was ordered to be printed in the *Record*, as follows:

U.S. Must Lead Efforts to Prevent Refugee Crisis in Afghanistan

by U.S. Senator Paul Wellstone, Chairman, Subcommittee on Near Eastern and South Asian Affairs, September 28, 2001.

The September 11 attacks in New York and Washington require our country to respond assertively and effectively against international terrorism. As the administration reviews all its options, it must consider the humanitarian consequences of any military action against terrorist sites in Afghanistan, and take urgent steps now to address them.

Even before the world focused on it as a sanctuary for Osama bin Laden and other terrorists, Afghanistan was on the brink of a humanitarian catastrophe, the site of the greatest crisis in hunger and refugee displacement in the world. Now the worsening situation on the ground is almost unimaginable. After four years of relentless drought, the worst in three decades, and the total failure of the Taliban government in administering the country, four million people have abandoned their homes in search of food in Pakistan, Iran, Tajikistan, and elsewhere, while those left behind eat meals of locusts and animal fodder. Five million people inside the country are threatened by famine, according to the United Nations.

As President Bush made clear, we are waging a campaign against terrorists, not ordinary Afghans, who are some of the poorest and most beleaguered people on the planet and were our allies during the Cold War. Any military action must thus be targeted against those responsible for the terror attacks and those harboring them; planned to minimize the danger to innocent civilians on the edge of starvation; and prepared to address any humanitarian consequences as soon as possible. Since it seems clear that a major international refugee influx will require a massive expansion of existing refugee camps, and creation of new ones, the U.S. and our U.N. Security Council allies should also be thinking now about how to protect those camps, including possibly using a U.N.-sanctioned military force drawn primarily from Arab nations.

Osama bin Laden is not a native of Afghanistan, but of Saudi Arabia. Most Afghans do not support bin Laden. Instead, ninety percent of the Afghan people are subsistence farmers struggling simply to grow enough food to stay alive. War widows, orphans, and thousands of others in the cities are dependent upon international aid to survive.

Now, anticipating military strikes by the U.S., hundreds of thousands of Afghan civilians are on the move, fleeing the cities for their native villages or for the borders. According to the U.N. High Commissioner for Refugees, nearly 20,000 have gathered at one Pakistani border crossing alone. The U.N. says it is the most tense border point in the world, with thousands of people out in the open, exposed to scorching days and frigid nights. Kandahar, the spiritual seat of the Taliban, is said to be "half empty." Those who are left behind are the most vulnerable—the elderly, orphans, war widows, and the mentally and physically disabled.

Inside Afghanistan, the U.N.'s World Food Programme (UNWFP) aid—much of it U.S.-donated wheat—is the sole source of food for millions. After the attacks on September 11th, the UNWFP was forced to pull out. It left two weeks of food stocks to be administered by local U.N. staff, but Taliban officials last Monday broke into the U.N. compound and stole thousands of tons of grain. Under intense international pressure, the UNWFP has announced it will resume shipments of grain to Afghanistan. Yet how it will be distributed is uncertain, as the Taliban has severed contact between international aid groups and their Afghan staffs, and taken over many of their facilities. To get needed aid in, and slow the outflow of Afghan refugees driven by a lack of food at home, the Pakistani government should immediately relax its border restrictions enough to allow the flow of food and other humanitarian aid into Afghanistan, while maintaining border security.

There is no easy solution to this building crisis, and yet our government must aggressively seek solutions to the critical needs of Afghan civilians. As one of its most urgent tasks, the

United States must do its part to shore up relief operations and help to again get aid flowing to refugees now. We also must prepare for an already critical situation to worsen as Afghanistan heads into its notoriously harsh winter. We must prepare now for huge numbers of refugees and humanitarian problems in the aftermath of military strikes, repositioning in the region the people and resources needed to deal with it.

The U.N. and several privately-funded aid groups are working frantically to set up new camps and bring in supplies and personnel to sites along the border. And yet, developing a stronger response to a massive outflow of Afghans into Pakistan is sure to put pressure on already over-burdened camps, and by extension Pakistani resources and patience. Pakistan is already host to over a million refugees from Afghanistan; 170,000 came as a result of recent drought in Afghanistan. Others fled earlier and have been in Pakistan for years.

The United States must do everything it can now to alleviate the suffering of ordinary Afghan civilians. We have agreed to participate in U.N. efforts to raise quickly almost $600 million in aid funds, a number likely to grow. We should be leading that effort, including by contributing substantially. The U.S. and our allies cannot afford to be indifferent to this humanitarian crisis, especially as we seek to build a coalition of moderate Arab and non-Arab Muslims around the globe for our anti-terror efforts. If a humanitarian catastrophe in Afghanistan is attributed to our military operations, it will weaken international support for our fight against terrorism, and may even make the American people more vulnerable in the end.

THE IRAQ WAR

> "The problem is that the actual resolution before us goes in a different direction. What this resolution does is give the president the authority for a possible go-it-alone, unilateral military strike and ground war. I think this would be a mistake. We should not go it alone." ~Senator Paul Wellstone, October 8, 2002

On January 29, 2002, President Bush gave his second State of the Union address. In this speech, he famously identified North Korea, Iran, and Iraq as the "axis of evil." President Bush further stated that Iraq has plotted to develop anthrax, and nerve gas, and nuclear weapons for over a decade: "This is a regime that agreed to international inspections—then kicked out the inspectors. This is a regime that has something to hide from the civilized world."

Weapons of mass destruction and the imminent threat Iraq posed to the United States was a cornerstone of the argument in favor of invading and overthrowing Iraqi President Saddam Hussein. Administration officials repeatedly warned that, although there will always be uncertainty, they did not want to wait for the "smoking gun to be a mushroom cloud."

The connection between Iraq and al-Qaeda was also one of the primary reasons for invading Iraq. Then-National Security Advisor Condoleeza Rice stated in an interview just a week before the United States Senate voted on whether to authorize the war:

No one is trying to make an argument at this point that Saddam Hussein somehow had operational control of what happened on September 11, so we don't want to push this too far, but this is a story that is unfolding, and it is getting clear, and we're learning more. We're learning more because we have a lot of detainees who are able to fill in pieces of the puzzle. And when the picture is clear, we'll make full disclosure about it. But, yes, there clearly are contacts between al-Qaida and Iraq that can be documented. There clearly is testimony that some of these contacts have been important contacts and there's a relationship here.

After the invasion, weapons of mass destruction were not found, and there has been extensive discussion related to whether intelligence officials in the United States and Great Britain were pressured to "hype" security reports and the imminence of an Iraqi threat. The connection between Iraq and al-Qaeda has also been largely dismissed. At the time of Senator Wellstone's vote against the war in Iraq, however, military action had popular support. Senator Wellstone was in fierce campaign for a third-term, and he was the only senator facing re-election to vote against the resolution. It was also one of his last major speeches, if not the last.

IRAQ
October 3, 2002

Madam President, I rise to address our policy in Iraq. The situation remains fluid. Administration officials are engaged in negotiations at the United Nations over what approach we ought to take with our allies to disarm the brutal and dictatorial Iraqi regime.

The debate we will have in the Senate today and in the days to follow is critical because the administration seeks our authorization now for military action, including possibly unprecedented, preemptive, go-it-alone military action in Iraq, even as it seeks to garner support from our allies on a new U.N. disarmament resolution.

Let me be clear: Saddam Hussein is a brutal, ruthless dictator who has repressed his own people, attacked his neighbors, and he remains an international outlaw. The world would be a much better place if he were gone and the regime in Iraq were changed. That is why the United States should unite the world against Saddam and not allow him to unite forces against us.

A go-it-alone approach, allowing a ground invasion of Iraq without the support of other countries, could give Saddam exactly that chance. A preemptive, go-it-alone strategy toward Iraq is wrong. I oppose it. I support ridding Iraq of weapons of mass destruction through unfettered U.N. inspections which would begin as soon as possible. Only a broad coalition of nations, united to disarm Saddam, while preserving our war on terror, is likely to succeed.

Our primary focus now must be on Iraq's verifiable disarmament of weapons of mass destruction. This will help maintain international support and could even eventually result in Saddam's loss of power. Of course, I would welcome this, along with most of our allies.

The president has helped to direct intense new multilateral pressure on Saddam Hussein to allow U.N. and International Atomic Energy Agency weapons inspectors back in Iraq to conduct their assessment of Iraq's chemical, biological, and nuclear programs. He clearly has felt that heat. It suggests what can be accomplished through collective action.

I am not naive about this process. Much work lies ahead. But we cannot dismiss out of hand Saddam's late and reluctant commitment to comply with U.N. disarmament arrangements or the agreement struck Tuesday to begin to implement them. We should use the gathering international resolve to collectively confront this regime by building on these efforts.

This debate must include all Americans because our decisions finally must have the informed consent of the American people who will be asked to bear the cost, in blood and treasure, of our decisions.

When the lives of sons and daughters of average Americans could be risked and lost, their voices must be heard in the Congress before we make decisions about military action. Right now, despite a desire to support our president, I believe many Americans still have profound questions about the wisdom of relying too heavily on a preemptive go-it-alone military approach. Acting now on our own might be a sign of our power. Acting sensibly and in a measured way, in concert with our allies, with bipartisan congressional support, would be a sign of our strength.

It would also be a sign of the wisdom of our founders who lodged in the president the power to command U.S. Armed Forces, and in Congress the power to make war, ensuring a balance of powers between coequal branches of government. Our Constitution lodges the power to weigh the causes of war and the ability to declare war in Congress precisely to ensure that the American people and those who represent them will be consulted before military action is taken.

The Senate has a grave duty to insist on a full debate that examines for all Americans the full range of options before us and weighs those options, together with their risks and costs. Such a debate should be energized by the real spirit of September 11, a debate which places a priority not on unanimity but on the unity of a people determined to forcefully confront and defeat terrorism and to defend our values.

I have supported internationally sanctioned coalition military action in Bosnia, in Kosovo, in Serbia, and in Afghanistan. Even so, in recent weeks, I and others—including major Republican policymakers, such as former Bush National Security Adviser Brent Scowcroft; former Bush Secretary of State James Baker; my colleague on the Senate Foreign Relations Committee, Senator Chuck Hagel; Bush Mid-East envoy General Anthony Zinni; and other leading U.S. military leaders—have raised serious questions about the approach the administration is taking on Iraq.

There have been questions raised about the nature and urgency of Iraq's threat and our response to that threat: What is the best course of action that the United States could take to address this threat? What are the economic, political, and national security consequences of a possible U.S. or allied invasion of Iraq? There have been questions raised about the consequences of our actions abroad, including its effect on the continuing war on terrorism, our ongoing efforts to stabilize and rebuild Afghanistan, and efforts to calm the intensifying Middle East crises, especially the Israeli-Palestinian conflict.

There have been questions raised about the consequences of our actions here at home. Of gravest concern, obviously, are the questions raised about the possible loss of life that could result from our actions. The United States could post tens of thousands of troops in Iraq and, in so doing, risk countless lives of soldiers and innocent Iraqis.

There are other questions about the impact of an attack in relation to our economy. The United States could face soaring oil prices and could spend billions both on a war and a years-long effort to stabilize Iraq after an invasion.

The resolution that will be before the Senate explicitly authorizes a go-it-alone approach. I believe an international approach is essential. In my view, our policy should have four key elements.

First and foremost, the United States must work with our allies to deal with Iraq. We should not go it alone, or virtually alone, with a preemptive ground invasion. Most critically, acting alone could jeopardize our top national priority, the continuing war on terror. I believe it would be a mistake to vote for a resolution that authorizes a preemptive ground invasion. The intense cooperation of other nations in relation to matters that deal with intelligence sharing, security, political and economic cooperation, law enforcement, and financial surveillance, and other areas is crucial to this fight, and this is what is critical for our country to be able to wage its war effectively with our allies. Over the past year, this cooperation has been the most successful weapon against terrorist networks. That—not attacking Iraq—should be the main focus of our efforts in the war on terror.

As I think about what a go-it-alone strategy would mean in terms of the consequences in South Asia and the Near East and the need for our country to have access on the ground, and cooperation of the community, and get intelligence in the war against al-Qaida and in this war against terrorism, I believe a go-it-alone approach could undercut that effort. That is why I believe our effort should be international.

We have succeeded in destroying some al-Qaida forces, but many operatives have scattered. Their will to kill Americans is still strong. The United States has relied heavily on alliances with nearly 100 countries in a coalition against terror for critical intelligence to protect Americans from possible future attacks. Acting with the support of allies, including, hopefully, Arab and Muslim allies, would limit possible damage to that coalition and our antiterrorism effort. But as General Wes Clark, former supreme commander of Allied Forces in Europe, has recently noted, a premature, go-it-alone invasion of Iraq "would supercharge recruiting for al-Qaida."

Second, our efforts should have a goal of disarming Saddam Hussein of all his weapons of mass destruction. Iraq agreed to destroy its weapons of mass destruction at the end of the Persian Gulf War and to verification by the U.N. and the International Atomic Energy Agency that this had been done. According to the U.N. and the IAEA, and undisputed by the administration, inspections during the 1990s neutralized a substantial portion of Iraq's weapons of mass destruction, and getting inspectors back to finish the job is critical. We know he did not cooperate with all of the inspection regime.

We know what needs to be done. But the fact is we had that regime, and it is important now to call on the Security Council of the U.N. to insist that those inspectors be on the ground. The goal is disarmament, unfettered access. It is an international effort, and with that Saddam Hussein must comply. Otherwise, there will be consequences, including appropriate use of force. The prompt resumption of inspections and disarmament, under an expedited timetable and with unfettered access in Iraq, is imperative.

Third, weapons inspections should be enforceable. If efforts by the U.N. weapons inspectors

are tried and fail, a range of potential U.N. sanctions means, including proportionate military force, should be considered. I have no doubt that this Congress would act swiftly to authorize force in such circumstances. This does not mean giving the United Nations a veto over U.S. actions. Nobody wants to do that. It simply means, as Chairman Levin has observed, that Saddam Hussein is a world problem and should be addressed in the world arena.

Finally, our approach toward Iraq must be consistent with international law and the framework of collective security developed over the last fifty years or more. It should be sanctioned by the Security Council under the U.N. charter, to which we are a party and by which we are legally bound. Only a broad coalition of nations, united to disarm Saddam Hussein, while preserving our war on terror, can succeed.

Our response will be far more effective if Saddam Hussein sees the whole world arrayed against him. We should act forcefully, resolutely, sensibly, with our allies—and not alone—to disarm Saddam Hussein. Authorizing the preemptive go-alone use of force right now, which is what the resolution before us calls for, in the midst of continuing efforts to enlist the world community to back a tough, new disarmament resolution on Iraq, could be a very costly mistake for our country.

Madam President, quite often at the end of debates on amendments, we thank our staffs for the work they have done and appreciate their hard work.

At the end of my statement today on the floor of the Senate as to why I am opposed to the resolution before us that we will be debating today and in the days to come, which is too open-ended and would provide the president with authority for preemptive military action, including a ground invasion in Iraq, I would like to thank my staff. I would like to thank my staff for never trying one time to influence me to make any other decision than what I honestly and truthfully believe is right for the state I represent, Minnesota, for my country, and for the world in which my children and my grandchildren live. To all of my staff, I thank you for believing in me.

VOTING AGAINST AUTHORIZATION OF THE USE OF UNITED STATES ARMED FORCES AGAINST IRAQ

October 8, 2002

Mr. President, I rise to speak for a short time today about the Iraq resolution, and tomorrow I will have a chance to speak at greater length. I thank Senator Kennedy for allowing me to precede him. I also tell my colleague from Georgia that his speech on the concurrent receipt was powerful and, having spent the whole day with veterans yesterday, is absolutely right. It is critically important that this defense appropriations bill go through with that provision.

Mr. President, I did not have a chance to hear the president speak last night, but I read the transcript. I think it is important that the president focus on obtaining international support. The military option should only be considered as the last option. I believe that people were glad to hear that last night in Minnesota and in the country.

The problem is that the actual resolution before us goes in a different direction. What this resolution does is give the president the authority for a possible go-it-alone, unilateral military strike and ground war. I think this would be a mistake. We should not go it alone.

There is a critical distinction between going it alone and taking action in conjunction with our allies. Our focus should be going to the United Nations Security Council and asking for a resolution that makes it clear to Saddam Hussein that he

must disarm. Saddam must give arms inspectors unfettered access. And, if he does not comply with this new U.N. resolution there will be consequences, including the use of appropriate military force. But we must do this together with our allies. We must bring the international community on board. This resolution allows for a preemptive, unilateral strike, which I believe would be a huge mistake.

When secretaries Kissinger and Albright testified before the Foreign Relations Committee, I asked both of them about the consequences of going alone versus working with the international community. First I asked: Shouldn't the goal be disarmament, and shouldn't we make every effort to try to make disarmament happen before taking military action?

They both were in agreement. Secretary Kissinger said: Yes, we need to play this out.

No one trusts Saddam Hussein. Everybody knows he is a brutal dictator. That is not the point. The point is how to proceed, how to do this the right way. The focus should be on disarmament and getting the support of our allies in the international community.

I do not think we should be approving a preemptive, unilateral strike by the United States, going it alone, or only with Great Britain.

I asked the former secretaries what the differences would be. They spelled out hugely different consequences between our going it alone, if, in fact, military action was necessary, versus taking action with our allies.

The former secretaries made the following points. If we take unilateral military action Saddam Hussein we will have a better chance of uniting the world community against us, rather than vice versa. Moreover, there could be grave consequences in the Near East and South Asia that could include energizing other radical elements and increasing support for al-Qaida. Would this not play into the hands of the radicals? This is a big question if we go it alone.

What about our men and women, our sons and daughters who would be put in harm's way? What would the consequences be on the ground for them if we go it alone versus with our allies?

What about this war against terror? As a father and grandfather of six children I take al-Qaida very seriously. Unfortunately international terror is a part of the world in which we now live. Will we have the same international cooperation to fight international terror if we go it alone? In many parts of the world we need the cooperation, assets, and on-the-ground intelligence of our allies for the continued war on terror. I think going it alone, a preemptive military strike, perhaps a ground war, could very well undercut that effort.

Mr. President, I have one more point. I am not going to talk at length about my interaction with people in Minnesota over the last several days since I announced my opposition to the first resolution, but I will tell my colleagues this: Many people have come up to me, and I had great discussions with people in Minnesota. I cannot thank them enough.

I do not really know what the breakdown is in terms of X percentage this way or that way, but I will say that the people in Minnesota and our country are worried about this issue. They are worried about us going it alone. They are worried about what might happen to our sons and daughters in Iraq. They far prefer we work together with our allies. They far prefer we have international support and that the focus be on disarmament.

I believe that is the direction in which we should go. That is not what this resolution before us asks us to do. Therefore, I will vote no on this resolution.

REMEMBERING SENATOR WELLSTONE

> "Now we must continue Paul's journey for justice in America."
>
> —Senator Tom Harkin (D-Iowa), October 29, 2002

STATEMENT FROM SENATOR PAUL WELLSTONE'S STAFF

October 26, 2002

Yesterday morning Senator Paul Wellstone, Sheila Wellstone, and Marcia Wellstone, along with Will McLaughlin, Tom Lapic, and Mary McEvoy of our campaign staff were traveling on a plane flown by Captains Richard Conroy and Michael Guess in northern Minnesota. The Department of Transportation confirmed that the identification number on the tail of the plane that went down southeast of Eveleth, Minnesota, matched the serial number of Senator Wellstone's plane. There were no survivors.

We are shocked and saddened by this horrible news. Our thoughts and prayers are with the family and friends of those who were on the plane.

This is an unspeakable loss of a leader and mentor we loved, and of friends and colleagues who were dear to us. The overwhelming number of messages we have received since the crash is a tribute to the kind of person Paul was: a passionate visionary who never gave up hope that we could make the world a better place for everyone,

a committed fighter for social justice who gave a voice to the voiceless, a man with a huge heart who lit up a room-and the hearts of others when he walked in.

He was a man who valued others for who they were, not where they came from, or what they wore, or their position or social status. We who had the privilege of working with him are confident that he will be remembered as he lived every day: as a champion for people.

We will miss Paul and Sheila and our friends and colleagues dearly. And we will remember them, fittingly, by picking up their banner and holding it high, in our work and in our lives.

STATEMENT FROM CONGRESSMAN JIM RAMSTAD (R-MINNESOTA)

(October 25, 2002)

I am completely overwhelmed by sadness at the tragic death of Paul, Sheila, and Marcia Wellstone and the others who perished. I join all Minnesotans in mourning our great loss. Minnesota has lost two compassionate and caring public servants. Nobody fought harder for the underdog than Paul and Sheila Wellstone.

Senator Paul Wellstone dedicated his life to serving others—and he was a passionate advocate for people in need. Sheila Wellstone was a true champion for battered women and their families. Both Paul and Sheila will be missed by all of us who knew and loved them.

I have lost my good friend and partner in the fight for people with chemical addiction and will always be grateful to Senator Wellstone for his tireless efforts to provide chemical dependency treatment for more Americans.

My heart goes out to the family members left behind and to Paul's dedicated staff.

DEATH OF PAUL WELLSTONE, A SENATOR FROM THE STATE OF MINNESOTA
October 28, 2002
Senator Mark Dayton (D-Minnesota)

Mr. President, I ask that the Senate observe a moment of silence in tribute to Senator Wellstone and his family. (Moment of silence.) Mr. President, it is with a profoundly heavy heart that I rise today to present this resolution honoring my colleague, Paul Wellstone. This is not the occasion in this brief session for eulogies. There will be other opportunities on the Senate floor for all of us to share our memories and our perspectives.

For myself, I cannot begin to do Paul justice in a few minutes or even a few hours. He was such an extraordinary, such a remarkable man, and he brought so much life and enthusiasm and passion and commitment to the public life he lived, and he touched so many thousands of Minnesotans and others across this country who mourn his loss as we do here today.

He died fearlessly, as he lived his life. In the resolution that was just read, the words "never wavered from the principles" will be words that I

will always associate with Paul Wellstone. He never ever blinked in the face of adversity. Courageous, difficult, perhaps at times unpopular positions were articles of faith for Paul because he believed in them.

It was not about polls. It was not about pundits. It was about the conviction he had about what was right for people, for his fellow citizens.

He was unpretentious, unassuming, just himself. He was no different as a senator than as a man, than as a political activist all in one. He was extraordinary, and he will never be replaced. In the hearts and minds of Minnesotans, he will never be forgotten.

Yet, Mr. President, he loved this institution. He respected enormously the traditions, the men and women who served here. They came to respect him for the courage of his convictions. I could see in the course of the two years I have shared with him in the Senate that he was respected by people who did not agree with him because they knew he was speaking from his heart, that he was speaking from his soul, that he was speaking what he truly believed.

One could ask for no more, no less from any of us than the strength of our convictions and our willingness to speak out about them regardless of political cost.

Paul and his wife, Sheila, at his side for thirty-nine years, died last Friday together, as they would have wanted it to be, not with their daughter, Marcia, who also was on that flight and three of their devoted aides and two pilots. It is an unspeakable tragedy and horror for all of us in Minnesota, but it will be for all of us, on behalf of Paul, to take a deep breath and carry on in behalf of our convictions and our causes—as he would want us to do.

I thank the Senate for this resolution on behalf of Paul. And for his two surviving sons, David and Mark, and their families I know it will be of solace to them in their hours of terrible grief.

Mr. President, I yield to my colleague, the Senator from California.

Senator Barbara Boxer (D-California)

Thank you very much, Mr. President. Senator Dayton, your remarks were beautiful, and Paul would have been so pleased to hear your tone and your spirit. And I can tell you, Senator Dayton, how much he loved you, how proud he was to have you here by his side.

Mr. President, I have flown in from California to be here on the Senate floor today to make just a few remarks about our dear friend and colleague, Senator Paul Wellstone. I want to start by reading two paragraphs written by his loyal and hardworking staff. After his plane went down, and they learned the worst, they wrote the following:

> Paul Wellstone was one of a kind. He was a man of principle and conviction, in a world that has too little of either. He was dedicated to helping the little guy, in a business dominated by the big guys. We who had the privilege of working with him hope that he will be remembered as he lived every day: as a champion for people.
>
> His family was the center of his life and it breaks our hearts that his wife of thirty-nine years and his daughter Marcia were with him. Our prayers are with Mark and David and the grandchildren he and Sheila cherished so much.

That was posted on the Wellstone Web site by Senator Wellstone's staff.

Mr. President, Senator Dayton, for me, the loss of Paul Wellstone cuts very deep. Kind, compassionate, self-deprecating, a passionate voice for those without a voice, enthusiastic, a bundle of energy—this was a unique man of the people.

When we learned that the tragedy of Paul's death was magnified by the death of the two women he cherished so much—his wife, Sheila,

and his daughter, Marcia—the wounds in our hearts cut deeper still, plus the loss of three staffers—Tom Lapic, Will McLaughlin, and Mary McEvoy—and the two pilots—Captains Richard Conroy and Michael Guess.

Mr. President, no words—no words—can possibly ease the pain of all the family members who were touched by this tragedy. No words can ease the pain of David and Mark, Paul's two sons, and their families. All we can do is let them know that we pray that they have the strength to endure this time for the sake of the Wellstone grandchildren: Cari, Keith, Joshua, Acacia, Sydney, and Matt. Let the record show that your grandchildren brought endless joy to you. And we say to the grandchildren, thank you for the joy that you gave to grandma and grandpa.

I want to say to the people of Minnesota, thank you, thank you for sending Paul to us, for sharing Paul with us these past twelve years. He loved the people of his state: the farmers, the workers, the children, the elderly, the sick, the disabled, the families. He fought for you all, so long and so hard, without stopping, in committees and subcommittees, in the Democratic caucus meetings, when he would get up and say: Just give me thirty seconds—just thirty seconds—to make my point about the people of Minnesota. He stood up at press conferences. He would grab senators, one by one, and fight for you, the people of Minnesota, who were always in his thoughts and on his mind. And I know he is now in your thoughts and on your minds.

In my own state of California—so many thousands of miles away from Minnesota—there are memorial services being set up for Paul. You see, his compassionate voice reached thousands of miles, and many people in my state are sending me condolence notes and flowers because they know how much I will miss working with Paul Wellstone, and so will all senators on both sides of the aisle.

As Mark said, Paul was never afraid to speak out when it might be unpopular, nor was he afraid to be on the losing side of a Senate vote. He had courage. And when you told him that, when you said: "Paul, you have courage," he shrugged it off. He would say something like: "What else could I do? It's just not right!" He would say that—determined, brave.

You see, Paul Wellstone could not vote against his conscience or for something he did not believe was in the best interest of the people he represented. He couldn't; he wouldn't—no matter what the consequences.

He cared about the underdog always. He cared about the victim always. He cared about peace always. And Paul, blessed are the peacemakers. Paul, blessed are the peacemakers.

Paul was a humble man. When his longtime staffer, Mike Epstein, died—and many of us knew Mike—Paul took to the Senate floor, and this is what he said, in part:

> Mike, I know you will not like me saying this, but I'm going to say it anyway because it's true. I believe from the bottom of my heart that everything I've been able to do as a Senator that has been good for Minnesota and the country is because, Mike, you have been right by my side, one inch away from me.

And he said: Mike was my tutor. He was my teacher. He was teaching me.

That was Paul Wellstone. He never bragged about himself. He loved his family so much. He loved his staff. He took time for all the Senate employees: the young people who work with us, the officers who protect us, the food service people, the elevator operators—all the Senate family, no matter what their status.

Mr. President, he wanted to give everyone—everyone he touched—his sense of optimism, his energy, his strength.

When Paul learned he had multiple sclerosis, I worried and I said to him: Are you okay? He said: I probably had it for a long time. I'm just not going to think about it. And off he went in his usual rush. There was so much to do. Off he went to his desk in the Senate, his desk now incredibly shrouded in black.

Paul loved that aisle desk. It gave him a bird's eye view of the Senate that he loved. And when he spoke from his desk, he could come out from behind it. He could leave his notes behind—arms gesturing, voice determined—and talk from his heart. He would say something like: I don't represent big business or big anything. He would say: I represent the people of Minnesota. And that he did every minute of his all-too-short life.

As our session wound down, Paul wanted to finish our business and go home. He told us all: I want to be with my people. I need to touch them. I need to look them in the eye. I can't wait to get home.

Paul was a powerful man. His power did not come from his physical stature. He was strong but he was slight of build. His power did not come from generations of family wealth. He was not a man of moneyed wealth. His parents were immigrants: Leon and Minnie Wellstone. His power did not come from political connections. His connections were with regular people.

Let me tell you from where his power came. It came from a fierce dedication to justice and truth and honesty and righteousness. He gave comfort and he gave hope to those he touched. And he gave them some of his power—the power to see the possibilities of their own lives. Paul died on his way to give comfort and hope to those facing death. He was flying to a funeral service.

Today we say to Paul: We will give comfort

and hope to those you have left behind by doing all that we can to continue your legacy and your dream. Together, we can build an America of fairness, of justice, of prosperity, a world of tolerance and a world of peace. And, Paul, may you and yours rest in peace forever.

I yield the floor.

Senator Patrick Leahy (D-Vermont)

Mr. President, I thank the senator from Minnesota and the senator from California for their words. I know and respect both the Senator from Minnesota, Senator Dayton, and the senator from California, Senator Boxer. I know them well enough to know this was a very painful moment for both of them—just as it is for the distinguished presiding officer and as it is for the senator from Vermont.

Mr. President, you and I have been here a long time in the Senate. With the senator from Minnesota, who is now—not at his choice—the senior senator from Minnesota, and the senator from California, I think we can all say that there is no sadder sight than coming on the floor and seeing a black drape on a senator's desk. The distinguished presiding officer and I have unfortunately seen that many times in our careers, for senators on both sides of the aisle. In every instance when we have entered the chamber and seen the black drape we know that there has been a death in the family.

We are privileged in this body, one hundred men and women—now ninety-nine men and women—to represent the greatest nation on Earth, a nation of a quarter of a billion people. But because there are only one hundred of us, no matter our political differences, when one is lost we all feel it. When I heard the news in Vermont, I was at a restaurant in Burlington with my son, Kevin. It was a small restaurant. There was a TV

going but with no sound. My back was to it. I saw the look of shock on Kevin's face. He spun me around, and I saw the news. We both left that restaurant in tears. The news spread quickly and as I walked down the street people—many of them I never met before—just came up and hugged me because they, too, lost somebody.

Paul Wellstone had come to Vermont and was greeted with great warmth. I vividly remember the evening he came to speak. Everybody came up to him. They didn't want him to leave. Paul Wellstone, like one of his predecessors, my dear friend, Hubert Humphrey, was a happy warrior. If people wanted to talk with him, he did not mind and would stay, the same way Hubert would have.

There is an affinity, I believe, between our state of Vermont and Minnesota. That is why there was a bond Vermonters felt with Paul Wellstone. Paul could sense it. And, we worked on many important issues as a team. During the recent farm bill debate he met with Vermont farmers and together we drafted a dairy provision that was beneficial to both of our states. I remember when he and Jim Jeffords and Bernie Sanders and I joined together to have a milk toast. We were joking around. Paul was not a tall man. I playfully stood blocking him from the cameras. And he said: "Hey, remember, I'm a wrestler," at which point I quickly moved aside.

Of course Paul was far more than a wrestler —but it is easy to make the correlation to the way he wrestled with issues here on the floor. He wrestled them down. I thought to myself: What a man to have on your side. What a man to be a friend.

Paul Wellstone served with powerful people but he was not intimidated by that. And, he never took on the airs of one who was powerful. He would introduce himself to people: Hi, I'm Paul Wellstone. And someone else would have to say: That's a U.S. senator.

I never went on an elevator with Paul without him calling the elevator operator by name. He would talk with the pages and give them tutorials. He knew everybody in the Senate and they knew and loved him.

It is impossible to talk about our colleague Paul Wellstone without mentioning Sheila Wellstone. They were inseparable. Whenever the Senate would have a late-night session Sheila would be in the galleries, waiting for Paul to leave.

Of all my memories of Paul Wellstone, the one I may remember the most is the last time I saw the two of them. It was a late night session. You know these gorgeous halls we have, with the chandeliers and everything else, and here is this couple walking hand in hand down one of the halls about midnight—Paul and Sheila Wellstone. I came around the corner and I said: "Hey, you teenagers," and they laughed and hugged each other. I saw them go out, down the steps into the night, hand in hand.

Let us hope that they have gone hand and hand into the light and that they are now together.

Marcella and I also extend our thoughts and prayers to Marcia, Paul and Sheila's daughter, and her family. And, as the Senate noted in the resolution that was just passed a few moments ago, we all grieve for the Wellstone staff who were on board the plane: Tom Lapic, Mary McEvoy and Will McLaughlin. Our thoughts and prayer are with their families in these trying times. Our condolences also go out to the families of the pilots on the plane, Richard Conry and Michael Guess.

Senator Christopher Dodd (D-Connecticut)

Madam President, first let me express my thanks to our colleague from Minnesota, Senator Dayton, and express our sympathies to him and through him to the people of Minnesota and to the Wellstone family, the extended family, for all that they are suffering in this particular time, and to express my grati-

tude as well to my colleague from California, Senator Boxer, and my colleague from Vermont, Senator Leahy, for their very moving and emotional remarks. I think they captured to a large extent the sentiments of all of us.

This is a difficult time. I suppose the American people see we are in session and wonder why only a few of us are here. Obviously, with a week to go before the congressional elections, not many are here in Washington. But suffice it to say, were ninety-six or ninety-seven other senators here today, you would hear much the same sentiments that have been expressed already by the now-senior senator from Minnesota, the senator from California, and the senator from Vermont.

So I join my colleagues, and all Americans, in mourning the very tragic and sudden loss of our dear friend and colleague, Senator Paul Wellstone, who will be forever remembered as a friend and patriot and true public servant, who fought each and every day of his public life—in fact, of his life—to improve the lives of average Americans. We got to know him here over the last ten or eleven years as a member of the U.S. Senate, but the people of Minnesota and the people of Carleton College, students who had him as a professor, people who knew him beforehand, they knew that Paul Wellstone didn't just become a fighter when he arrived in the Senate of the United States. He dedicated his life to it. It is what his parents taught him. It is what he believed in passionately as an American. We became witnesses to that sense of passion and outrage about wrongs in this country and around the world as we served with our colleague, Paul Wellstone, for the last decade.

So, like my colleagues, I was stunned and deeply saddened by the enormous scope and tragedy of this loss. Obviously, the entire Wellstone family has suffered an unfathomable loss, as have the families of other victims of this horrendous accident.

His wife, Sheila—I join my colleagues in expressing our deep sense of loss. Sometimes, although we get to know members, we don't get to know the spouses of our colleagues very well, but Sheila Wellstone really became a member of the Senate family aside from being a spouse. She was an unpaid volunteer in her husband's office.

If there are women today who are suffering less because of domestic violence—and they are many who are not, but many who are—you can thank some colleagues here. But I suspect one of the reasons they became so motivated about the issue was because there was a person by the name of Sheila Wellstone who arrived here a decade ago and wanted to make this a matter of the business of the U.S. Senate.

So they became partners, not just over the almost forty years of love and affection for each other, but partners in their sense of idealism, sense of values, and sense of purpose.

Marcia I did not know very well but certainly heard Paul and Sheila talk abut her with great admiration and affection. In the loss suffered by her family, with young children, it is just difficult to even come up with the words to express the sense of grief that I feel for her and her family. And obviously the staff: Will McLaughlin, Tom Lapic, and Mary McEvoy, along with the pilots who have been mentioned already: Richard Conry and Michael Guess, we didn't know, but I suspect on that flight up there they had gotten to know the Wellstone family and the staff. And so we want to express our deep sense of loss to their families.

I ask unanimous consent to have printed at the end of my remarks a wonderful editorial by David Rosenbaum in the *New York Times* on Saturday which I thought captured perfectly the image of Paul Wellstone, who he was and what he tried to do, better than any words I could possibly express here today.

Madam President, William Shakespeare once wrote, "No legacy is so rich as honesty." I have never met, let alone worked with, a more honest or noble man than Paul Wellstone.

His rich, rich legacy will be that of an honest, passionate and tireless fighter on behalf of justice and fairness for all Americans, especially those less fortunate than himself.

Paul suffered a lot. He had this bad back. He would hobble around. He had this gait that if you didn't know he was hurting was almost an affectionate gait. He sort of limped around at various times; he would stand a lot at times in meetings because sitting would be so painful for him as a result of injuries he suffered. He had MS which he sort of shrugged off, as my colleague from California said. He grew up in a situation where his family were immigrants who came from Russia. They grew up actually in Arlington, Virginai, a short distance from here. A former staff member of mine was a neighbor of theirs. He knew Paul as a child growing up. They had their own burdens to bear aside from being immigrants, problems of those newly arriving, with the language barriers. Trying to get acclimated to a new society such as ours is not easy. So Paul understood the issues of those who suffered more than in just an intellectual effort. This was something he deeply felt and had grown up with and appreciated immensely.

When he came to this body and we got to know him as someone who would fight tirelessly on behalf of those who did not have lawyers, lobbyists, and others to express their concerns, to bring their issues to the debate of the Senate, we found in this individual just a remarkable voice and a remarkable fight. Like many of my colleagues, I might be home or completed the evening and turned on the television and the Senate would still be in session, and there would be Paul Wellstone, standing at that desk in the rear of this chamber, speaking to an empty place except for the millions of Americans tuned in to C-SPAN who would hear someone talking about subjects that were affecting their lives.

Single moms, working families, children without health care, the homeless, international victims of torture—these were among Senator Paul Wellstone's core constituencies, and they could not have had a better spokesperson.

A lot of times we spend days here talking about issues that might seem terribly arcane to the average citizen in this country, matters that don't seem terribly relevant to their daily lives, and yet Paul Wellstone never let a day go by that he didn't give voice to the concerns of average Americans or those who are, as Hubert Humphrey would talk about, in the shadows of life or the dawn of life or the dusk of life—Paul Wellstone giving voice, that great Minnesota voice to those who needed to have their concerns raised in chambers such as this. And so for all of those people who are wondering today whether or not their concerns, their hopes, their fears will find expression, it is hard to find any silver lining with the passage of someone you care about so much, but I suspect as we reconvene here on November 12 and again with a new Congress coming in in January we will hear the words of Paul Wellstone repeated quite frequently. We will hear the passion that he brought to the issues raised maybe more frequently than they otherwise might be. That's because we will remember an individual we had the privilege and honor of serving with who reminded this institution of what its role ought to be, not just to those who are well heeled, those who can afford to acquire the access, but those who need to have their issues raised—that their concerns and their worries, their hopes, their dreams for this country and their own families will be once again a part of the mainstream of debate in the Senate.

Paul Wellstone fought some awfully tough battles. He fought a tough battle to get here, a man who was told he could not possibly get elected to the Senate, who was being outspent by overwhelming odds.

I rode with him in that bus—I am sure my colleague from Minnesota, maybe my colleagues from California and Vermont remember—that rattly old green bus, in the freezing cold, bitter cold, cold months of Minnesota. I remember going with him to some big fair or festival that he was holding on behalf of poor farmers and family farmers in Minnesota. Just a few weeks ago, Madam President, I campaigned with him in Minnesota, with some of the medical-device companies around Minneapolis and St. Paul. This was supposed to be about a twenty-minute meeting we were going to have at one of these firms to talk about the medical devices that Paul played a major role in working to see to it that they were going to become a reality for people who would use them. We were supposed to leave in fifteen or twenty minutes but the room was packed; the people wanted to talk about other things. And Paul Wellstone stayed for about one and one-half hours just engaging with the people in this room. They went far beyond the medical device issues. The people in that room wanted to talk about health care; they wanted to talk about education; they wanted to talk about the environment; they wanted to talk about prescription drugs and the elderly; they wanted to talk about issues affecting Native Americans and minority groups; they wanted to talk about foreign policy. And he engaged, engaged and engaged for an hour and a half. He would have stayed longer. Staff had to almost drag him out of the room. But it was so reflective, standing in the back of the room watching Paul Wellstone with great passion and clarity expressing where he stood.

He didn't sit there and try to figure out

where the question was coming from based on the tilt of their rhetoric. He answered them how he felt as their senator, their representative, so they would know where he stood.

Madam President, I apologize for sort of meandering here, but it is how I feel. I have a great sense of loss and also a sense of joy. Paul Wellstone had a great sense of humor. He cared deeply about issues, but he also had the wonderful ability to laugh at himself, to appreciate the humor that only this institution can provide in some of the more bizarre moments, a wonderful relationship with virtually everyone here. It didn't happen automatically or initially. Paul came here determined to change the world; if not the world, change the United States; if not that, maybe his Minnesota. Along the way and in the process he probably rubbed some people the wrong way, but those very people became the people who cared most about him in many ways in the final analysis because they realized that everything he said and everything he did was not about himself but about the people he wanted to represent. And so I know there are members who are not here today because of other obligations, but who, when the opportunity comes, will express their own thoughts and feelings, but don't be surprised—Madam President, I know you will not be, nor my colleagues from Minnesota or Vermont— that some of the heartfelt remarks about Paul will come from people who disagreed with him vehemently on substantive matters, but appreciated immensely his sense of conviction, something we can do a lot more of in politics in America today.

Frederick Douglass once said, "The life of a nation is secure only while the nation is honest, truthful, and virtuous." For fifty-eight years, Paul Wellstone lived a life that was honest, truthful, and virtuous. For twelve years, he personally lent those characteristics to the heart of the United States government.

America, Minnesota, and this institution have suffered a terrible loss at the death of Paul Wellstone, but there is a silver lining in all of this; that as a result of his service this country is a better place, there are people who are living better lives; this world with all of its difficulties has been a better world because Paul Wellstone was a part of it.

I am confident as I stand before you today, Madam President, that in the weeks, months, and years ahead, his memory and legacy will live on in the debates, the discussions, and actions we take in this body.

For that, Paul Wellstone, you ought to know that your service continues and your words and your actions will have a legacy borne out by those who come after you in the service of your state and the thousands of young people you motivated.

Madam President, if you could only see, as many have, the hundreds of young people throughout Minnesota who Paul Wellstone energized and brought to the public life of this country, people who otherwise would not have paid any attention. Paul Wellstone said: You ought to be involved; there is a reason to be involved.

His ability to attract people to come to a cause and to fight for the good cause will live on. I suspect one day this chamber will have people who will serve in it who cut their teeth in politics working on a Wellstone campaign.

Paul, the campaign goes on. Your battles will go on, and we are going to miss you. I yield the floor.

IN REMEMBRANCE OF PAUL WELLSTONE
November 12-13, 2002
Senator Tom Daschle (D-South Dakota)

I begin our remembrance of Paul Wellstone with the recognition that at times such as this it is more important to celebrate a life than to mourn a death. I will do my utmost in the next couple of minutes to remember my own advice, the importance of celebrating a life.

We mourn the loss of Paul Wellstone, his wife, Sheila, their daughter, Marcia, the staff, and the pilots who lost their lives. It has been a shock from which we have not yet fully recovered. Sometimes in these difficult moments, I turn to the Bible, sometimes I turn to expressions offered to me by others, and sometimes to poetry.

An old Irish text was found in a Carmelite monastery in Tallow County, Wicklow, Ireland. The text was entitled "Togetherness." I find solace in the words of "Togetherness."

> Death is nothing at all—I have only slipped away into the next room. Whatever we were to each other, that we are still. Call me by my old familiar name, speak to me in the easy way which we always used. Laugh as we always laughed at the little jokes we enjoyed together. Play, smile, think of me, pray for me. Let my name be the household word it always was. Let it be spoken without effort. Life means all that it ever meant. It is the same as it always was: There is an absolute unbroken continuity. Why would I be out of your mind because I am out of your sight? I am but waiting for you, for an interval, somewhere very near, just around the corner. All is well. Nothing is passed, nothing is lost. One brief moment, and all will be as it was before—Only better, infinitely happier, and forever—We will all be one together . . .

Paul was all of five-foot-five. But I remember what someone once told me: someone certainly more than five-foot-five. He said it is not the size of the man in the fight, it is the size of the fight in the man. Paul Wellstone by that measurement was a giant. He fought. He spoke. He challenged us all. But he did so in a way that made him a friend, not an enemy, a friend with people on this side of the aisle and a friend, of course, with those on this side, too; he had friends.

While he walked in this chamber small in stature, everyone recognized that if you measure a man and, in so doing, measure the true weight of his being, you don't measure his size, you measure his heart.

Paul Wellstone inspired me. With his physical challenges—his back, his knees, his legs from wrestling injuries, and then later with MS—I never once heard him complain. Never once did he come to me saying, Tom, you have to give me an opportunity to recover, to rest. He had an energy, a dynamism, that overcame all of those ailments. He seemed more well than those who are well. He inspired all with his joy, with his passion, with his energy.

For those of us who believe in public service, there was no greater evidence of his deep sense of commitment to public service than his advocacy for mental health parity. Again, working across the aisle with Senator Domenici, that passion, that energy, that commitment, that determination, that persistence, all that was Paul Wellstone, flowed right up there from that desk. We knew he cared about mental health parity. I can think of no better monument, no better memorial, no better way to honor him than by passing mental health parity soon.

We were all the beneficiaries. Perhaps those who will benefit most by his memory, his example, by his commitment, are our youth. I spoke to his staff on the Sunday following his passing. I reminded them that in the course of five years in my early life, I, too, lost heroes. Their names were John F. Kennedy, Robert F. Kennedy, and Martin Luther King. While I recognize their physical being is no longer here, as our poem said, I recognize, too, that they only slipped into the next room, and their spirit was very much alive. And that burns within me with my understanding and my belief in our democracy in this commitment you must make to public service.

In remembering the Wellstones, we must

also pay tribute to that remarkable woman, Sheila Wellstone, for her advocacy, her leadership, her commitment to abolishing domestic abuse. The commitment she made, the lives she saved, her willingness to be engaged, the extraordinary effort she made and the example she set, too, is something we will always remember and for which we will always be indebted.

On this new day, let us not think of sadness but of celebration. Let us celebrate the life of Paul Wellstone as we acknowledge the loss of his physical being. Let us extend our heartfelt condolences to David, to Mark, and to Todd, to Cari, Keith, to Joshua and Acacia, Sydney and Matt, his family. The hole in their hearts is large. The hole in their lives may never be fully filled.

To them I ask they, too, find solace in the words of "Togetherness."

Death is nothing at all—I have only slipped away into the next room. Whatever we were to each other, that we are still.

Senator Trent Lott (R-Mississippi)

Mr. President, I will begin by thanking Senator Daschle for his remarks so well delivered just now and also for conversations that he and I experienced in the aftermath of this tragic loss.

I rise today also to pay tribute to the life and the service of Senator Paul Wellstone of Minnesota. He had a real impact on this institution. He was a committed warrior to things he believed in. He did it not only with compassion but with sincerity and also generousness and geniality. He never failed to take the time to tell a story, to explain why he felt so strongly about these issues. He was unfailingly willing to be considerate of others, to seek an agreement as to how the process would work, even when it led to a battle of words and of votes. He also had such an upbeat, optimistic view of that process, that

battle, and the next one.

He would come over and say: "Good job, I'll get you next time," if he hadn't won. Even when he might be the single vote, or one of a couple of votes—just a few—he was undaunted. You cannot help but admire that approach to life and to the Senate. I not only understand when senators take a different view, I appreciate it when they take that view—the way Paul Wellstone did.

I have learned over the years that the saying that seems trite is so true in life and in this institution: You can disagree without being disagreeable. He was the master at that.

I appreciated the friendship we developed. I loved to pick at him. I loved to go over and kid him about the little extra face hair that he had for a while, and I would tell him he was my man for the nomination for presidency. When other potential candidates would come up, I would say: Oh, no, I am already committed to Paul. He loved it, actually.

He was very kind to me. When I faced difficult tragedies—as with Paul Coverdell, when I stood here with tears rolling down my face, announcing the loss of that great senator—he would always be one of the first to come over and engage and say how he felt. Sometimes in difficult straits that the Senate has had to go through, when Senator Daschle and I had to make difficult decisions, he would be the only one who would come over and say: It was tough, I know, but you did the right thing. I remember that.

So I think the people of Minnesota have an awful lot to be proud of in their senator. When I went there to pay my respects to the people of Minnesota and to the family and to his friends and supporters, Senator Kennedy was on the bus as we were leaving the airport. He said: We appreciate the fact that you are here. I know you are here not just because you are the leader of the party, but because you wanted to pay proper respects.

I said: I am here because it is the right thing to do, but also because, if the tables had been reversed and this was for me, Paul would have been there. I really believe that.

So I take my hat off, I salute the senator. He will be missed. The Senate will be different. But to the people and his family who are so heartbroken, to his friends and supporters and the people all over his state, our memory of him and his service will not be forgotten. He will go down in history as a truly unique Member of the Senate. I guess we all are in some respects but Paul more so than others.

Senator Ted Kennedy (D-Massachusetts)

Mr. President, Paul Wellston was an extraordinary leader with a common touch. His dedication to the well-being of average Americans was unparalleled in Congress.

He believed all of our citizens, no matter how humble their beginnings, or difficult their plight, had an equal right to happy, healthy, and full lives. He always made the time to hear the real needs of the people, and he always took the time to speak up for them in the U.S. Senate.

For Paul, core beliefs were not something to be compromised. He understood as well as anyone in this body the give-and-take of legislation. But we always knew his values were at the forefront of every battle, and the people of Minnesota could count on him to fight for them with every ounce of his considerable energy and ability.

Paul and I were seatmates. His desk is right beside mine on the Senate floor. But we were more than neighbors. Paul was our conscience, our guiding light. He turned overlooked needs and forgotten causes into real hopes for millions of Americans. For them, Paul Wellstone was their champion, their senator.

Earlier this year, Senator Wellstone chaired a hearing in the Labor Committee on an issue of great concern to American workers. A group of low-wage men and women were so excited by the prospect of the hearing that they took a day off from work, boarded buses, and headed for the hearing. When they arrived, they found the room full and the door barred. But Senator Wellstone heard about the workers who were waiting in the hallway, unable to get in. He invited them in and seated them on the dais among the senators attending the hearing. For Paul, this was the way it was intended to be. For him, there was no distance, no barrier between the people and their elected representatives.

Senator Wellstone did his homework. He knew the facts and he also knew the reality of everyday life for the people he cared for so deeply and served so well. When the Senate debated education policy, we knew Paul understood the issues thoroughly. We also knew Paul had spent more time visiting the public schools than any other senator. He knew the challenges firsthand because he had taken the time to listen to parents, teachers, and schoolchildren so he could be a true voice for them in Washington.

He taught us all by his example that Americans face challenges together. He was the embodiment of *e pluribus unum*, that out of many peoples in America, we are one nation. He lived every moment of every day fighting to make our nation even stronger, ever the beacon of opportunity for all of our citizens.

Paul, we will miss you. You and Sheila and Marcia leave an extraordinary legacy for millions of Americans to honor, to cherish, and to carry on. Your outstanding contributions to the Senate, to Minnesota, and to the Nation will always be remembered.

Senator Byron Dorgan (D-North Dakota)

Mr. President, life gives no joy like that it takes away. As always, the poet said it best. All of us in the Senate were suddenly and tragically reminded of that on a Friday morning two and one-half weeks ago—a cold, gray, dreary October day. I was in a van driving between Fargo and Grand Forks, North Dakota, when I received a call saying that an airplane had crashed in northern Minnesota and that Senator Paul Wellstone, his wife, Sheila, staff, and others were on the plane. To say that I and others have been deeply saddened, in fact devastated, by the loss of one of our colleagues is perhaps to even understate it.

Paul Wellstone and Sheila Wellstone died as they campaigned throughout Minnesota for another term in the Senate. It was a tough campaign, a close campaign, a hard-fought campaign. And yet Paul Wellstone never complained about that. He seemed to relish it.

One of the last things he told me on the floor of the Senate several weeks ago about this campaign was, with a sparkle in his eye: We are going to win this campaign. He said: Byron, I have 4,000 volunteers—4,000 volunteers—who are going to be working election day in Minnesota for me, getting people to the polls, driving people, calling people.

That was so typical of Paul Wellstone. It was always about citizen action, about people rising to the passion of an idea. That was typical Paul Wellstone.

Paul and Sheila Wellstone were wonderful friends to many of us in the Senate, and our thoughts and prayers go to the family, the families of the pilots who lost their lives, the families of Paul's daughter and the three staff people who were on the plane as well.

As my colleague from Minnesota, Senator Dayton, said in what I thought was a wonderful tribute to his friend and colleague, all of us would be remiss if we did not say to Paul's staff: Paul would want first and foremost for us to recognize you today. Paul attracted to his service in the Senate men and women with the burning in their soul to do good things, who cared about fairness and justice and who cared about public service.

All of us who work here know Paul Wellstone had a wonderful staff, and they have been through some very difficult times, about as difficult as it can get for a Senate staff. Our thoughts and prayers go out to them and for strength as well.

Today let me for a moment remember Paul and Sheila for their service to our country. This is a rather small community in the Senate—men and women who love this country, fellow travelers who want to make democracy work. What the American people see are some pitched battles during the day and the early evening hours in the middle of a debate in which there are different philosophies and ideas that clash on the Senate floor. What they do not see is we are colleagues and friends, first and foremost.

I think the entire Senate membership would say: We have, indeed, lost a couple of good friends, Paul and Sheila Wellstone. Our country has lost two tireless fighters for justice. The Senate has lost its strongest voice for those who do not have it so good in this country. And American politics has lost the true champion for the little guy.

If ever a man and wife were a team, it was Paul and Sheila Wellstone. They did everything together. Sheila's public service, as Paul would be the first to tell you, was every bit as important as his. That public service was marked by a green bus, and that green bus meant in Minnesota and our part of the country citizen action, people empowerment, and something that was on the move, a mission, a campaign on the move.

It is true, as my colleague said, Paul was different. He would not have been caught dead in Ferragamo shoes, even if he wanted them, and he did not. He was not a man to wear Brooks Brothers suits. He was short of stature and tall of ambition with a power and passion of ideas, as my colleague from Nevada just described, that would at the end stage of any debate leave him sitting at that chair with two more amendments to offer—the hour was late, patience was short. Imploring him made no difference. You could say: Paul, Paul, we are just out of time; can you just not offer one of these amendments? The answer was always the same: Absolutely not.

I am here to offer this amendment. This amendment is important. I came here to do that work and there are people who depend on me to offer this amendment—people whose lives were changed because of this amendment.

It was always with Paul: No. And we always turned away understanding the passion that burned in his soul to do the right thing, to do the thing he felt was important for our country.

Paul was different in a much more significant way as well. In today's modern politics, it is so often the case that politicians with a sophisticated network of pollsters and advisers are able to evaluate exactly which way the wind is blowing, to be able to set their sail to get maximum capability from that wind. It is a constant job of tacking for some into or with that wind to find out exactly where the maximum wind will be. Paul was not interested in sailing or winds. Paul was only interested in the rudder. He set the rudder and he did not care where the wind was: This is the direction I am going and it does not matter whether it is a favorable wind or an unfavorable wind. This is where we are headed and this is why—very unusual in modern politics but also very refreshing.

I found it interesting that those newspapers that were not very good to his ideas in life, in death gave Paul great credit for raising ideas, for standing by his principles, for never wavering and never causing for a moment any constituent anyplace to wonder where he stood. You knew where Paul Wellstone stood.

There are two things, of a great many, that stand out in my mind. One day I sent around a memorandum to senators saying we were going to visit a youth detention center in Maryland and I wanted to know if anyone wanted to come along. Paul Wellstone called me and said: I would like to come.

The two of us, with some staff, went out to a youth detention center and spent the entire morning sitting in that youth detention center talking to kids, kids who had committed murder, kids who were drug addicted, kids who had been in the worst kind of trouble one could possibly imagine. Driving back to Capitol Hill after this visit, I once again got another glimpse of Paul Wellstone's soul. He said: If someone had cared about those kids early in their lives they would not be there today. Someone needed to help those kids at the right moment, and we can do that in the Senate.

To Paul, that visit was, how can we reach out to help people who need help at a time when they desperately need that help?

In the last couple of months, Paul came up to me while we were in the well of the Senate, and he said: I was campaigning in Minnesota and I went to an independent auto repair shop, and the major automobile manufacturers would not give the computer codes to these independent auto repair shops. These small independents are telling me they cannot work on the new cars. They do not have the computer cards for the carburetors and all those things they have to have to work on those cars.

He said: That is unfair, and it is going to drive those folks out of business. This is going to kill the little guy.

He asked if I would hold a hearing on this in

my Consumer Subcommittee. I said of course I will. We put together some information on it. The day of the hearing came and Senator Wellstone was to be the lead-off witness. That was not enough for Senator Wellstone. As was his want, in the way he did politics, the hearing room was packed. It was full of mechanics and independent repair shop owners from all across this country. I guess that hearing room holds probably 100 people, and there were 150 people there. Paul had brought his people, the independent repair shop folks, to that hearing room as a demonstration of this problem, to say this problem ought to be fixed.

Paul was the lead-off witness and, as was typical with him, with great passion he made the case about the unfairness to the little guy, about the independent repair shops trying to make a living, and how what is happening is unfair to them.

About three weeks ago, right before we completed our work and left for the election, Paul came up to me on the floor of the Senate during a vote. He was holding a sheet of paper. He was flashing this paper and saying: We won. His point was that the automobile manufacturers had reached an agreement with the independent repair shops, and that problem had gotten solved. For Paul, it was about the little guy versus the big guy, about those who did not have the power and those who did.

It was always that he wanted to stand on the side of those who did not have the power, those who needed help. That was so much of Paul Wellstone's life.

There is much to say, and my colleagues, I am sure, will say it when we talk about his service to our country. It is sufficient now to say that one of our Senate desks is empty. The Senate has lost a wonderful friend.

I conclude by quoting Thomas Moore, if I might, and relate it to Paul's service:

Let fate do her worst; there are relics of joy,

Bright dreams of the past, which she cannot destroy; Which come in the nighttime of sorrow and care, And bring back the features that joy used to wear. Long; long be my heart with such memories fill'd! Like the vase, in which roses have once been distill'd You may break, you may shatter the vase, if you will, But the scent of the roses will hang 'round it still.

Paul Wellstone is no longer in the Senate, his desk is empty, but the passion of his ideas most surely will remain for years and years to come.

Senator Russ Feingold (D-Wisconsin)

Mr. President, I rise to pay tribute to our colleague, Paul Wellstone. As with the loss of anyone so vital, so full of energy, and so dear to us, it is hard to believe that Paul is really gone. But as with a brother, or a father, or a great teacher, even if they have died, they leave a part of themselves with those who carry on. They are never really gone.

I first met Paul before either of us had been elected to the Senate. I was meeting with different people as I considered a run for the Senate, and I heard about this professor in Minnesota who was planning to run in 1990. I had a chance to visit him at his home. When we met, we laughed at the idea that the two of us or either of us, would ever have been elected to the Senate.

But then Paul went on to run a terrific campaign, without a lot of money, but with a whole lot of energy. When he won, he helped me and others to believe that we could do the same. I will always be grateful to him for that example, as I am sure are many others across the country who were inspired by Paul and the exceptional life that he led.

So now we know that whenever a candidate runs a scrappy populist campaign, Paul Wellstone will be there.

Paul Wellstone believed in clean elections.

Paul was a strong, stalwart ally over the years that we served together in the Senate, working for campaign finance reform. He was an original cosponsor of the first McCain-Feingold bill—one of a handful of us, along with Senators Claiborne Pell and Fred Thompson, and he was there all the way. Some have said that the law that we enacted this year went too far. Characteristically, Paul thought that it did not go far enough.

Paul Wellstone wrote: "The way in which money has come to dominate politics is the foremost ethical issue of politics of our time. We need to invite ordinary citizens back into American politics to work for what is right for our nation."

Whenever Americans reform our election campaigns, Paul Wellstone will be there.

Paul Wellstone said: "I don't represent the big oil companies. I don't represent the big pharmaceutical companies. I don't represent the Enrons of this world. But you know what, they already have great representation in Washington. It's the rest of the people that need it." That's what Paul Wellstone said.

So, whenever there are voices standing up for the little guy, Paul Wellstone's voice will be there.

There is a role that some senators play of leading where not many follow because they know that it is right. Paul Wellstone had the courage of his convictions. He was not afraid to stand alone. Now that he is gone, there may come more times when some of us will be counted as the only vote against something.

But whenever a senator stands alone in the well of the Senate and casts a solitary vote because that's what he or she believes, that senator won't really be alone because Paul Wellstone will be there.

There is a role that some senators play of reminding the rest of us of what is right, even when we don't necessarily like to hear it. It has been said many times, and it is nonetheless true,

that like Paul Douglas, Phil Hart, and Paul Simon before him, Paul Wellstone was the conscience of the Senate.

Whenever political expediency pulls us to vote one way, but our consciences pull us back the other, Paul Wellstone will be there.

Paul Wellstone was a dear, sweet man, and a good friend to those of us who knew him. Yes, he had a puckish grin and a ready sense of humor. His passing brings a tear to our eyes.

But whenever we think of that smile of his, Paul Wellstone will be there.

The Bible says: "Justice, justice shall you pursue." Paul didn't need to be told. That was who he was. Paul Wellstone believed in justice with every fiber of his being.

Paul fought for justice for children who didn't have enough to eat. He fought for environmental justice, even for the poor side of town. He fought for social justice when it came to access to health care. He fought for economic justice when it came to a fair minimum wage and the ability of working families to protect themselves under the bankruptcy law. And he fought for justice among nations, and for peace. Paul Wellstone was the very embodiment of justice.

And so, Paul Wellstone, here on the Senate floor, there is a hole in our hearts. We will miss you, dear friend.

But we will still look for you. For wherever it is on this Senate floor, at a political rally, or at a town hall meeting somewhere on a cold, windy day in the heartland of America whenever someone speaks for justice, Paul Wellstone will be there.

Senator Arlen Specter (R-Pennsylvania)

Mr. President, the Senate is greatly diminished with the passing of Senator Paul Wellstone. As we see the bouquet of flowers on his desk, we can see

Paul in action, speaking out, speaking up indefatigable on the issues of concern to him.

He undertook a very difficult campaign back in 1990 against the odds, against a popular incumbent senator. He was able to mobilize students, activists, people who believed in what he believed in because he was always a man with a cause. All the time he had a point. He did not mind being a dissenter.

People who may be listening to this session of the Senate do not know, but there is a little card at the desk on each side, Republicans and Democrats. When the senators come in and vote, there is a check. It is not easy, when, say, there are fifty members of the party and forty-nine checks are on one side, to vote against the forty-nine, to have your name stand out in marked contrast as a dissenter, but Paul Wellstone did not mind that a bit.

I believe in the history of our country the dissenters are vitally important, sometimes more important than the majority. Oliver Wendell Holmes, a Supreme Court Justice, was a prime example. He did not mind speaking out in dissent. And then he got another Supreme Court Justice, Louis Brandeis, to join him. So then instead of one to eights, it was two to seven. The brainpower of the two was characteristically better than the seven. For that matter, the brainpower of that one, Justice Oliver Wendell Holmes, was greater than the eight of many occasions.

Plessy v. Ferguson was a decision establishing the principle of separate but equal, having segregation in America, in a decision shortly before the turn of the twentieth century, I believe in 1896. John Marshall Harlan was the one dissenter. That dissent became a clarion call for Brown v. Board of Education. Similarly, I think the dissents that Senator Wellstone registered have the potential to become a majority point of view.

It was said earlier today, and I think with real meaning, that the legislation to establish parity for mental illness with physical illness would be an appropriate tribute for Senator Paul Wellstone. That legislation came within a hair's breadth of being passed in the spring of 2001 on an appropriations bill.

Technically, we are not supposed to legislate on an appropriations bill, but that rule is honored and then breached very often, maybe not more often than it is observed, but it is breached very frequently.

We had passed it through the Labor, Health, Human Services and Education Subcommittee which I had chaired. It was a health bill. Senator Domenici was the principal champion on the Republican side, and Senator Wellstone was the principal champion on the Democratic side. I was long a cosponsor of the matter. In chairing the conference, we pushed very hard. It came within one vote on the House side—we had the Senate—of getting that legislation passed.

It ought to be passed as a tribute to Senator Wellstone. It also ought to be passed for the benefit of the people who suffer from mental illness, which is every bit as debilitating as a physical illness.

On October 25, I was campaigning, as I think most people were. I had just come from a political rally in Reading, Pennsylvania, where Vice President Cheney had spoken for Congressman Gekas who was running in a hotly contested election against Congressman Tim Holden, two incumbents pitted against one another. I turned on the radio at about 1:30 eastern time and was shocked to hear the news that Senator Wellstone's plane had gone down. It brought memories of the plane that went down on April 3, 1991, with Senator John Heinz, a vibrant, young senator who had great potential, as did Senator Paul Wellstone.

Flying small planes is an occupational hazard, and everybody in this chamber, all 100 of us, as well as the 435 members in the other chamber, and many other legislators and governmental officials, climb into small airplanes every other day. We all hold our breath as to whether we will be successful on the flight. Regrettably, we fly in bad weather, which sometimes we should not do but there is always a big crowd waiting and always some reason to finish.

It was a great tragedy. Paul's wife, Sheila, was with him in the plane. One seldom saw Paul in the Halls of Congress without Sheila. She was not on the floor of the Senate, but she was with him constantly, holding hands, a very devoted couple. Their daughter, Marcia, was with them, also devoted in the campaign, a brilliant young woman at the age of thirty-three.

Senator Wellstone will be sorely missed in the Senate. There are many Paul Wellstone stories. I will mention one. I was managing the appropriations bill for Labor, Health, Human Services and Education. Senator Wellstone was in the chamber bright and early. We started at 9:30. He had an amendment. Sometimes it is hard to get amendments up onto the floor. His amendment provided that no member of Congress should have a health insurance policy at government expense that was superior to what every other American had available to him or her.

When that amendment was brought up, it was through the distinguished senior senator from Minnesota, who was smiling broadly. It was a very extraordinary amendment to make. It is pretty hard to make an amendment like that stick because it would have made President Clinton's national health insurance policy look entrepreneurial to the nth degree. It did not pass, even though the Democrats controlled the House and the Senate. Senator Mitchell, the majority leader in 1993, was a major proponent of health care, but the Clinton plan with its bureaucracy went down to defeat. To have a requirement that no member of Congress could have a health plan that was superior in any way to what the

government provided for every citizen was really an extraordinary idea, to characterize it very mildly.

I did not have to debate Senator Wellstone for very long before there was an avalanche of senators who came to the chamber. He really struck a nerve, and he struck a nerve because many people think that senators and members of the House have health insurance which is paid for by the government, which is not true. We pay for the health service which we have, but we also have additional health service policies, Blue Cross and Blue Shield. To have legislation limiting what a member could have to that which every other citizen would have at government expense would be a great inducement to pass a widespread health insurance benefit, and perhaps we ought to do that. That was Senator Wellstone's idea. He debated it with fervor and intensity.

It was an extraordinary debate. I do not think he got too many votes for his plan, but that did not diminish it in any way. That is the great quality of a dissenter. This chamber will not be the same without Senator Wellstone.

Senator Hillary Clinton (D-New York)

Mr. President, I join with my colleagues in taking these few moments to pay tribute to an extraordinary man and a great senator. It is hard to come back to the Senate floor this afternoon and not be overcome by a sense of loss because this desk behind me, with the flowers, will never again serve as the launching pad for one of Paul Wellstone's memorable and impassioned speeches.

Every American who shared Paul's determination to make our country all that it should be, all that it can be, all that Paul thought it must be, felt that same sense of loss. The Americans who only knew Paul Wellstone through tuning into C-SPAN or seeing the evening news, watching that energy flow, those arms flail about, that pacing up and down, may not have known the man but they too saw, as we his colleagues saw, that deep abiding love of our country. That is what motivated Paul Wellstone. He would come onto this floor, sometimes bursting through those doors, having to speak out, making it clear that there was some injustice that had to be righted, some problem that had to be solved, in order for us all to be the best we could be.

That wrestling spirit that never let go really was with him in every encounter. He was a bear hugger. He was a caring, loving man, as well as a great advocate.

His determination to improve our nation, our education system, our health care system, our employment system, to strengthen civil and human rights and provide opportunities to those who live on the outskirts of American life, was unparalleled. Every one of us who knew him, and the millions who did not, were heartbroken by his untimely death.

I had someone say to me that the voice for the voiceless has been silenced. That is not only a tribute to Paul but it can also be heard as a rebuke to us. Was there only one among us who spoke for the voiceless, who hurt for those who were hurting, who carried the pain of injustice and exclusion under which so many suffered? One hopes that is not the case, but the only way to prove it is not is to ensure that our voices are heard loudly and clearly.

This floor will seem empty without his words of conviction unless we fill it with our own. The ideals he represented and his steadfast belief that we, the people, through our government, acting together, can be a positive force, literally to change the future for those who might otherwise be left in despair, that commitment motivated every aspect of his daily life.

Our Senate family and the people of Minnesota not only lost Senator Paul Wellstone, but we lost a great advocate in Sheila Wellstone and

we lost a great teacher in Marcia Wellstone. His family shared his passion and his drive for justice. His staff were with him every step of the way and some tragically even gave their lives in service. Our thoughts and prayers are certainly with all those, along with the Wellstone family, who lost family members, friends, and colleagues.

Before coming to the Senate, I had the great pleasure of working with both Paul and Sheila Wellstone. I admired Sheila greatly. Just as her husband, she was made of steel. That little package of energy that propelled her down these corridors and throughout the State of Minnesota looking for ways to help and to shed the spotlight she could bring into the darkest corners of human misery set her apart. She especially became a champion of those women and children who were victims of domestic violence. The stories she heard from women all over Minnesota and America did not stay her property; she told them to anyone. She would come to the White House and button hole me or the president. She would go anywhere to see anyone to make sure that someone whose small cry for help that she heard in St. Paul or Margie would be heard in Washington as well.

She believed that the idea of violence-free families should be a reality in every home in our nation.

She and Paul, together, believed the diseases, the illnesses of the mind, should no longer be relegated to some back room where they would be brushed aside, ignored because of the stigma, the embarrassment attached to them historically. She encouraged Paul to join forces with Senator Domenici to transform each of their families' experiences into a national campaign to improve the lives of the mentally ill.

Sheila and Paul were also instrumental in bringing to international awareness the horrific problem of trafficking in human beings, the modern form of slavery by which young women, young girls, are literally sold into bondage, into the sex trade, into domestic servitude. Sheila and Paul Wellstone were absolutely committed that this practice of degradation would end.

When each of us heard the news that the plane carrying Paul and Sheila and Marcia went down, time seemed to stop. Many did not want to believe it. We kept asking our staff and others how it could be true. How could this have happened? Horrible events, tragedies of this magnitude, have a way of stopping time. But then we have to return. The clocks have to start moving again. We have to continue our journey into the future. But if we remember what that moment in time felt like when we realized our friend, our colleague, a great senator, would no longer join us for our debates, then perhaps that tragedy can change the tone and landscape of our politics and our debates. Perhaps Paul's example in life, his legacy in death, will compel all to look inward, to ask ourselves what are we doing today with the same energy, the same good humor, the same fighting spirit that Paul Wellstone embodied to make life a little better for the people we represent, to give voice to the voiceless.

Over the past weeks I have thought a lot about Paul Wellstone. I remember so many incidents and so many of his triumphs. He was there day in and day out. No issue was too small that it did not have his commitment behind it if he thought it would make a difference in someone's life. The Senate passed expanding insurance coverage for the mentally ill. I hope Senator Domenici's heartfelt plea and his long-time commitment will help finally to pass his and Paul's dream into law.

We increased access to child care for the working poor because Paul Wellstone knew what it meant to worry about your children while at work because you did not know the conditions

they would be in, whether they would receive the quality of care they should.

One of my favorite Paul Wellstone moments was that Paul and I were at a hearing he was chairing the Subcommittee on Employment and Training. We had been receiving reports about a sharp increase in the numbers of unreported deaths and injuries among immigrant workers—many of them illegal, who found their way to our country and were put to work, despite the laws against it, for the cheap labor they provided—who were not given the protection or the support or the respect they should have for the dangerous jobs they were performing.

One of my state's newspapers, *NewsDay*, ran a powerful investigative report about the conditions in which immigrant workers labored in New York. Paul read it and contacted me right away. He wanted us to work together to find out what we could do to stop people from dying, literally dying, in New York and around America.

Many who go to hearings around here know that not many people, except the paid lobbyists for the various industries affected, show up for the committee hearings. The lobbyists fill the chairs. They take the notes. They rush out to make the cell phone calls to report to their superiors and employers what is going on. But unfortunately, except on rare occasions, other people do not come.

On that day, to our surprise, hundreds of workers flooded the halls of the Dirksen Building trying to get into our hearing, trying to tell their stories. Unfortunately, we had no idea this would draw such a crowd. The room the hearing was being held in was not big enough to accommodate everyone waiting.

Paul and I conferred, and Paul said: I can't believe it. There are all these people outside. Some of them came from miles away. You can see his arms, as you hear those words, going back and forth. What are we going to do?

Before I could answer, he got up, and in that bow-legged wrestler's stance and walk he had, he walked down from the platform, through the crowd, threw open the doors, told the Capitol police that everyone was coming in and that there would be room. They could sit on the floor, they could sit in the senators' chairs because he and I were the only senators there. He would not keep the very people we were having the hearing about out of the hearing room.

That was Paul. He was a people's senator. Everyone was welcome. Every door was open. It was an unusual hearing, but it was a memorable one. Afterwards, he greeted each and every person who was there.

It was this passion that got him up and fighting every day, even when he was in such pain, as some of us can remember, seeing him in pain on this floor, remembering how last year the pain was so intense he literally dropped to the floor of the Senate. He later learned that he was not just contending with the aches and pains of a Hall of Fame wrestling career but that he had multiple sclerosis. That did not stop him either.

For any of us who inquired how he was doing, he brushed it off. He was not interested in any way or concerned about his own health. He wanted to talk to you about what we were going to do about unemployment insurance, what we were going to do about education, how we could turn our backs on all these children who would not get the resources they needed.

During the debate on the education bill, Paul was the only member of our Education Committee to vote against it. We knew why. He warned that focusing our education system solely on improvements in standardized tests without a major increase in federal funding was wrong. I agreed with that. I said so at the time in our committee. I will vote for

this bill, but only if we have the funding.

Here we are, a year later. We got the funding for one year and then the administration came in and no more funding.

Paul was right, as the distinguished senator from West Virginia knows.

Trust, but verify, when it comes to such promises.

Senator Wellstone always stood by his beliefs. His last big fight, as Senator Byrd has so eloquently reminded us, was over two big issues: Certainly Iraq, what should be done, what will be done, what our obligations as senators are to hold this administration accountable; and, here at home, the fight for unemployment benefits to be extended. For the life of me and for Paul Wellstone, with whom I spoke about this at length time and time again, it made no sense. How could we turn our backs on people who were out of work through no fault of their own, who needed a little bit of a helping hand? He would come to the floor, he would make that case, and we wouldn't go anywhere with it. We couldn't get our colleagues to support extending unemployment insurance one more time.

Along with what I hope will be a lasting legacy of mental health parity, I truly request our colleagues and the administration to extend unemployment insurance, Paul Wellstone's last domestic battle, for people who will otherwise have nowhere to turn when those benefits are gone.

I want to say also a word about Senator Wellstone's staff, because he certainly loved and respected his staff. As Senator Byrd has mentioned, his staff was a loyal, hard-working group who often accompanied Senator Wellstone to the floor and sat there watching him, getting energy from his excitement and passion. I want to name some of the names of those men and women who helped him do the work we honor today. Colin McGinnis, his chief of staff, and Brian Ahlberg, his legislative director, are two extraordinary public servants. My staff has enjoyed the privilege of working with them.

My staff and I have also had the opportunity to work with Marge Baker, who led Senator Wellstone's efforts on the Subcommittee on Employment and Training, with Jill Morningstar, who was his legislative assistant on education and women's issues, with Rachel Gregg, who led his efforts to assist the working poor, as well as Patti Unruh, Ellen Gerrity, and Richard McKeon, who made up his team of health care advisers.

I offer my condolences to each of his extraordinary staff members, and I want them to know how much we appreciate the work they did for Paul.

On October 15, at the close of his last debate, here is what Senator Wellstone said:

I don't represent the pharmaceutical companies, I don't represent the big oil companies, I don't represent the big health insurance industry, I don't represent the big financial institutions. But you know what, I represent the people of Minnesota.

That may be his most fitting tribute—the honor, the ability, the results he brought to the way he represented the people of Minnesota. He did it with passion and principle. We join in saluting his life and his service and we challenge ourselves to remember the reasons why so many are mourning him today. Each of us, try to live up to the standard Paul Wellstone set.

Senator Sam Brownback (R-Kansas)

Mr. President, I rise to speak in morning business to pay tribute to Paul and Sheila Wellstone. It is a difficult thing to do. It is a difficult thing for all of us to do. It is easier for me, right now, to imagine Paul standing over there and articulating a great point, a great point that would be for the consideration of some group of people or an individual about whom he would be deeply concerned—he was clear, passionate, and very forceful in his advocacy for them—rather than to think of him as being gone but he is.

You cannot really measure the height of a tree until it is down. That is, unfortunately, again, the case for Paul and Sheila Wellstone. He was a really tall man. They were really tall trees in what they did.

I had the great fortune to be able to work with both Paul and Sheila on an issue we cared a lot about—the trafficking of individuals across country borders, generally for reasons of prostitution but also for other purposes. We found this was going on.

Actually, Sheila discovered this was happening by visiting with a number of Ukrainian women, some of whom had been trafficked themselves when the Soviet Union fell, when the superstructure that was the Soviet Union came down.

It turned out that gangs, groups came in, the Mafia-type organizations, to operate in the former Soviet Union, and they would run a number of different things. They would run drugs, they would run weaponry, and they would run people. It turned out the trafficking of people was actually their third most profitable operation. It was a real despicable thing they were doing. They would actually go into communities, trick young ladies, generally—sometimes young boys, but generally young girls—saying: We have this great bit of excitement for you. We are going to be able to have you travel to Europe or to the Middle East.

With the fall of the Soviet Union, they didn't see hope or opportunity in their own country, and they would sign on, only to have their papers taken away once they crossed the border. They would be put into a brothel, in some cases chained and tortured until they would submit to prostitution. And then they would even be moved from brothel to brothel. It was a real seamy, dirty, ugly thing that was taking place. It was a dark side of the globalizing economy. It was a dark side of the fall of the Soviet Union. And Sheila found out about it by meeting with Ukrainian women.

Now, I am sure there were not many votes at all in Minnesota that were going to hinge on whether or not Paul or Sheila were going to work on the issue of the trafficking of young girls from the former Soviet Union, Nepal, and India, or from other places. Generally, there was trafficking from poorer countries into richer countries. But Paul was such a champion of the value and the beauty of each person and the needs and the dignity of that individual, and Sheila was as well, that they were willing to put this issue forward and fight for it over a period of a couple years, until we could get the bill passed.

Sheila found out about it. She brought it to Paul's attention. He learned about it and talked with some of these women who had been trafficked. I started to hear about it. I met with women who had been trafficked and found out about the despicable nature of this new form of human slavery, a human slavery of which one person even wrote a book entitled, *Disposable People*, because it happened in a situation where they would be moved from one brothel to another, and then, as they would get sick or diseased—in some cases they would get tuberculosis, AIDS—the owners would even throw them out on the street and say: Well, we are done with that one. It was just the most ugly act.

I remember being in a home for girls who had been trafficked and returned to Nepal. There were fifty girls, sixteen to eighteen years of age. Many of them had been trafficked when they were twelve to fourteen years of age. And a lady was helping run this home. This was a recovery house for girls after they would come back from the brothels. This woman was trying to teach them a trade, trying to get them back into the community in Nepal. She would point around the room and say: That girl has tuberculosis and AIDS and she is dying. This girl is dying. That girl has this disease; I don't know if she is going to make it. These were girls who were sixteen years of age who should have been in the very flower of their lives, and they were all dying.

They saw it. They were willing to fight for these other people. And we were able to get through legislation on sex trafficking.

Paul joked with me afterwards. He is a more liberal member, and I am a more conservative member. After that legislative session, he commented that he moved from being the most liberal member to the second most liberal member of the Senate, and he blamed it on working with me. I said: Well, just hang around with me, Paul, and we will get you reelected.

He had that kind of humor. He was a friend. He was a friend that was not scared of ideology splitting people apart. He had his beliefs; I had mine. We all do. But he did not let that separate him. He did not judge a person's soul by their ideology. He judged people by their character and their heart, where they would be willing to stand.

I would often see him come over to greet and talk with Jesse Helms. He and Jesse disagreed on a number of issues, but they both had passion, soul, and heart. That is what they respected and loved about each other, and that is what I continue to see and love about Paul and Sheila Wellstone, that passion, heart, and soul that would carry them forward.

I do not know that there is a better quote one could put forward than from Dr. Martin Luther King. He once noted that the ultimate measure of a man is not where he stands in moments of comfort but where he stands at times of challenge and controversy.

If we measure Paul and Sheila by that measurement, they stand as a very tall tree. Paul knew controversy. He knew difficulty. He knew challenge. It rallied him. It made him taller. It made him stronger. It was not comfort that he sought. It was not comfort that he wanted to have. I have often thought that in this life it is challenges that build us, it is not comfort that builds us; that God has created us to meet challenges, not to sit back and to eat bon-bons or to let things go by in a measurable way, but He puts challenges in front of us. The more we are willing to accept, the more He is willing to give, and the more He is willing to test us.

Paul and Sheila accepted challenge after challenge, controversy after controversy, always with a pure heart, wanting to do the right thing to help people, regardless of what it might mean to themselves. They were there to do it and they wanted to do it. They relished doing it and they grew in doing it. He was a spirited fighter.

I remember reading about—certainly I was not in this body then—when Hubert Humphrey served in this body and was dying of cancer, and they had a tribute to him in *Time* magazine. I remember so vividly reading about it. The title of it was "Happy Warrior," because he was a warrior and he was happy about it, that his course, his challenge, in life was to be a warrior. He relished in the opportunity to be a warrior.

I did not know him personally, but he could not imagine, as I understand his personality, that there would be any calling any better than to be a warrior.

Paul followed in those footsteps in a great and magnificent way. He was a happy warrior, happily fighting for his cause, happily pressing forward, knowing that people disagreed with him. I disagreed with him often, but I could never disagree with that passion. Nor could I ever disagree with that heart. We developed a really good friendship.

He is a man I was very fond of and I am fond of even now. As I say, it is hard to think of him being gone. I suppose that is because he and Sheila really probably still are here.

My prayers have been with them, with the other people who went down in that plane. So tragically their lives were ended early. None of us will know why on this side of eternity, but we can always learn and grow from him. We are caused to grow in our life by each person with whom we come in contact. I was caused to grow in a very profound and very personal way by my contact with Paul and Sheila. I am indebted to them. I pay tribute to them and what they have done. God bless them.

SOURCES

> "In the last analysis, politics is not predictions and politics is not observations. Politics is what we do. Politics is what we do, politics is what we create, by what we work for, by what we hope for and what we dare to imagine."
>
> ~Senator Paul Wellstone (Frequently used quote)

Burg, Steven L. and Paul S. Shoup, *The War in Bosnia-Herzegovina*, M.E. Sharpe, March 2000

Clark, Wesley K., *Waging Modern War: Bosnia, Kosovo, and the Future of Combat*, Public Affairs, 2001

Gydson, Terry, *Twelve Years and Thirteen Days*, The University of Minnesota Press, 2003

Hersh, Seymour M., *Chain of Command: The Road from 9/11 to Abu Ghraib*, Harper Collins Publishers, 2004

Holm, Bill, *A Liberal with a Wrestler's Stance*, The New York Times, October 26, 2002

Lewis, Jack, *The Spirit of the First Earth Day*, EPA Journal, January-February 1990

Lofy, Bill, *Paul Wellstone: The Life of Passionate Progressive*, The University of Michigan Press, 2005

Malcolm, Noel, *Bosnia: A short history*, New York University Press, 1994

McGrath, Dennis J. and Dane Smith, *Professor Wellstone Goes to Washington*, The University of Minnesota Press, 1995

The National Commission on Terrorist Attacks, *The 9/11 Commission Report*, W.W. Norton & Company, 2004

Nelson, Gaylord, *Earth Day '70 What It Meant*, EPA Journal, April 1980

Rockefeller, Jay, *Rockefeller Travels to Minnesota to Pay Tribute to Senator Wellstone*, Press Release, December 29, 2002

Rosenbaum, David E., *A Death in the Senate: Paul Wellstone, 58, Icon of Liberalism in Senate*, The New York Times, October 26, 2002

Wellstone, Paul and Barry M. Casper, *Powerline: The First Battle of America's Energy War*, University of Minnesota Press, September 2003

Wellstone, Paul, *The Conscience of a Liberal: Reclaiming the Compassionate Agenda*, Random House, 2001

Wellstone, Paul, *How the rural poor got power: Narrative of a grassroots organizer*, The University of Minnesota Press, September 2003

Wilgoren, Jodi, *Mourning in Minnesota*, The New York Times, October 30, 2002

Woodward, Bob, *The Commanders*, Simon & Schuster, 1991

ACKNOWLEDGEMENTS

"People have to hear words that not only sound right but feel right. I think it's in part the economic message, but it's also in part a message about community, about who we are as a nation, about how to live a life in which you don't have to separate the life you live from the words you speak, be that in your relationship with your family, your community, your country or your world. I don't want to give an inch on a 'family values' agenda . . ." ~Senator Paul Wellstone (*Tikkun* magazine, August, 1998)

I want to thank my wife, Amy, for her patience, support, and love. She is the best partner, friend, and spouse a person could ever have, in addition to being a great immigration attorney. I also hope the words of Senator Paul Wellstone inspire our two daughters—Ella and Johanna—to dream, and then fight for that dream to the very end.

My parents, Rick and Nancy, and my sisters, Mari and Cristi, have always supported my various interests and never knocked me down (even when I deserved to be knocked down). To my Grandpa Wayne for his love of knowledge—here's another book for your collection. To my brother, Darrin Friedman, thank you for being who you are. And, also my teachers and mentors: Mrs. Clemons, Mrs. Schmitz, Mrs. Heuser, Mr. Peterson, Mr. Nordstrom, Herr Kauls, Dr. David Patterson, Dr. Hal Williams, Professor Prentiss Cox and all those in between.

I want to acknowledge Terry Gydesen. She is a true artist and spirit, who graciously donated the cover photograph for this book. Please check out her photographs at www.terrygydesen.com,

and purchase her wonderful book of photographs, *Twelve Years and Thirteen Days: Remembering Paul and Sheila Wellstone*.

I also want to say a few words about the friends, staff, and supporters of Senator Paul Wellstone. I still remember going to the Minnesota State Fair and buying my green t-shirt that featured Professor Wellstone and his bus. It was 1990. I was sixteen years old. He was the first politician who connected with me. Paul Wellstone was smart, funny, rebellious, and broke the anchorman-as-politician mold. In hindsight, it isn't hard to understand why those characteristics appealed to a weird kid like me. But, it wasn't that simple.

Paul Wellstone made that connection to me with the help of thousands of volunteers, friends, and staff that amplified his spirit of hope and renewal. You are the unsung heroes that carry on his message and work, and I want to thank you for sacrificing your time so that I could be inspired. I hope the speeches collected in this book inspire you to continue to stand up and keep fighting.